WORLDS APART

Acting and Writing in Academic
and Workplace Contexts

RHETORIC, KNOWLEDGE, AND SOCIETY
A Series of Monographs Edited by
Charles Bazerman

WORLDS APART

Acting and Writing in Academic and Workplace Contexts

Patrick Dias

Aviva Freedman

Peter Medway

Anthony Paré

Routledge
Taylor & Francis Group

NEW YORK AND LONDON

First Published by
Lawrence Erlbaum Associates, Inc., Publishers
10 Industrial Avenue
Mahwah, NJ 07430

Transferred to Digital Printing 2009 by Routledge
270 Madison Ave, New York NY 10016
2 Park Square, Milton Park, Abingdon, Oxon, OX14 4RN

Cover design by Kathryn Houghtaling Lacey

Library of Congress Cataloging-in-Publication Data
Worlds Apart: acting and writing in academic and workplace
contexts / Patrick Dias ... [et al.].
      p. cm.
Includes bibliographical references and index.
ISBN 0-8058-2147-3 (cloth : alk. paper)
— ISBN 0-8058-2148-1 (pbk. : alk. paper)
English language—Rhetoric—Study and teaching. 2. Aca-
demic writing—Study and teaching. 3. Technical writ-
ing—Study and teaching. 4. Business writing—study and
teaching. I. Dias, Patrick.
PE1404.W665 1999
808—dc21   98–49931
                                      CIP

CONTENTS

EDITOR'S INTRODUCTION

Charles Bazerman
University of California, Santa Barbara

Worlds Apart: Acting and Writing in Academic and Workplace Contexts is an impressive multisite comparative study of writing in different university courses and matched workplaces: law and public administration courses and government institutions; management courses and financial institutions; social work courses and social work agencies; and architecture courses and architecture practice. The study, carried out across 7 years by a dozen people, looked intently into how writing functions within the activities of each of these various settings. The study, despite its size and multi-authorship, avoids the simplifications that typically are needed to generate consistency and comparability across extensive data. Rather than looking for easy points of comparison, the authors sought to understand each setting through detailed ethnography and found comparisons only by understanding how writing is operative within the particularities of settings.

This revealing theoretical understanding was developed in a conversation among the four lead investigators over the years of the project, a conversation that I saw as a distant onlooker and then as an editor. Although there are numerous other products of this research project, this book is a culmination of that theoretical discussion about the overall meanings of all of the findings. What they found at each of the sites was that learning to write in the locally relevant genres was a means by which individuals were socialized into the particular activities, ideologies, identities, meaning systems, power structures, institutional goals, and cooperative endeavors enacted in each place. Furthermore, those genres became the site of tension among the various motives, perceptions, and goals of different individuals as those in institutional power tried to regulate others into particular ways of life, and others insisted that important motives were being lost if they wrote as they were directed, as in the case of the social work agency. Yet, in many of the sites the generic shaping of the communal activity and way of life went uncontested as individuals wanted to become creative architects, competent lawyers, recipients of contracts, contributors to a well-analyzed monetary policy, or just students with good grades.

Each of these settings offered different pathways of explicit and implicit instruction, mentoring, disciplining, accountability, and evaluation. In schools, no matter what the subject area, the socialization into practice predictably appeared as pedagogy directed toward student performance of known practice, for which students were held accountable—what the authors here have called *facilitated performance*. Although workplace internship experiences carried important elements of learning, these still became framed as facilitated performance when returned to the classroom. In the workplace, the focus was on the work task at hand, rather than the overt instruction and evaluation of the learner; the learning was in the doing and the accountability was in the accomplishment of the work; insofar as there was overt training, it was built around the learner's actual participation in the work, either through what the authors call *attenuated authentic performance* (where mentors limit, focus, advise, and themselves remain responsible for the tasks of the novices) or through legitimate peripheral participation (Lave and Wegner's term here used to indicate the novice's actual responsibility and accountability for limited tasks performed).

In each of the classroom and workplace sites, the writing was integrated with relevant practices, modes of expression, and material realities, but most of the classrooms were so fully devoted to textual practices that the world of student production was tightly framed by the written and spoken texts that made up the course. The most notable exception was in architecture, where the writing was integrated with, and subordinated to, visual and material design; internship courses also provided some contact with the social, material, and representational complexity of the workplace, although students' papers remained the central form of evaluation and responsibility. In the workplace, however, the writing was integrated with many forms of experience and representation in the course of the work—relationship with and responsibility toward clients and the dramatic realities of courtroom proceedings; economic data and the actual economic well-being of a nation; and, again most strikingly, in architecture, the visual design and material construction. These issues are made most explicit in the chapters on architectural education and practice, but they are an undercurrent throughout the book.

In coming to understand the writing process and writing learning in these various sites, the authors have developed and refined activity theory as a tool of analyses. The theoretical discussions in this book are clear and illuminating, and lead to a widely applicable and easily intelligible way of approaching writing in any school or workplace setting.

The ultimate effect of the theoretical clarity evolved through the long conversation of the authors, however, is the surprising illumination of the details of how writing works in each of these settings and the kinds of demands and opportunities each presents for the developing writer. The theoretically illuminated case studies reveal the rich and multiple contours of writing within each situation and thereby help us to see similar dynamics in other situations. The authors have used theory to help them figure out what they have seen and thereby have given us sharper theoretical lenses to see what is occurring in other places. That is among the best uses of theory.

PREFACE

It is largely in academic settings that writing calls attention to itself and, more often than not, is regarded in isolation from the larger social and communicative action to which it is so intrinsically bound. On the other hand, in non-academic workplace settings, writing is seldom regarded (when it is regarded at all) as apart from the goals, occasions, and contexts that engender writing. In these settings, writing is a means, a tool in accomplishing larger goals, which may involve actions other than writing and other participants who function in a variety of roles. It is just this kind of disjunction between academic and workplace settings that occasions the study from which this book derives.

This 7-year collaboration between researchers at Carleton University, Ottawa, and McGill University, Montreal, involves several different academic and workplace settings. It draws on a wide variety of theoretical approaches to make sense of what was observed and recorded in these locales and the written material and interview data that emerged. Begun largely with the intention of understanding the relationships between writing in academic and workplace settings, the research has evolved to examining writing as it is embedded in both kinds of settings—settings where social relationships, available tools, historical, cultural, temporal and physical location are all implicated in complex and intricate ways in the decisions people make as writers. Each setting in its uniqueness makes salient different aspects of writers and writing with complex and probably unsettling implications for writing theory and the teaching of writing.

ACKNOWLEDGMENTS

This long and multifaceted study has relied on the generous assistance of several people and agencies. We are deeply indebted to the Social Sciences and Humanities Research Council of Canada for funding the research that provides the material for this book. We also wish to thank the several partners in our research, benefactors who remain anonymous, who afforded us the time of their employees, access to records, and the space to carry out our inquiries: the educational institutions, teachers and students, governmental and nongovernmental organizations, the commercial and professional firms and their employees. We hope these results justify, to some degree, the patience, trust, and collaboration they so freely gave us. We are especially grateful to the people who helped collect, assemble, and analyze the considerable data for this study: Christine Adam, Dawn Allen, Natasha Artemeva, Jane Ledwell-Brown, Stephen Fai, Jennifer Fraser, Danica Robertson, Tariq Sami, Graham Smart, and Scott Weir. We thank particularly Carole Kleivstul, Avigail Ram, and Michael Beddall for their secretarial help. Much of this work was presented at several professional meetings and university seminars, where colleagues and students asked us the questions and provided the suggestions that have helped shape this book. Alas, there are far too many such occasions to list here. Finally, this book has profited considerably from the perceptive readings of both Charles Bazerman and David Russell; to them our sincere appreciation and warmest thanks.

—Patrick Dias
McGill University, Montreal

—Aviva Freedman
Carleton University, Ottawa

—Peter Medway
Carleton University, Ottawa

—Anthony Paré
McGill University, Montreal

INTRODUCTION

I

1

INTRODUCTION: RESEARCHING WRITING AT SCHOOL AND AT WORK

When we began the research from which this book derives, our major question was about the relationships between writing in school and writing in the workplace. Our answer to that question, and the conclusion we reach in this book, is summed up by our title: school and work are worlds apart. That conclusion, simple as it looks, was not easily come by, since it is contrary to all appearances. The book can be seen in one light as a documentation of the evidence and theoretical perspectives that led to our growing realization of this apartness and its consequences for the teaching and practice of writing. But the title of this book does double duty; for it is through our perception of writing as acting that we are able to justify our account of difference. Because writing is acting, it is highly contextualized, and it is the character of this contextualization that turns out to be the burden of this book.

Our question about the relationships between writing at work and at school arose from some dissatisfaction with the performance of universities in preparing their graduates for the changed writing demands of professional workplaces. Thus, one of our concerns is pedagogical, to do with evaluating and, if necessary, addressing the ways that universities prepare writers. There is also a disciplinary history, within writing research, that gives rise to a second set of questions, not pedagogical but theoretical, that we address both in the research and in the book. In fact, the pedagogical and the theoretical concerns are closely linked, reflecting the fact, as we explain below, that writing research grew fairly recently out of issues related to the teaching of writing.

Both our pedagogical and our theoretical interests are informed by one major question: What are the relationships between writing as it is elicited in the university and writing as it is generated in the workplace? A particular stress we give to that question is: how and to what extent can we speak of writing in school settings as preparation for writing at work? Or, as writers, what adjustments, if any, must university graduates make when they move into the workforce? This is not to imply that we regard all or even most university education as preparation for the workplace. We must also make it clear that the question we are asking is not about the effectiveness of courses concerned specifically with the teaching of writing; rather, our question is about all practices related to writing in university courses, about how writing is defined and valued by such practices, about how these practices relate to writing practices in the workplace, and about the place and value accorded writing in the workplace. We will be more specific below about the theoretical issues, and about what relevance they might have to those who are not researchers into or teachers of writing.

We bring to our study a body of understandings about writing developed in the fields of linguistics, rhetoric, cognitive, social and cultural psychology, composition studies, and education. We will say more below, in this chapter and the next, about the nature of those understandings, but let us first characterize them briefly so that readers have some idea of the sort of account they may expect from us. The accounts that we find persuasive acknowledge that writing is not a single clearly definable skill acquired once and for all; that writing is shaped fundamentally by its sociocultural context; that writing is often more than transcription or communication, and that, certainly in school, writing functions as a way of learning and knowing (and not just a way of demonstrating learning and knowing); that the functions of writing vary widely—from making discoveries to imparting knowledge, from persuading to asserting status, from establishing credibility to negotiating power; that there is considerable variation in strategy—by individual and by task or context; that, in some settings, composing is an intensely collaborative activity, involving intricate layers of responding and revising, each with its own complex political and social dimensions. Writing, in other words, is a very complex act; to understand what is being accomplished in writing in any social setting requires lengthy in-depth observation and analysis. Without such understanding, it is impossible to make any useful or meaningful suggestions (which we hope to do within the more pedagogically oriented aspect of our purpose) with respect to easing the transition between one social context and another.

WHERE OUR PERSPECTIVE COMES FROM: A BRIEF HISTORY OF RESEARCH ON WRITING

Let us now explain that perspective more fully, locating it in its historical context. The story of writing research, at least in North America, is that it arose in the context of problems encountered in the teaching of writing and sub-sequently developed into a more general study that embraced manifestations of writing outside as well as inside education. We hope our account will help readers who are not in the community of those who study and teach writing understand how we locate ourselves in that story and the contexts of those issues that are central in our inquiry.

Most academics, we believe, are used to thinking of writing as a regular everyday activity that occupies both students and teachers. It is just as pervasive an activity in school as it is in the world outside school, and similarly treated as transparent; that is, it is regarded less as an activity in itself and more as a means, a seemingly inert tool *through* which activities are carried out. Students write to take notes from lectures and the books they read, to reflect, to record information, to carry out their research, and to record and organize their findings for presentation to professors and in many cases their peers, to demonstrate their learning in tests and examinations —in short, they write in order to learn and to demonstrate that learning. Students may also write otherwise: they may keep personal diaries, logs, and journals; write poetry, fiction, and plays; correspond formally and informally, including letters to newspapers and complaints to landlords; and they have increasingly taken to writing on the Internet. When we then contrast writing in school with writing at work, it appears at first glance that although purposes and modes might differ, at heart, to borrow from Gertrude Stein, writing is writing is writing; so that the passage from writing in the university to writing at work ought to be unproblematic.

But, as a perennial chorus of complaints from the business world (and some assenting voices from in the university as well) attests, such is not the case. The writing abilities of students graduating from universities are increasingly in question when they move into the workplace. For many reasons, which this study investigates, writing practices in the university do not translate into effective writing within the work setting (Bataille, 1982; Rush & Evers, 1986). A large number of people believe that they learned to write on the job rather than in school or university (Anderson, 1985; Brown, 1988; Rush & Evers, 1991). Universities, it appears, have failed to prepare their students to write at work. From such a point of view, writing, far from being regarded as transparent, becomes opaque, draws attention to itself as a tool and medium that does not work well or is improperly employed by its users. So we are forced to ask, wearing our pedagogical hats: In what ways is writing in university preparation for writing at work? What deficiencies, if any, need to be made up in such preparation? Can universities, indeed, by whatever means prepare students to write at work, and is that a realistic expectation? Recent developments in the teaching of and research into writing have in part been occasioned by such anxieties.

School Writing Practices

Early responses to such questions, at least in North America, were focused on changing practices in the university, and those changes were concentrated largely in 1st-year composition courses, where it seems the task of teaching students to write for academic purposes was concentrated. Until the late 1960s, teaching writing in university was largely a matter of introducing students to rhetorical structures and models and urging imitation. Some courses stressed forms of argumentation and techniques liberally illustrated with examples from contemporary essayists. In fact, the goal of writing in such writing courses was the production of essays or "themes" on topics usually based on personal experience with an emphasis on presenting an insightful and coherent argument, and generally requiring little or no investigation. Handbooks of style, grammar, and usage enforced rules and conventions considered desirable and seemingly unchanging. As Faigley (1992) puts it, given such tasks, both "the writer and potential readers are removed from any specific setting and are represented as living outside of history and having no investment in particular issues" (p. 15). Such tasks, moreover, define writing as primarily an academic enterprise, without regard to the traditions of writing in the workplace and in other nonacademic settings.

But with rapid university expansion in the early 1970s and changes in the socioeconomic makeup of the population that traditionally gained university entrance, particularly in universities that had introduced open admissions policies as a way of righting past discriminatory practices, traditional approaches to teaching writing were increasingly in question (Berlin, 1987; Russell, 1991; Shaughnessy, 1977).

Supported by research that focused on understanding the processes involved in writing rather than studying finished products as exemplars (Britton, Burgess, Martin, McLeod, & Rosen, 1975; Emig, 1971; Flower, 1977; Flower & Hayes, 1981; Sommers, 1980), writing pedagogy began to attend to students' writing processes; for instance, what enables and what inhibits invention, or how successful writers anticipate the needs and concerns of readers as they write. Writing was taught as a process involving exploration, drafting, and revision, a process involving multiple drafts with opportunities for feedback from peers and teacher. Teachers became empathetic and supportive readers rather than expert correctors and assessors. Topics were self-initiated rather than imposed, classrooms became workshops, writing moved toward publication through a process of being read and revised with the help of encouraging peer editors (Graves, 1984; Murray, 1980).

The idea of writing as discovery paralleled a renewed interest in the traditional notion of *invention* as one of the five arts in rhetorical discourse (Freedman & Pringle, 1979; LeFevre, 1987). Writing is not simply communication or translation of something already extant in the world or in the mind. The composing process itself is a way of making meaning. This is a key thread in the argument for a view of writing as *epistemic* or knowledge-making, and an underlying justification, as we point out below, for the promotion of "writing across the curriculum."

The teaching of writing as entrusted to the 1st-year composition program, housed largely in English departments, was regarded largely as a service industry, intended to train competent writers for other courses, familiarizing them with academic practices and conventions. In some programs, English departments collaborated with engineering and business schools to design and teach specialized courses in technical and business writing respectively; in some other cases, engineering and business schools developed their own writing programs. By and large, such courses, seen as foundational, were offered at the 1st-year level; an unstated assumption was that once taught, writing need not be a matter for concern and inquiry at upper levels.

A boost to making writing in schools more visible as a medium and less transparent was provided by Britton (et al., 1975) and his colleagues at the London Institute of Education in the 1970s, who argued the close link between writing and learning. Their Language across the Curriculum movement (more commonly adopted in North America as Writing across the Curriculum or WAC) provided a rationale for instituting writing-intensive courses in the disciplines as opposed to teaching writing *per se* as a discipline-neutral skill within English departments. Where they were promoted, WAC programs were also instrumental in helping teachers in all departments accept some degree of responsibility for the literacy of their students.

WAC movements also instigated investigations of writing within specialist disciplines, toward identifying those discipline-specific features that could then be taught to students in those disciplines. However, there was a growing realization, exemplified especially in the work of Bazerman (1979; 1988), that such features ought not to be regarded as isolated conventions but as part of a larger context of disciplinary activity, conditioned by historical, social, and psychological factors. As Bazerman (1988) put it, one "could not understand what constituted an appropriate text in any discipline without considering the social and intellectual activity which the text was part of" (p. 4). Such a recognition is a key instance of the widening perspectives emerging in the teaching of writing. Instead of domesticating workplace texts for academic purposes, some writing theorists were redefining writing as situated practice, a point to which we return often in this book.

A related development in the teaching of writing is linked to a newer understanding of the role of readers. From the 1930s to the 1960s, New Criticism occupied a dominant position in North American literary criticism and exerted a strong influence on how literature was taught in the university. New Criticism or the formalist approach accorded the literary text the status of an autonomous object, fixed and unchanging, regardless of the reader and the situation in which it was being read. Meaning, it was assumed, was located entirely in the text. The counterpart of such a position in the teaching of writing would be that all texts should aspire to a condition of being stable, conventional, self-contained, and separable from a consideration of the writer's intentions and situation. Increasingly over the 1970s, such New Critical positions were displaced by the notion of reading as an event in time, of meaning as continually recreated in each act of reading and subject, therefore, to the knowledge and intentions the reader brings to the text (Rosenblatt, 1978; Suleiman & Crossman, 1980; Tompkins, 1980). And in the teaching of writing, with the increasing attention to process and the several variables that figure in that process, such as the writer's situation and intentions and the role of readers, formal and structural features of written products are no longer the primary determinants of how writing should be taught. Moreover, such formal and structural features are seen not as intrinsically fixed and immutable, rather they emerge and become salient in recurring rhetorical situations that justify their usefulness, and continue to evolve or decline in use. It follows that the knowledge necessary to produce effective texts within a setting is not a static entity but a fluid set of variables continually revised in the flux of textual and contextual demands.

As studies of nonacademic writing proliferate, it is possible to see the extent to which writers rely on situation-specific knowledge in the preparation of texts. This "local knowledge" (Geertz, 1983) concerns all aspects of the writing situation, from disciplinary and institutional regulations governing the form and substance of texts to relationships among writers and readers. Such a view of writing has been confirmed in the growing consideration of genre theory in theorizing about writing (Bazerman, 1988; Bazerman & Paradis, 1991b; Berkenkotter & Huckin, 1995; Cope & Kalantzis, 1993; Freedman & Medway,

1994a, 1994b; Swales, 1990). This expansion of studies of writing to nonacademic contexts has been accompanied by the gradual abandonment of the notion of writing as the solitary act of the autonomous individual. A major development over the last decade in writing theory and research is the notion of writing as both discipline specific and socially defined (Bazerman, 1988; Freedman, 1987; Herrington, 1985; Myers, 1985, 1989; Paré, 1991a, Selzer, 1983; Smart, 1989; Winsor, 1989). Studies have variously demonstrated the strong link between successful writers at work and their knowledge of readers and situations (Odell & Goswami, 1982; Spilka, 1990), explored the enculturation of new employees (Hebden, 1986), and studied the writer's transition from an academic to a work setting (MacKinnon, 1993).

What this research has in common is an attention to the settings in which writing is produced, a concern central to an emerging social theory of writing, a theory that explains written communication by reference to its social contexts: the procedures, regulations, relationships, and activities that influence (and, in turn, are influenced by) the production of texts (Berlin, 1987; Clark, 1990; Faigley, 1986; LeFevre, 1987; Rafoth & Rubin, 1989). This perspective challenges many of the assumptions of contemporary writing theory and pedagogy. Perhaps one of the most important understandings to emerge from recent studies is the degree to which workplace writing is a collaborative or social activity (Ede & Lunsford, 1990; Odell & Goswami, 1985; Reither & Vipond, 1989). Many individuals write as members of a group, such as a discipline, organization, or institution; a full understanding of writers' processes and products cannot occur without close reference to their place and role in their particular contexts. Many texts have multiple readers, all of whom have different reasons for reading, and each of whom may pay heed to different parts of the text. Such texts must often stay within strict guidelines (stylistic, legal, procedural) and the consequences of ignoring those rules can be severe. Case studies of writing contexts describe situations of complex interaction: writers often work with others in the preparation of texts within a wide variety of co-authoring arrangements; scheduled revision cycles are common (Ede & Lunsford, 1990; Paradis, Dobrin, & Miller, 1985; Smart, 1993). At the same time we need to be aware that workplaces can be places of contestation and disagreement, where writing practices must eventually cooperate with institutional interests and sometimes compromise socially responsible goals (Fairclough, 1992; Herndl, 1993; McCarthy & Gerring, 1994).

To sum up: Writing is a complex act, integrally related to learning and knowing, and performs a variety of functions. It is not a discrete clearly definable skill learned once and for all; moreover, both in school and at work, writing is seldom the product of isolated individuals but rather and seldom obviously, the outcome of continuing collaboration, of interactions that involve other people and other texts. Writing practices are closely linked to their sociocultural contexts, and writing strategies vary with individual and situation.

THE STUDY

As stated earlier, the goal of the study is to develop a more complete and more refined picture than currently exists of the relationship between the writing elicited at university and writing generated in the workplace. We hope that the value of this picture will be both practical and theoretical. On the one hand we hope to provide a basis for more effective planning for the formation and development of writers in both domains—a pedagogical aspiration. On the other hand, we hope to draw the various threads of our research into an account that confronts some key questions about writing as communicative means, as sociocultural practice, and as a means of learning and definition.

The emerging social perspective on writing made it clear that academic and workplace writing must be considered in context, within the complex political and social dimensions that influence and define writing practices and expectations. Thus it was imperative that we examine *in situ* the writing elicited currently in university and the writing typically engaged in at the workplace, and plan for lengthy in-depth observation and analysis.

We selected four matching university and professional settings: public administration courses and Federal government institutions, management courses and corresponding work settings, architecture courses and a firm of architects, social work courses and social work agencies. These were disciplines that were considered to be strong in the two universities we chose to work in, and appeared to offer a range of writing practices. Each discipline and its cognate work sites call for distinctive genres of writing, so that there is little or no overlapping in the kinds of texts we examine. Our choice of architecture has an extra justification. Although writing is a major means of communication and documentation in the fields of social work, management, and public administration, it is ancillary to graphical representation in architecture. Thus, academic and workplace architecture settings allow us to examine how writing articulates with graphical communication to produce nonverbal artifacts. These settings also provide a useful counter to the logocentric bias that may still direct our thinking about writing despite the increasing use of multimedia presentations and the fact that so much of what we read is interspersed with visual images.

The means by which we would answer our question about the relationship between the writing practices in the two domains was obviously to compare the two. Since this entailed constructing descriptions of each, our separate case studies in workplaces and in universities could not be conducted as free-standing projects solely in the light of the issues that presented themselves in the specific sites. Instead, to ensure comparability, they needed to be framed around a common set of procedural goals and questions, though we also had specific questions that applied only to one domain or other. In fact a large measure of commonality across the studies in fact arises from the underlying theoretical frame in which the whole of the research was conceived.

The aim in each setting was to produce an account that addressed a number of key issues: the kinds of writing produced; how writing tasks originate; how writing is generated and proceeds; the place writing occupies in that setting (salience, frequency, time allotted to it); the relationship between written and spoken transactions; constraints on writing; the place and effect of deadlines and document guidelines; the expectations of readers; how writing is responded to and evaluated; the ways of beginning writers and experienced writers; acquiring the language of the field; writing in collaboration.

There were two questions that emerged and became central as our study proceeded, questions that helped us frame the description of practices at the different sites. The first was, what functions did writing perform: social and cultural on the one hand (for instance, induction into the ways of thinking and language practices of a disciplinary or professional community), and epistemic on the other (that is, supporting thinking, planning, knowing, and learning). The second was, how do sociocultural settings shape writing practices? In other words, how is writing defined by the values and practices that prevail in university settings and in the workplace?

In the university settings, additional domain-specific objectives were to compare writing in different disciplines, to discover how students learn to do what it is that they are expected to do in each course (how much explicit teaching there is, what use is made of models, what other resources students draw on). And we were interested in what we call the climate for writing in the particular programs of study.

Issues that related more specifically to workplaces included the range of readerships for each individual document; the place of writing in maneuvering within the political hierarchies, and the effect of hierarchy on the composing processes and products; the nature of collaboration in composing; and the extrainstitutional contextual and disciplinary factors that shape the writing.

By answering such questions, we hoped to identify commonalities and differences: distinguishing between university and workplace writing, on the one hand, and among the disciplines and professions, on the other. We approached the study with certain expectations, derived from the research literature referred to above and from our own earlier work. We were confident that the relationships would be far more complex and subtle than conventionally conceived. Certainly, workplace writing cannot fail to be radically different in some ways from university writing given the significant difference in its social context: for example, university students typically write solo to audiences of one, who quite likely know more than the writer about the subject, who, nevertheless, by convention are committed to reading the entire text (whatever its length) within specified time frames, and who value the writing insofar as it reveals and enacts the students' learning. In the workplace, writers may prepare documents collaboratively, for complex and varied audiences, who often know considerably less than the writers about that subject, who will read only what is useful to them, and who will ideally use the document themselves for a variety of political and communicative purposes. All these factors, and many more, are endemic to the institutional situations and necessarily affect the form and the process of writing in fundamental ways. On the other hand, certain habits of mind, certain ways of marshaling data or constructing arguments (i.e., aspects of the writing that are more fundamental to its role in creating and transmitting knowledge and less immediately apparent from the surface of the texts) may very well be transferred from university to workplace and vice-versa—according to the discipline.

Research Activities

Given the scope and objectives of this research program (which began in 1992), we decided to use a multiple-case study approach to study writers and writing in both academic and workplace settings. The case study approach was necessary in order to ensure that participants' perspectives were an integral part of the data. Our major operational concern was to derive rich and contextualized records of communicative transactions (primarily written, but in many cases, oral, and especially with architecture, graphical). To that end, and depending on the setting, our data-gathering activities included the following.

Data Gathering

1. *Inventorying the genres in each domain*: Constructing catalogues of text-types in the different workplace and academic settings, and classifying the

text-types according to a) function or purpose, b) readership, c) nature of task, d) rhetorical form.

2. *Document tracking*: In each setting and for each discipline, the history of specific typical texts was traced from the first specification of the task to the text's completion and dissemination (its composition, dissemination, and various readerships; how the writing originated, what works or people were consulted, what kind of collaboration or feedback took place and when, who were the interim and final readers, etc.).

3. *Conducting reading protocols of designated readers*: Supervisors in the workplace or instructors responded to texts—articulating aloud (into a taperecorder) their immediate responses to the written piece (Dias, 1987; Ericsson & Simon, 1985; Flower, Hayes, & Swarts, 1980; Ledwell-Brown, 1993; Smart, 1989; Waern, 1979). This procedure reveals similarities and differences in expectations and tacit criteria for writing in different settings.

4. *Ethnographic observation of writers involved in tasks of composing*—from first assignment to final completion of task. We asked students and professionals to keep logs of all activities related to writing that were conducted in private and save all notes and drafts; we observed group work and conducted regular interviews with writers concerning their goals, strategies, and decisions. Recording techniques comprised audio taping, video recording, and field notes.

5. *Interviews*: These occurred in relation to all of the activities described above. Early interviews helped identify participants for more intensive study. Most interviews were open-ended and nondirective (Mishler, 1986).

6. *Participant validation*: Selected participants were asked to review and confirm the case-study descriptions of their settings.

The above represents something of the range of our inquiry processes. Whereas the research was unified by a common theoretical approach and shared questions (see below), our data gathering had to be responsive to the particularities of the contexts we encountered, which varied strikingly. Our data is not all of a piece: there are similarities in observations that span the various sites and disciplines; there are significant differences regarding writing practices that are directly attributable to the specific discipline of study or area of work.

Data Analyses

These included textual analyses of the writing collected (syntactic, rhetorical, and conceptual); that is, analyses aimed at defining the modes of argumentation (Toulmin, 1958; Toulmin, Reike, & Janik, 1979) and of categorizing experience; analyses of oral discourse surrounding production of texts using categories based on systemic linguistics (Halliday, 1985); and sociolinguistic analyses of production and reception of texts, framed within the contexts within which the acts of speaking, reading, and writing occurred, drawing on methods of text analysis developed by Brandt (1992), Huckin (1992), and MacDonald (1992).

More recently we have been looking particularly at how novices are initiated into workplace settings and at transitional programs, such as internships, within university programs. In the first case, all pieces of writing done by selected workplace novices over a period of months were collected, and regular interviews conducted before, during, and after the composing of a number of tasks. This analysis enabled us to pinpoint gaps in performance and expectation, common misconceptions, and ad hoc intervention strategies on the part of supervisors that appeared to be successful, as well as common false starts and blind alleys in the trial-and-error attempts of unguided novice writers.

The transitional programs we looked at were of various kinds. Thus, in one 4th-year business course, students were assigned to real worksites and asked to do a real writing project for the enterprise. Social work students spent approximately 700 hours in field placements. Similarly, students in a Masters of Public Administration program were placed as full-time interns (for one or two semesters) in a variety of governmental settings. Observation of the students, and discussions with the instructor, the students, and their employers enabled us to determine the success of the programs as well as the areas that need strengthening.

The team met regularly to agree on the instruments, questions, and approaches to analysis. Members shared logs and field notes, put forward and refined hypotheses, considered emerging data in the light of those hypotheses, and reviewed research strategies. What we report in this book arises from the comparisons we have been making among the data we have obtained from the various sites. In fact, writing this book together has been very much a continuation of the collaborative exchange that has characterized our research process throughout.

Hopeful Outcomes From the Research

Through the understanding that the research is yielding about the relationship between academic and professional writing, those involved with professional education and development in both spheres will, we hope, be better able to develop appropriate programs to help facilitate the transition between the two environments. In the university, instructors who administer internship programs, for example, will be better able to design, sequence, and facilitate the kind of writing normally expected in the workplace. Similarly, personnel officers dedicated to training in the workplace, will be better able with such knowledge to design relevant and helpful programs. Finally, a variety of joint endeavors are possible, in which this new knowledge can be used as a basis for the collaborative development of new co-operative programs. This is not to imply that all writing in the university, even within professional programs, has to justify its place by the contribution it makes to the ability to write at work; certain needs are specific to each domain, so that the practices that address them are not appropriately or usefully transferred to the other.

THE RESEARCH AND THE BOOK

Those are our practical hopes for bringing help to writers and to those who depend on the skills of writers. At the same time, as we have made clear, we locate ourselves in a research tradition and wish to contribute to it. This book, however, is not addressed to teachers and writing researchers alone. To our other readers we want to suggest that the interest of our work is not limited to its practical implications for improving the state of affairs associated with writing skills. We believe that our findings throw light not only on the nature of writing but also on the nature of disciplines and professions; to understand what writing does in either context is to understand a great deal about how the various enterprises keep themselves on track, secure the allegiances of newcomers, and maintain power relations in and outside their boundaries.

In the chapters that follow we attempt to answer the following general questions. We see answering these as a potential contribution to both theory and practice.

- How do university writing practices relate to writing in the workplace?
- In what sense and to what extent is writing in university a preparation for writing in the workplace?

At the same time we hope to throw light on a number of areas of practical concern, by indicating areas of potential intervention to provide for more effective development of the writing potential of students and professionals. The following sorts of question relating respectively to university and workplace arise from that aspiration:

- What changes need to be made in university teaching practices in order to exploit more fully the potential of writing as a tool for learning, and to prepare students to enter more easily into workplace writing practices? Can universities prepare students to write for work?
- What workplace practices inhibit the full development and use of writing for productive work? What practices support the use of writing to promote workplace goals?

We begin in the following chapter by introducing the theoretical principles that have guided our inquiry and define the terms that recur frequently in our discussion. That chapter ought to help readers identify and track the key strands of our argument through the following chapters. Those chapters are arranged in three parts: discussions of university writing and related practices, workplace writing and how it differs from writing in university, and writing in transitional programs between university and workplace. A concluding chapter considers the understandings that have emerged in this study and their meaning for writing practices in the university and the workplace, as well as the questions they raise for further research.

2

SITUATING WRITING

In this chapter we describe briefly theories that we have studied and drawn on in different ways throughout the book. We said earlier that our perspective on writing was a social one and need to explain what we mean by that. That writing is social is not news. Of course it is used for social communication and learned from other people. But we have a stronger, less commonsensical sense of social in mind, one that we can perhaps indicate with the term *situated*.

WRITING AS SITUATED ACTIVITY

Again, this at first looks like a common sense notion. We maintain that writing does not occur in a social or institutional vacuum, that the context in which any given writing occurs (with all its particularities) is integrally part of that act of writing. We are all familiar with experiences that confirm this, and know how situations and particular relationships can constrain or facilitate inventiveness. Where the writer is, when he or she is writing, and who he or she is writing to or for, may precipitate inarticulateness or give rise to apparently serendipitous or inspired formulations. Looking at our own past writings we realize how some of the freshest and most powerful parts of our texts are the product of specific situations and exigencies.

Along with other writing researchers of the last 10 or 15 years we want to push that notion beyond its everyday consensual application, and to claim that the contexts of writing not only influence it (facilitating it or frustrating it or nudging it in a particular direction) but are integral to it. The context is not simply the contingent circumstances within which we happen to switch on the writing motor. Writing is not a module that we bring along and plug into any situation we find ourselves in. Rather, the context constitutes the situation that defines the activity of writing; to write *is* to address the situation by means of textual production. Just as there is no such thing as just writing, only writing *something*, so all writing is a response to, and assumes as starting point, a situation. Or, rather, an interpretation of a situation, because what determines the writing is less the objective state of affairs than the writer's understanding of it. Situation in this sense has, clearly, to be defined quite broadly and does not simply or necessarily refer to the immediate social context; the situation that is psychologically most real to some writers might be that of membership of a community of poets stretching back hundreds of years (though they will inevitably be influenced too, consciously or not, by aspects of their contemporary world).

Situation is a psychological reality, but in this book we will be stressing social reality, situation as a shared, communally available, culturally defined reality. Our view of the situatedness (alternatively, embeddedness) of writing is well caught by Lave's (1991) account of "situated social practice:"

> This theoretical view emphasizes the relational interdependency of agent and world, activity, meaning, cognition, learning, and knowing. It emphasizes the inherently socially negotiated quality of meaning and the interested, concerned character of the thought and action of persons engaged in activity.... [T]his view also claims that learning, thinking, and knowing are relations among people engaged in activity *in, with, and arising from the socially and culturally structured world.* (p. 67, emphasis in original)

It is because writing is so embedded in situations that we normally experience it as transparent (in the sense that it is not the focus or point of our attention). Writing dissolves into the action, more or less disappearing as anything separately identifiable—there is only the attending to the tone, avoiding touchy subjects, finding an appropriate phrase, and so on.

GENRE STUDIES

To see writing as situated in the way we have indicated is to take a rhetorical view. Rhetoric in the classical sense is the art of using language to persuade; more generally, to act on a situation by acting on people by means of words. In modern rhetorical theory what a situation presents to us that elicits a verbal response is an exigence (Bitzer, 1968).

The most developed and comprehensive rhetorical theory to address writing in recent times goes by the misleadingly limiting name of genre studies. This approach is central to our own work; we will return to it repeatedly, and will discuss specific aspects in more depth in chapter 3. The term is limiting because the theory is not just an account of genres but is also, more generally, a situated account of writing *per se*. As we say below, it ties the textual to the social, sees texts as action and texts as in dialogue with each other; none of those strengths relate specifically to explaining genres. In attempting to account for genre, theorists have developed a position that is capable of much more. Genre in this view has two aspects: social action and textual regularity. In accounting for the first of these we have potentially dealt with most texts, and not only those that we would regard as instantiations of a genre.[1]

We will now proceed to give an account of genre studies that will give the background needed for reading this book and for understanding the increasingly frequent references to genre that are cropping up in quite diverse places. We will then go on to describe some other theories and theoretical ideas, but must make clear that their status is rather different. Because of its comprehensively rhetorical character, as we have just indicated, genre studies constitutes the main framework of our discussion (even when we are not talking about genres). The other ideas will be used by way of elaboration and extension; thus, for example, concepts of *situated learning* will help us to understand how genres are *learned*.

In our discussion of genre studies, then, consideration of the textual regularities (similarities or family resemblances) that are the most obvious feature of genres will get us quickly into the other aspect of writing, writing as *action*, which in turn will lead us to the crucial notion of *social motive*.

Genre studies offers a way of dealing at the same time with textual and contextual regularities, repeated actions, both across texts and across "the composing practices involved in creating these texts, the reading practices used to interpret them, and the social roles performed by writers and readers" (Paré & Smart, 1994, p. 147).

Most readers will recall the more familiar meaning of *genre*, as referring to generally unchanging regularities in conventions of form and content, usually with reference to literary works, allowing readers to identify, for example, classes of work such as poetry, fiction, and drama, and within such classes, sub-categories such as the ballad or sonnet, romance or detective fiction, and tragedy, comedy, or absurdist theatre. Such classification of texts has extended as well to prescriptive classification in school writing and thus the familiar categories of exposition, description, argumentation, and narration, with sub-categories such as the book report, the business letter, and the lab report. In the workplace we have such familiar genres as the memo, the progress report, minutes of meetings, and the annual report. The definite article that designates these genres is telling in that it seems to prescribe an unchanging, fixed, and authorized rubric, with the strong implication that adherence to form is tied in with effective writing. Because "they treat socially constructed categories as

---

[1]This is a tricky matter. In the strong view of genre as set out by Miller (1994) in her original account, genre is a level of the system of language discourse, so that an utterance can no more avoid making genre choices than it can avoid mood choices at the level of grammar. For our purposes in this book we fortunately do not need to take a position on this.

stable natural facts [,]" such formalist and essentialist approaches to understanding genre, according to Bazerman (1988, p. 7), provide inadequate accounts of the semiotic reality.[2]

The conception of genre we work from acknowledges regularities in textual
form and substance as the more obvious features of genre, but goes on to
examine the underlying, non-textual regularities that produce these regularities
in texts. These underlying regularities have to do with typical ways in which
writers engage rhetorically with recurring situations. In her seminal article,
"Genre as Social Action," Miller (1994) lays out much of the theoretical
groundwork underlying current reconceptions of genre. Genres, she explains,
are typified rhetorical responses to situations that are socially interpreted or
constructed as recurrent or similar; genres are thus social actions. As in Burke
(1950), the notion of *action* (with discourse seen as symbolic action) is central
for Miller, as are the notions of *situation* and *motive*: "human action, whether
symbolic or otherwise, is interpretable only against a context of situation and
through the attributing of motives" (Miller, 1994, p. 24). From Bitzer, Miller
borrows the term *exigence*, but radically reinterprets it to refer not to an
objective external state of affairs but to a "form of social knowledge—a mutual
construing of objects, events, interests, and purposes that not only links them
but also makes them what they are: an objectified social need" (p. 30).
Exigences for Miller are what everyone agrees are exigences. There are social
categories of exigence, and if someone interprets my text as a response to one
of these, then they will find my text rational and intelligible. (Conversely, if I
write something that does not identifiably address a recognized type of exigence, then I will fail to communicate; exigence is one way in which *situation*
inserts itself into the essence of writing and is not just circumstance—which is
why we insist on the strong sense in which writing is a social activity.)

Crucial terms in Miller's discussion are situation and social motive. The
latter needs some explaining, since motive is something we think of as pertain-
ing exclusively to individual psychology. Social motive means not a motive
about the social or a motive shared by the group but a motive that is socially
recognized and allowed for. It is the sort of motive that the culture acknowledges you may have and allows you to have, and the culture's arrangements,
such as genres, are means of legitimately acting on these motives. An example:
having had a claim for a veteran's pension denied, we perceive it is now the

---

[2]We briefly discuss a semiotic view of communication toward the end of the chapter. The
central point is that meanings are not built into signs (which may be anything from individual
letters of the alphabet to words to texts to genres) but are brought to them from repertoires of
cultural knowledge (and individual idiosyncratic association) by writers and readers. Thus,
meanings are therefore inherently unstable.

moment to write a letter of complaint, institute a lawsuit, or petition our representative in Parliament or Congress. Social motive "is clearly not the same as the rhetor's intention, for that can be ill-formed, dissembling, or at odds with what the situation conventionally supports" (Miller, 1994, p. 31). This distinction is equally important for understanding the difference between the actual players in a scene and the social roles they must inhabit to perform appropriately. Genres ascribe to those involved distinct personae and social roles so that, depending on the recurring situation and genre, Jane Doe writes as professor, consultant, mother, or irate customer.

Social motives, and the genres that provide for their enactment, are thus both enabling and constraining, depending on how closely they map onto our individual motives. In Miller's (1994) words, "what we learn when we learn a genre is not just a pattern of forms or even a method of achieving our own ends. We learn, more importantly, what ends we may have" (p. 38). An implication of her account is that socialization into a "community of practice" (see below) is "learn[ing] to adopt social motives as ways of satisfying private intentions through rhetorical action" (p. 36). If what we want above all is to *belong* to a particular group but do not know what specific things we ought to do in order to act as members, the genres of the group will tell us both what to want to do as member and how, rhetorically, to achieve it. We can be easily persuaded that we thus submit ourselves to the cultural imperatives of the group or the system, so that private intentions may be constantly frustrated by the available and required genres, and writers within an occupational culture may experience its genres as straitjackets. Later, in chapter 6, we report on hospital social workers, some of whom were unhappy with aspects of the required genre for recording cases. These individuals would mainly go along with the genre, having no choice in the matter, but there would be little likelihood of any deep reshaping of individual desires in the process; learning a genre does not always involve pervasive secondary socialization. Authoritative discourse does not become internally persuasive discourse (Bakhtin, 1981).

But we need to argue also for the potentialities of genres for creating spaces for forming and realizing new versions of self as one discovers new motives and transforms the self in response to the new communicative needs and opportunities. We report in chapter 5 on the sketchbooks kept by architecture students and how they provide the "opportunity space" (Bazerman's phrase) to participate through acts of private inscription in the diverse ways the architectural community act and represent themselves. But we must acknowledge here that our account documents far more the controlling than the identity-forming and self-realizing possibilities of genre participation.

It ought to be clear now why genres, as opposed to other linguistic phenomena (word definitions and syntax rules), are far more fluid, flexible, and dynamic; and why their number is indeterminate. For genres respond to social interpretations and reinterpretations of necessarily shifting, complex experiences. This refocusing of genre away from regularities in form and substance toward the social action a particular discourse is used to accomplish is the strength of this particular approach, which we should distinguish in this respect from one other theoretical position.

A group of scholars drawing on the systemic linguistics tradition developed by Michael Halliday at the University of Sydney have also emphasized the social dimensions of genre, pointing out the political and ideological implications of genre, and, in some cases, how the values of particular ruling elites are embodied in certain genres. Some of these scholars, such as Jim Martin, Joan Rothery, and Frances Christie (as for instance in a collection of papers edited by Cope & Kalantzis, 1993), advocate teaching the textual features of such genres to disadvantaged students in order to empower them. This seems like a move back to the traditional notion of genre with its concern for unchanging regularities of form and content, except that these scholars do not focus on literary texts; rather they are concerned to identify, describe, and teach the generic structures that occur differently in different school subjects, in order to provide those who have traditionally been excluded from full participation in school textual practices an entry into the curriculum.

Again, we reject this reification of genre as a primarily textual matter, as if one can learn the text type in one context and then transport it into the context to which it properly applies. An implication of the Sydney position would seem to be that genres of workplace writing can also be made available to those who seek jobs that assume at least a beginner's facility in using such genres. But such an approach would normalize workplace genres as somehow fixed, unchanging, and accessible to newcomers in an organization. To anticipate the argument we will be setting forth extensively later in the book, our own contrasting view is twofold. First, we hold that the knowledge that one needs in order to write effectively in a particular work context is not simply of the textual aspect of the accepted genres, in the general form in which it can be imparted outside the specific site; one also needs knowledge of the culture and the circumstances, and one needs to understand and take on the local *purposes*, the social motives that prevail in that setting. Participating in a genre means not just producing a text that looks like the ones that are usually produced in that milieu but having purposes, for action and, therefore, communication, that are recognized and allowed for within that context and for which the genre has emerged adaptively as the appropriate vehicle.

Our second point is that genres are always in flux, "stabilized–for–now," as Schryer (1994, p. 107) puts it, provisional and open to contestation and change, adaptation to or displacement by new technology, or decay from disuse and irrelevance. A brief case in point is the increasing competition for space in some research journals of papers based on ethnographic research, and how these journals must adapt to create room for such necessarily extensive accounts, and how the reporting of such research must trim unnaturally its bulk and quite likely the cogency of its arguments in order to be considered for acceptance in such journals. Determining the shape and content of such articles are also readers' beliefs, including those of reviewers and editors, about what counts as research. One might also consider that publishers of manuals and other stakeholders have some interest in conserving and consolidating research–reporting genres.

To sum up, the value of genre studies as the main conceptual frame for our inquiry lies primarily in the stance it enables us to adopt toward written discourse: regularized but not fixed; fluid, flexible, and dynamic; emerging and evolving in exigency and action; reflecting and incorporating social needs, demands, and structures; and responsive to social interpretations and reinterpretations of necessarily shifting, complex experiences.

We now turn to a consideration of certain other ideas that have influenced us and we draw on in the accounts that follow. Nearly all may be seen as supplying elaboration of or a parallel take on concepts that are present in genre theory. So Activity Theory will offer another perspective on social motive, and on the action aspect of genre; ideas about Situated Learning in "communities of practice" will provide ways of accounting for the learning of genres; and Distributed Cognition draws attention to the way that writing functions within sociotechnical systems of knowledge and action. Our remaining topic of Semiotic Approaches to writing is less directly related, though not unrelated, to genre studies.

ACTIVITY THEORY

Activity Theory (AT) derives from the Vygotskian school of Soviet psychology, especially through the work of Leont'ev (1981).[3] In proposing a new unit of analysis, *activity*, AT can be regarded as a counter to the tendency within western cognitive psychology to focus on mental operations of individuals, for example, problem-solving, in isolation from the larger human activity in which

---

[3]" ... colleagues and students of Vygotsky have emphasized that most of the essential roots of the theory of activity may be traced to Vygotsky's own writings. Various hypotheses have been advanced for why Vygotsky himself did not reformulate his ideas into a theory of activity. Some scholars have argued that he would have moved in that direction had he lived longer. Others ... have claimed that Vygotsky was in fact very close to proposing such a theory" (Wertsch, 1985, p. 200).

it is situated. More relevantly for our purposes, however, activity theory turns out to be highly congruent with the genre theory approach we have presented thus far.

Briefly, Leont'ev proposes three distinct but interrelated levels of analysis, each level associated with a specific unit of analysis (Wertsch, 1985). In other words, Leont'ev proposes three distinct ways of answering the question: what is an individual or group doing in a particular setting? The first and most global is the level of activities (the term *activity* as used in *a unit of activity* refers to specific human activities, and ought not to be confused with its use in "activity theory," which applies to human activity in general). Examples of a unit of activity are playing, learning, working, and eating, and apply to individual as well as collective functioning. Activities are distinguished on the basis of their motive and the object (this could easily translate to our sense of *objective*) toward which they are oriented. Thus the activity of going to school may be motivated by the object of getting an education. As Renshaw (1992) states:

> *Motives* (such as work, education, or play) are the taken–for– granted frameworks that organize participation in everyday activities and social institutions. A motive, like Goffman's notion of a frame, provides a socioculturally defined milieu where participants are able to coordinate their purposes and maintain a predictable sense of the ongoing interaction. (p. 55)

It is important to remember that it is the subject or subjects (the person or persons engaged in the activity) who interpret what activity they are involved in. The action of reading a novel, which is essentially a recreational activity in most settings, is regarded in most school settings as a learning activity, as work in a magazine's book editor's office, and very different work in a professor's study. Renshaw's point is that motive is socioculturally defined. While this does not exclude the possibility of individual definition, it is the concept of social definition that we find particularly relevant to our inquiry. Wertsch, Minick, and Arns (1984) make the same point in this way:

> The theory of activity in Soviet psychology suggests that … the organization of systems of activity at the societal level establishes important parameters that determine the manner in which an individual or group of individuals carries out and masters a particular type of goal-oriented action. (p. 171)

The parallel with Miller's (1994) "social motive" is obvious. Cultures have repertoires of socially recognized activities; engaging in them is a motive in itself. Playing, learning, working, and eating are just "things that we do," that require no further explanation; they are not pursuits that we see ourselves as engaging in primarily in order to achieve some other end; no ulterior motive is looked for without which these activities do not make sense. In the same way, socially institutionalized genres are activities one engages in, without need of further explanation, as part of what one does as a member of a particular cultural milieu; they are enactments of recognized social motives, and are activities in Leont'ev's sense.

The second level of analysis is at the level of action. Actions are "goal-directed processes that must be undertaken to fulfill the object [of the activity]. They are conscious (because one holds a goal in mind), and different actions may be taken to meet the same goal" (Nardi, 1992, p. 353). Actions may be driving a car, completing a puzzle, writing a letter, or reading a newspaper. Wertsch et al. (1984) point out that the need for distinguishing the level of activity from the level of action is apparent in the fact that an action can vary independently of an activity. To cite Leont'ev (1981):

> an activity and an action are genuinely different realities, which therefore do not coincide. One and the same action can be instrumental in realizing different activities. It can be transferred from one activity to another, thus revealing its relative independence. Let us turn once again to a crude illustration. Assume that I have the goal of getting to point N, and I carry it out. It is clear that this action can have completely different motives, i.e., it can realize completely different activities. The converse is also obvious: one and the same motive can give rise to different goals and, accordingly, can produce different actions. (p. 61)

Thus, the *action* of reading, depending on the goal, can realize the *activity* of play, or work, or learning.

The third level of analysis is concerned with *operations*, the conditions under which the action is carried out and the means by which it is carried out. A goal of getting to school can command different sets of operations, depending on the conditions involved: the distance, the weather, time available, traffic conditions—all these will determine whether one walks, uses public transportation, or drives a car. As long as the goal remains the same, the changed operations do not determine a different action. With practice, operations may become routine and automatic, requiring no conscious effort; so that specific steps (walking to the bus stop, having exact change ready, depositing change, obtaining a transfer) are subsumed under one operation; for example, taking a bus. Wertsch (1981) summarizes the distinctions among the three levels of analysis:

> Leont'ev points out that *activities* are distinguished on the basis of their motive and the object toward which they are oriented; *actions*, on the basis of their goals; and *operations*, on the basis of the conditions under which they are carried out. (p. 18)

Thus the *activity* of work may involve the action of writing a report, which itself will include several subactions such as reading, note-taking, interviewing, a computer-search, consulting company guidelines, and circulating drafts, all intended to meet the goal of writing a report. These *actions* are distinguished from the *operations* that enable one to perform those actions: typing, reading, writing, telephoning, faxing (routinized, requiring no conscious attention).

One can see how the question, "What is the writer doing?" can be answered differently depending on the level of analysis one is using. In the report-writing situation much of the actual writing (getting words on paper, transcribing) is merely *operational,* a means needed to fulfil an *action* rather than a goal-directed *action* in itself. For people who are learning to use a word processor as a tool for writing, the act of getting letters and words on screen remains a goal-directed *action*, until the process has been mastered and become automatic and routine. Such a development is easily visible in children learning to write. At one stage, merely holding a pencil in order to create shapes on paper is an *action*. As experience sets in, getting recognizable letters down on paper is moving into the category of an *operation*, a means, but the matter of forming words and sentences is now the goal-directed *action*. In time writing words and sentences has become largely *operational,* and developing and shaping one's thoughts on paper, composing, constitutes the goal and *action*. Russell (1997) suggests that writing routinely in a familiar genre is an instance of how a complex action in time and with repeated use becomes operational. But, occasionally, even for experienced writers, forming words and letters does become the substance of an *action* rather than a routine, automatized *operation*: when one enters letters into boxes on forms for instance, or when a pen begins to run out of ink and making marks on paper becomes a prime goal, or when a minor hand injury makes holding a pen awkward.

Leont'ev (1981) nicely makes the point about how "actions and operations have different origins, different dynamics, and different fates" (p. 64) by describing the operations required for driving an automobile:

Initially, every operation—for example, shifting gears—appears as an action subordinated to a goal. Such actions have their conscious "orienting basis" (Gal'perin). Subsequently, this action is included in another complex action, such as that of changing the speed of the automobile. At this point, shifting gears becomes one of the methods for carrying out this action—that is, it becomes an operation necessary for performing the action. It is no longer carried out as a special goal-directed process. The driver does not distinguish its goal. So far as the driver's conscious processes are concerned, it is as if shifting gears under normal circumstances does not exist. He/she is doing something else: he/she is driving the automobile from place to place.... Indeed, we know that this operation can "drop out" of the driver's activity entirely and can be performed automatically. It is generally the fate of operations that, sooner or later, they become a function of a machine. (p. 64)

In our example of report writing, writing was categorized as a goal-directed *action* at times, and at other times an *operation*, a routinized means to the end of producing a report. Depending on the subject's orientation and motivation, the activity could be regarded as work or learning. Again, a reminder that naming an activity "is a sociocultural interpretation or creation that is imposed on the context by the participant(s)" (Wertsch, 1985, p. 203).

On the other hand, a subject involved in the *activity* of school going may be writing a report directed by the object of a good grade and select *actions* whose goals are to meet the instructor's criteria for that particular assignment: not more than 1000 words, provide an outline, and include at least five specific references to related periodical literature, marks deducted for late papers. The specific actions that meet such goals may differ according to the writer's experience, the time available for researching and writing this paper, and the availability of library and other resources—generally whatever strategic actions the writer conceives as necessary to meet those goals.

Writing occurs in both settings but it is clearly not the same kind of event or activity in both settings. The contexts, and hence the tasks, as they are interpreted by writers define what that writing will be, and to use AT terminology, will determine different *actions* and *operations*. In both the work and in the school setting, writing is a "a mediating tool," an extension of the person, "mind in action," as James Wertsch might say. But the mind is not necessarily working toward the same goals. People who write at work, for instance, are unlikely to speak of themselves as doing writing as opposed to preparing reports. Social workers, who claim to do little or no "writing," admit that they spend much of their time "recording." Jane Ledwell–Brown, a member of our research team, reports that all of the people she observed in two departments of a pharmaceutical company did a significant amount of writing as part of their daily routine; yet none of their job descriptions specifically listed writing as one of their job requirements. It is only through the research interviews that the individuals discovered how much writing they actually did. To borrow from Michael Polanyi (1958), writing is held in *subsidiary awareness* rather than in *focal awareness*. As the writer encounters difficulty, writing may shift from being *operational* (or subsidiary) to being *action* (focal).

What does AT's tri-level categorization afford us? For one, it enables an analysis of human actions in context. For another, we are able to see an ecological interrelatedness among the three levels along which we can view activity, how activity is distributed along so many covarying strands in its fabric. Activity Theory, as we show in chapter 4, also uncovers internal contradictions in our practices, which with our attention to individual processes and textual products we normally tend to overlook.

In the analysis we present below we do not regularly make direct reference to AT. It is nevertheless part of our intellectual resource, and in numerous instances would have provided an alternative perspective in which to make similar points about our material. We do use it in chapter 5 to make the point that some of the private design notebook writing we have studied in a school of architecture realizes a different *activity* from writing that is done to be assessed in conventional courses. Similarly, the difference between a university classroom business simulation (chap. 3) and the related exercise in a firm (chap. 9) can well be described in AT terms.

One specific use of the theory could be as further grounds for objection to the Sydney view of genre. When they teach a genre we might argue that they are teaching an action, not an activity; in our terms that amounts to saying they are not teaching the genre. What people need to learn is to engage in the activity. It might be argued that familiarity with contributory actions is at least a great help in acquiring an activity, and in principle that is true. In the case of much situated writing, however, the action has to be customized to suit the situation through a form of intelligent reconstruction in the light of the sort of knowledge, for instance of values and local histories, that genre teachers cannot impart. The actions in question are not ones that, like gear-shifting, can simply be called up and run as sub-routines (to adopt programming lingo).

SITUATED LEARNING IN COMMUNITIES OF PRACTICE

Whereas academic institutions and classrooms have received the bulk of attention in studies concerned with learning, very few studies have attended to learning within groups and communities outside educational institutions. Even when studies have focussed on non-school contexts, they have generally regarded and assessed such learning from a school-based perspective. By far the most significant work in out-of-school learning comes from Jean Lave and her associates. As we explain more fully in chapter 9, in our own research Lave's insights illuminate the processes by which people learn the genres of the social milieu in which they find themselves, in school as well as out. Our use of the term, communities of practice (COPs), comes from the work of Lave and Wenger (1991) and their associates and refers to contexts for learning that operate successfully outside the classroom and provide the contrasting back-drop against which we can examine classroom activities.[4] (Lave and her colleagues did not, we should add, have the learning of writing in mind.)

In his *Keywords,* Williams (1976) speaks of the complexity of the word *community* because, on the one hand, it suggests "common concern," and on the other, "various forms of common organization." It is in the latter sense, the less rosy view, as Paré (1993) puts it, that Lave (1988) uses the term. We considered adopting the term spheres of practice as a substitute for communities of practice, in order to avoid the warm overtones usually accompanying *community* and discounting any notion of conflict and exclusiveness; however, *sphere* does not carry the notion of *peopled* with the same force as *community* does. By Lave's (1988) definition, a "community of practice is a set of relations among persons, activity, and the world, over time and in relation with other tangential and overlapping communities of practice" (p. 98). In foregrounding relationships, Lave foregrounds situatedness, emphasizing the interrelatedness of, the need to consider in context, the activity of participants. COPs describe members of a group involved in a common activity over time (these could be, for instance, members of a scout troop, tailors, or warehouse workers). In relation to other COPs, there is a shared understanding within a COP of what they are doing and who they are. Within the COP there is a relationship of experts and novices, oldtimers and newcomers; so that members, participating at multiple levels, are engaged in a process of learning. A COP need not be homogenous in its makeup; it is more likely to involve people with different interests, viewpoints, and abilities. "It does imply participation in an activity system about which participants share understanding concerning what they are doing and what that means in their lives and for their communities" (Lave & Wenger, 1991, p. 98). At the same time, we ought to note that as activity systems overlap, so do COPS; and these points of overlap can be critical and defining. Child welfare workers, for instance, may find themselves at points of conflu-ence and collision, where they must contend with the often competing claims of the medical profession, the judicial system, the social work agency, and the child's family members, and know the institutionally more powerful interests will have decisive say.

---

[4]For people familiar with composition and rhetorical theory, the term discourse community (Swales, 1990) immediately comes to mind. The notion has, however, been questioned because it implies static, unchanging modes of discourse as dominant and uncontested; whereas, as with any such active group one can assume competing discourses and interests (Faigley, 1992; Herndl, 1993; Paré, 1993) as well as emerging genres. We find "communities of practice," despite the problematic term "community" (see main text, below) both more general, in that it covers activity beyond language, and more precise, since it centers on what groups of people *do.*

The notion of COPs as we have described it thus far calls for illustration. A COP that also involves writing as one of its major activities is that of social workers who monitor and prepare regular reports on court-referred children in families designated as dysfunctional, or other such cases of children requiring care and attention. A newcomer will, on his induction into the job, work generally with an experienced social worker, observing and, in some cases, assisting her in writing up such reports. He will study his supervisor's and others' files of similar cases and be encouraged to ask questions and consider alternative accounts. At times, he may assist other workers in transcribing case notes, updating files, and tracking related documents. He may attend courtroom arbitration sessions where case-workers' reports are entered into evidence. Eventually he will write solo, with an understanding that he can count on oldtimers to review his work and suggest improvements, and typically cosign the document. Lave and Wenger (1991) describe a process called "legitimate peripheral participation" (LPP) to explain how newcomers "inevitably participate in communities of practitioners and the mastery of knowledge and skill requires newcomers to move toward full participation in the sociocultural practices of a community" (p. 29). LPP, they insist, is "a way of understanding learning," not a teaching strategy (p. 40); and learning is best viewed "as participation in the social world" (p. 43).

Legitimate and *peripheral* are carefully chosen words. *Legitimate* because participants feel they have access to and belong to a community, that they can observe and participate in the practice of the community. Lave and Wenger insist that peripherality does not imply a center and central participation. What they contrast with peripheral participation is full participation.

The notion that classrooms can model such real world settings and become COPs is difficult to resist. Brown et al. (1993) propose that schools should be communities "where students learn to learn.... graduates of such communities would be prepared as lifelong learners who have learned how to learn in many domains." They argue that by "participating in the practices of scholarly research, they [children] should be enculturated into the community of scholars during their 12 or more years of apprenticeship in school settings." They propose to do so by trying to create "a community of discourse ... where the participants are inducted into the rituals of academic and, more particularly, scientific discourse and activity" (pp. 190–191). It is tempting to reproduce the workplace within the classroom in order to have students learn to write professional discourse. If discourse is embedded in social situations, do simulations provide sufficient and contextually valid settings? It is precisely questions such as this that this study is designed to answer; and the notion of COPs may provide useful directions for classroom practice.

DISTRIBUTED COGNITION

Whereas the theoretical notions considered so far mainly address writing from the point of view of writers, explaining what it is they have to do in order to be writers within a milieu and how they learn to do it, the concept of distributed cognition gives us a way to think about the way in which writers' acts and texts are integrated into wider systems of actions. The unit of analysis is not the individual but the group and the mediating artifacts, including the language, they use. Cognition in the term *distributed cognition* refers to the knowledge and knowledge-making on which a group or organization depends in order to accomplish its activities; it includes both consciousness and storage of information and ideas. The idea is that this knowledge, in the words of Jean Lave, "is distributed—stretched over, not divided among—mind, body, activity and culturally organized settings (which include other actors)" (p. 1). It is, as signaled in the title of Resnick, Levine, and Teasley's (1991) collection of papers, socially shared.[5] But it is also important to note that the knowledge is dispersed not only in different people's heads but also in "culturally organized settings," including the routines and habitual practices of the group. The relevance to genre is clear; genres embody the experience of previous writers, allowing it to be reactivated on each new occasion of writing. This is stored knowledge, even though the individual writers who use the genres would generally be unable to say what that knowledge is. The stored knowledge is inherent in the reiteration of genre: textual regularities of form and category, habits of information collection and archival practices, patterns of writing and reading.

The work on distributed cognition gives us two useful perspectives on writing, one (the main one) to do with the manner in which writing contributes to the work of an organized group, the other to do with the social component of individual writing. Hutchins (1993) illustrates the first aspect of distributed cognition with an analysis of the activity of ship navigation, in this case, a crew working together to guide a naval vessel into San Diego harbor and the systems of socially distributed cognition they rely on. It is not just the activities and knowledge of the captain on the bridge that bring about the passage of the ship into the harbor. Similarly, we can see how the writing of an organization or community functions as an element within that structure, as one medium in

---

[5]In the final paper of that collection, Cole (1991, p. 398) points out that *shared* in *shared cognition* means both having in common and divided up or distributed. We prefer to think of *distributed cognition* as participating in both notions of *shared*.

which its important knowledge, about its core activities and not just about writing, is formulated, developed, shaped, and reshaped for different applications, communicated and stored. Hutchins (1993) further explains:

> socially distributed cognition can have a degree of parallelism of activity that is not possible in individuals. Although current research tells us that much of individual cognition is carried out by the parallel activity of many parts of the brain, still, at the scale of more molar activities, individuals have difficulty simultaneously performing more than one complex task or maintaining more than one rich hypothesis. These are things that are easily done in socially distributed cognitive systems. Ultimately, no matter how much parallelism there may be within a mind, there is the potential for more in a system composed of many minds. (p. 60)

One medium through which separate minds come together in a system of minds is clearly written communication. [6]

By the same token, the system is not merely external to the individual but enters into and contributes to the formation of his or her operations, including writing. Hutchins (1993) argues that "when the context of cognition is ignored, it is impossible to see the contribution of structure in the environment, in artifacts, and in other people to the organization of mental processes"(p. 63). The distributed cognition model enables us to see writing, too, as not enclosed within the mind of the knower, but extended in a complex of relationships and interactions that includes other people and artifacts. Thus a report produced by a newly hired employee of a small company may have been commissioned as a result of a meeting at which several questions driving this report were discussed. Earlier reports may have been consulted, relevant information may have been garnered from fellow workers via e-mail, a spreadsheet program may have produced informative tables and up-to-date analysis, and the structure and organization of the report, initially derived from company guidelines and model reports, may have been shaped by unexpected contingencies and inquiries and suggestions from coworkers and managers. The sense in which the production of a piece of writing is distributed is not just that of a mechanical division of labor. It is also that other people's contributions, not only via direct inputs and suggestions, but through their experience as stored in genres, existing texts, and cultural forms, are integral to the apparently individual production.

---

[6]"Systems composed of many minds" may be an apt designation for the operations of the workplace; the question then suggests itself, how well does that phrase apply to what goes on in classrooms, and whatever the advantages of such distributed cognition systems, to what extent should classroom organization and practice aspire to such a designation? We give some attention to this later in the book, in chapter 7.

In addition to those key points about the writing within systems of activity, Wertsch, Tulviste, and Hagstrom (1993) offer an interesting suggestion about the implications of distributed cognition for learning. They first cite Russian psychologist Vygotsky's (1981a) formulation:

> Any function in the child's cultural development appears twice, or on two planes. First it appears on the social plane, and then on the psychological plane. First it appears between people as an interpsychological category, and then within the child as an intrapsychological category. (p. 163)

Wertsch et al. (1993) then goes on to argue that Vygotsky

> was not simply asserting that mental processes in the individual somehow emerge out of participation in social life. Instead, he was making the much stronger claim that the specific structures and processes of instrumental functioning can be traced to their developmental precursors on the intermental plane. (p. 338)

Vygotsky is speaking of the mental development of children, specifically in so far as such development is integrally tied in with their social transactions with adults or more knowledgeable peers. But such an argument applies just as much to the learning relationships between skilled or experienced and less skilled or inexperienced adults. Socially distributed cognition represents the kind of functioning on the intermental plane out of which can evolve "the specific structures and processes of instrumental functioning." Such a claim provides further warrant for our belief that we cannot fully understand the processes by which individuals become writers in either academic or work settings, unless we look at these learners acting in context, their co-participants, and the mediational means involved.[7]

The constructs, situated cognition and distributed cognition, seem so common-sensical that we might legitimately ask what in them is so insightful that they might advance our inquiry. Thus Nickerson (1993), speaking of distributed cognition, asks:

> Does anyone doubt that the same people act differently in different situations, that people are influenced by the social and cultural contexts in which they live, that what one can do depends to a large degree on the tools and materials at one's disposal, that there are countless useful tools in the world including many that

---

[7]The use of wordprocessors and the facility they afford to incorporate other texts, revise, and format to print publication standards, the use of complex statistical analyses packages and other computer-run analytic tools, and the use of electronic mail and FAX to provide feedback at a speed undreamed of a decade ago are three well-worn instances of how mediational means are implicated in making a significant difference to how one defines and approaches a writing task, and to what one writes.

simplify cognitive tasks, that what skills people develop depends in part on the kinds of artifacts they must use, that it is easier to do certain things in some environments than in others, that two heads are (sometimes) better than one, that specialization of function within groups is often useful, that it is a waste of time and effort to keep some types of information in one's head ...? (p. 231)

All true and self-evident, it would appear. But then we need to consider how writing, and cognition in general, have been studied and taught as though they involve operations that occur entirely within an individual, as though "this individual existed in a cultural, historical, and institutional vacuum" (Wertsch, Tulviste, & Hagstrom, 1993, pp. 336–337). The main body of research into the "composing process" certainly exemplifies this ideology. And how much teaching of writing does *not* proceed as if learning to write were a matter of developing an individual's ability? How often in looking for ways to help a struggling writer do we look to the mode and quality of the writer's connectedness with the community within which the writing finds its purpose and resources?

Wertsch et al. (1993) go on to trace the roots of this view, drawing on the work of philosopher Charles Taylor (1985, 1989) and his argument that social science theory is "grounded in a certain tradition of individualism that permeates our personal and professional lives ... a social science that takes the atomistic agent as its basic building block" and leads "to accounts of human mental functioning in which such agency is viewed as being analytically and developmentally prior to sociocultural life" (Wertsch et al., 1993, pp. 337–338). However much we may view collaboration and exchange among individuals as a necessary part of writing processes, the default mode in our thinking about writing and its practices tends to be that writing is primarily and ultimately the product of individual minds. Such a notion is so deeply embedded in our consciousness that the question of what constitutes intellectual property or plagiarism is seldom subject to radical reexamination.

In chapter 7 we make use of the concept of distributed cognition in accounting for the way that writing worked in a government office we studied. We have not found that it illuminated much about classrooms, which leads us to an awareness that the presence of developed networks of distributed cognition may be one of the important criteria differentiating educational from workplace writing.

SEMIOTIC THEORY: THE MEDIATING ROLE OF SIGNS

The central tenet of semiotic theory, as it derives, via separate streams, from Peirce (1931–1958) and Morris (1971) on the one hand and from Vygotsky

(1978, 1986) and Bakhtin (1986)/Voloshinov (1986) on the other, and in distinction from Saussure's (1967) theory of signs that he called semiology, is that signs, linguistic and other, have no inherent meaning or value but are just things (literally, in the sense that they always have material reality as physical phenomena or events) to which we attribute meaning. Communication is possible because to some extent we agree, by convention, to accord the same meanings to the same signs. So dictionaries, for instance, are possible; these give us the core meaning of certain verbal signs, though semioticians such as Vygotsky, like literary scholars too, are aware of the cloud of other associated meanings, some of them highly personal, that are always also *read into* signs.

There are three ways in which this area of thinking is relevant for our study. One is about the relationship between written and other signs, a second concerns our use of signs as mediating means for communicating and thinking and the third relates to the way signs get their meanings within particular discursive settings.

Linguistic and Other Signs

Language is clearly not the only sign system we use, and its relative importance depends on context. Vygotsky (1981b) offers an intriguing list of other symbol systems, including, maps, diagrams, art, and mechanical drawings, "all sorts of conventional signs" (p. 137). In the contexts we have studied, writing often occurs in close relationship with, and sometimes as an optional alternative to, other sorts of inscribed signs, and especially drawings, diagrams, and charts. Understanding these settings requires us to look at the entire communicative matrix, with all the sign systems it employs, and not to single out writing as special in a way that the participants clearly do not. The need to consider semiotic activity as a whole with writing as one constituent of it has been increasingly recognized in the last few years (Ackerman & Oates, 1996; Smagorinksy & Coppock, 1994; Winsor, 1994; Witte, 1992).

Language (and Writing) as Mediating Tool

This set of insights is not of the kind that will reveal its utility overtly by being referred to in the specific analysis we will report, but constitutes an important element of our background understanding. In his *Voices of the Mind*, Wertsch's (1991) central claim is that "human action typically employs 'mediational means' such as tools and language, and that these mediational means shape the action in essential ways." (p. 12). His point is that we ought to think of "the person(s)-acting-with-mediational-means as an irreducible agent" (p. 120). He explains:

it is possible, as well as useful, to make an analytic distinction between action and mediational means, but the relationship between action and mediational means is so fundamental that it is more appropriate, when referring to the agent involved, to speak of "individual(s)-acting-with-mediational-means" than to simply speak of individual(s). Thus, the answer to the question of who is carrying out the action will invariably identify the individual(s) in the concrete situation *and* the mediational means employed. (p. 12)

Thus we can speak of language as an extension of the actor, "not bounded by the skin," as Bateson puts it (1972, p. 319). In this sense, language (writing in our case) is imbued with intention, situation, affect, attitude, and purpose.

Moreover, not only is the self extended in the mediational process, but to quote Wertsch (1991) again, the "incorporation of mediational means does not simply facilitate action that could have occurred without them, instead" (p. 32), and here Wertsch cites Vygotsky (1981b):

By being included in the process of behavior, the psychological tool alters the entire flow and structure of mental functions. It does this by determining the structure of a new instrumental act just as a technical tool alters the process of a natural adaptation by determining the form of labor operations. (p. 137)

Tool" may not be the happiest image to convey the nature of language as a mediating resource, but we accept Wertsch's point that the nature of this external resource has cognitive effects. Language as mediational means or tool is not a mere neutral conduit; it also puts its own mark on mediated action. Thus, in our case the genres that constitute the mediating communicative means of a community may affect thinking by constraining the sort of thought that can be expressed (and by creating a need to have certain kinds of thoughts in order to fulfill the requirements of the genre). And in general we concur with his insistence on regarding agent, means, and action as integrally bound and irreducible.

This line of thinking of course ties in very neatly with the idea of distributed cognition, because cognition can only be distributed via the mediation of signs. The distribution is then channeled and shaped by the particular mediational tools—genres imply particular social flows, interactions, informational, and communicative needs.

How Signs Get Their Meaning

Signs, including the verbal formulations conveyed in writing, do not have their meanings built in but acquire them from the cultural associations that writers and readers bring to bear on them. In any particular text or utterance, part of the meaning derives from the dialogic context: what has been said or written before to which the text is an explicit or implicit response, and what future utterances it anticipates by way of response. This insight has been most fully developed by Bakhtin (1986), who observes that "the utterance is filled with *dialogic overtones*" (p. 92, emphasis in original), that it "is a link in the chain of speech communication, ... related not only to preceding, but also to sub-sequent links ... that the utterance is constructed while taking into account possible responsive reactions, for whose sake, in essence, it is actually created" (p. 94). As we discuss below, the term *intertextuality* captures the manner in which texts allude to each other, deriving and giving meaning, in an intricate tissue. To be a successful user of a genre within a setting involves not just formal knowledge but an awareness of the dialogic chains, both immediate and local and those that have continued over a longer period and stretch into remote quarters of the professional community and wider culture. Writers need to know how to insert themselves into such a chain, reactivating certain of its latent meanings and leaving others well alone, referring explicitly to some existing texts and allusively evoking others; these are not matters of textual knowledge that can be taught in genre school.

It turns out that one of the features that distinguished at least some of our workplaces from all of our classrooms was the density and complexity of the intertextual connections within which writers were operating—how many textual strands a writer was simultaneously participating in, whether texts contributed to more than one strand at once (e.g., via multiple readership), and how much of a previous history of communication about a topic had to be implicitly alluded to in each fresh message.

WRITING IN RELATION TO OTHER MEDIA

There is one other element of our general perspective that we should describe at this point. Only in part is writing a linguistic phenomenon. A written text instantiates a linguistic system, certainly, but never only that. In order to write it is never sufficient to know the grammar and orthographic system of the language, not even with additional knowledge of the conventions and devices that create coherence. Choices are always made within other symbol systems, too, choices that have meaning that is not linguistic. There are times in our analysis where we have needed to take conscious account of this aspect, not normally obvious, of the act of writing.

There are two ways in which other forms of semiosis manifest themselves in the context of writing. The first way relates to the physical medium through which written or spoken language is actualized. Features of the medium unavoidably carry significance in our culture, so that it is impossible to speak or write without conveying, alongside the meaning encoded in language, other meanings that derive from characteristics of the material embodiment of the language. The voice quality, loudness, speed of utterance, breathiness and affective tone of our speech as well as the words as lexical items "speak" to our listeners. Similarly, writing participates in a variety of non-linguistic symbolic systems because of its need to take material form. Both the materials themselves—the surfaces and the marking substances, paper, screen, sky and T-shirt, pixel, tattoo dye, spray paint, and pencil—and the available forms of visual array—the fonts, orientations, and patternings—are already as heavily coded as the verbal signs they inscribe. Choices of writing surface, marking device, handwriting style or typeface, weight and quality of paper, letter size, degree of tidiness, and style of layout have semiotic weight and carry meanings that would often be impossible to render in verbal form (Kress & van Leeuwen, 1996). There are good reasons why university diplomas are not scribbled by the President in pencil on the back of an envelope, why mortgage documents eschew some of the typefaces employed in *Wired* and why many writers value in their drafting the variability in positioning, sizing, and styling of words and text that handwriting easily affords and word processors do not, or only with difficulty. Although the same words may be written in either medium, the richer visual system of handwriting enables more meaning to be encoded through a single act of inscription (Chandler, 1992). These meanings are often metatextual, in that they are about the status and significance of that part of the communication—its tentativeness or definiteness, its status as central or incidental in the argumentative structure, and so on.

If, as we have suggested, writing participates in certain symbolic systems simply by virtue of being written in a particular visual form and in and on a physical medium, it can also—and this is the second manifestation—participate *alongside* forms of semiosis that operate in their own separate space but work with writing in the *co*-production of a meaning. A communicated meaning can be the product of a combination of writing and other semiotic forms such as, most obviously, graphical, or mathematical representations, but also speech and gesture. We take the view that acts of writing represent decisions not just to write rather than not communicate but also to write rather than to speak, draw, or communicate by some other means. Alternative media are always present as potential choices, and sometimes as choices that are actually taken up alongside writing.

In most of our analysis this general view will remain tacit because it offers no specific purchase for the cases under discussion, which are mainly ones in which writing is customarily and conventionally expected and other modes are not actively entertained as alternatives. In some areas, however, and particularly in relation to architecture, it will be necessary to make explicit the nature of the choice involved when a participant opts to write at one point and to draw at another.

We will be suggesting that the way writing relates to other semiotic forms is an important differentiating feature both between academic and workplace writing and between the writing of different workplaces.

Here we briefly map the main ways in which different symbolic media may be combined in the communications we have observed. Because the professional workplace typically exploits symbolic communicative systems more flexibly and diversely than does the university classroom (a point we will argue in later chapters), we will illustrate the functioning and mutual relations of these systems mainly with examples from practice at work.

Spoken discourse is, not surprisingly, central to all the professions we have looked at. Only in architecture do we find graphical representations of the visual and spatial aspects of phenomena, but graphical presentation of quantitative relationships and data is indispensable in financial institutions and in business management (two of our other cases), while in the former mathematical symbols also comprise a significant proportion of many texts.

Types of Relationship Between Media

In all the workplaces that we have investigated, speech and gesture at least, if not other symbolic processes, are found alongside writing. The relationships between writing and these other processes are of three types.[8] In the first, there is no immediate or direct connection between them. In the second, the text in one medium makes reference to a text in a different medium. In the third, there is simultaneous mutual reference across media. To discuss these briefly in order:

1. As one would expect, each process can occur independently, without direct or obvious reference to either of the others. There are times when architects are just writing, just drawing, or just speaking, or when economists are just working calculations on a computer. (Indirect reference—by association or echo, for instance, or simply by virtue of addressing the same topic—is of course always potentially present.)

---

[8] These ideas are more extensively developed in Medway (1996).

2. Alternatively, there may be connections of a referential nature across media. A communication in one medium can be about something that has already been given expression in another. For instance, an architect may talk or write about something shown in a drawing or about the contents of a written text. A social worker can get on the phone about information just received in a fax message or can jot down what a client just said in an interview. Economists can gather round a screenful of figures and discuss them. An architect may also sit down and draw a feature that was suggested by the client in a meeting.

In these cases of references to what has already been in some way encoded, the relationship to the earlier text (using that term to mean any semiotic event or product, including spoken utterances) may or may not be explicitly signaled. The existing text or pre-text to which the new text refers may be one of the practitioner's own written or graphical or spoken productions, or it may have been generated by an outsider, as when a fax or phone message is received from an external agent such as a consulting engineer or the social work client's teacher. The reference text may equally be a public or semi-public document such as the printed regulations of government bodies or suppliers' catalogues. Equally it may be a point remembered from a talk at some professional conference. This sort of connection between new and existing productions is well addressed through the notion of *intertextuality*, which is Kristeva's (1986) term for Bakhtin's (1981) idea that utterances and texts cannot help reflecting what has been said or written before (and also what is expected to be said or written in the future; see also Todorov, 1984). As suggested above, it is useful to extend the sense of "text" in "intertextuality" to include non-written communications.

3. A third possible relationship is simultaneous occurrence of encoding in two or more media. Semiotic production can, and routinely does, proceed at more or less the same time in at least two media. An assessment report, for instance, may be distributed and/or read aloud during social work assessment meetings.

The permutations of possible interrelationships are numerous, and these possibilities offer "rich affordances" (Wood, 1992, p. 2), constituting a delicately graduated semiotic resource. One medium may be dominant, as when speech offers a sporadic commentary on the architectural condition one is sketching for a coparticipant, or when the social worker scribbles occasional notes while listening to the nurse's telephoned explanation of a client's stage of recovery from an accident; little sketches in the margin of a note to be faxed to the supplier of door furniture may be incidental and inessential to the main message. At other times the message formulated in one medium may be fundamentally defective without the meanings to be taken in parallel from the second channel. Thus, the spoken accompaniment may convey the significance of what is simultaneously being sketched, or the sketch may supply the material configuration of a design idea that is being represented verbally in some other terms, such as anticipating the experience the eventual user will have of the building.

In general, the advantages of each medium are exploited in the interests of efficient and convenient production, and a medium is not preferred if a purpose may be more easily achieved through a different one. Preference, however, may be outweighed by constraints that dictate the use of a less convenient medium, as when the law requires a written record.

As we suggested above, most of the time our awareness of the range of possible symbolic media makes little difference to our analysis. This is partly because of the nature of the written texts, the production of which has been the object of our study. Following the tradition of genre studies, we have tended to concentrate on substantial texts that are central to the core tasks of the classroom and work sites we have investigated, and have paid less attention to those fragmentary and very short texts that may display more interesting relationships with other semiotic phenomena. On occasion, however, we need to note that the essential characteristic of a particular piece of writing is precisely that it is not a phone call or a sketch, or that it adds to a drawing or to a conversation something unattainable by graphical or spoken means.

In some of our work places we found the choice of media to be improvisatory, opportunistic, adaptive, and fluid; we are impressed with the ease with which professional communications switch channels or proceed by using two or more media in parallel. When the need is to give expression to an idea, our workplace participants often exploit whatever communicative means come to hand, abandoning them when the communicative demand shifts and another medium becomes more convenient.

Through the discussion thus far, we keep returning to the various ways in which writing is situated: within Activity, work or learning groups, by the tools employed and the cultural artifacts and practices drawn on, and through genre-making practices. All these ways of situating writing imply writers' participation in sociocultural activity: in school or outside school, at home or in the workplace, or linked electronically across settings. We have as yet said little about the nature of that participation and what it might mean for the development of writing competencies. These are the topics we explore in the following chapters.

II

UNIVERSITY WRITING

From its very beginning, the resurgence of interest in rhetoric described in chapter 2 has focussed in particular on school writing. Theoretic and pedagogic issues have been framed within that context, and considerable research has been deployed to investigate the nature of student composing processes, the range of written products, and the nature of school contexts.

Insofar as our research adds to this literature, it does so because we have been able to define by contrast: that is, to look at school writing, and in particular university writing, by comparing it to discourse produced on similar topics in very different contexts—those of the workplace. In making these comparisons, we have been afforded an understanding of the tremendous shaping power of context and of the consequent radical and, as we shall argue, essential difference in the nature of the discourse produced.

Social and pragmatic perspectives on discourse and genre theory, in particular, have allowed for new insights into the nature of student and workplace writing, highlighting fundamental similarities and differences. By tying the textual to the social, by seeing texts as ways of doing things with words, by recognizing the dialogism and the continuous interplay among texts, we have been able to understand the degree to which texts both respond to and exist in potential inventive tension with their contexts. With respect to university writing, the notion of context has been expanded to include not just the assignment and feedback, not just the course lectures and the classroom interaction, but also the entire discursive and ideological context therein evoked (through readings, lectures, seminars) as well as the institutional and hence political, social, and cultural forces that shape and constrain each utterance.

GENRE STUDIES AND "SOCIAL MOTIVE"

A construct that has offered particularly rich explanatory power has been the notion of "social motive," as developed by Miller (1994). Our discussion of her work in chapter 2 outlines her central thesis that genres are best understood as "typified social actions." More germane to our purpose here is her discussion of motive: for Miller, action implies both situation and motive, both of which are interpreted as being socially and communally constructed.

Social motive is consequently a central construct: a key to understanding the nature of the potential differences between university and workplace writing lies in discriminating the social motives at play, recognizing that these social motives may not be easily available to, or expressible by, the players, especially in institutions whose values are so naturalized to the participants as to become tacit.

Our central argument is the following. The social motive of student genres is characterized by an inherent and inevitable duality. On the one hand, such writing is "epistemic"—in the sense of enabling students, through the discourse production, to take on stances toward and interpretations of realities valorized in specific disciplines. At the same time, however, another fundamental activity of the university is sorting and ranking its students, and scripts are produced as ways of enabling such ranking. A second social motive for university discourse, then, is to enable students to be graded and slotted.

The duality of this social motive is pervasive and inescapable. This is true even when instructors attempt simulations in which workplace motives are specified and workplace tasks carefully constructed. As long as the writing is elicited by and handed in to a professor, it is the institutional and ideological constraints of the university that continue to govern the whole.

THEORETIC BACKGROUND

To clarify our use of the term *epistemic*, we need to refer to the work of two philosophers: Stephen Toulmin and Charles Willard. Toulmin's work (e.g., 1958) is central to the philosophic field of argument theory. His seminal thesis is that the logic of argumentation is not universal; different disciplines as well as different forums of discourse all develop different modes of argumentation. Certain basic elements are available for use in any piece of discourse that can be classified as argument. These include the claim made, the evidence adduced to support the claim, the lines of reasoning connecting the evidence to the claim, et cetera. But the nature of these elements, and the degree to which they are called on in different fields varies considerably.

In his work on argumentation, Willard (1982) makes a further distinction. Within specific disciplinary fields, one can further distinguish between discourse whose goal is to get things done (instrumental or practical) and discourse whose goal is epistemic (i.e., knowledge oriented), where the discourse is an end in itself. Thus, he distinguishes legal briefs used to persuade a judge or jury from scholarly writing for, say, legal journals. Although this classification, like most, can become fuzzy at the boundaries and evaporates when pushed too far (knowledge ultimately may be applied, and some discourse has dual goals), nevertheless, we find valuable that central distinction he is making.

Our argument relies both on Toulmin's work and Willard's distinction. Part of the social motive of university writing is for students to be able to argue appropriately within the forums that they enter: be they law, management studies, architecture, or literature. Much of the work of each course—the work undertaken collaboratively by instructor and students—is focused on enabling students to learn the appropriate argumentative stance of their fields of inquiry.

Willard's distinction helps to define how this university writing differs from workplace writing in the same fields. At university, the goal of the writing and the writer is not practical, in Willard's use of the term, but rather epistemic. We need to acknowledge here that we are using Willard's term in a more specialized sense. School writing whose goal is epistemic is very different from that writing whose goal is to produce new knowledge for scholars. In school genres, the notion of epistemic applies to the writer: the writing is assigned as an occasion for his or her learning; it is typically not taken on as an opportunity to extend the knowledge of a discipline or of a community of scholars—at least at the undergraduate level. The idea that student writing will make a "contribution" to a discipline's knowledge does not arise until graduate work.

OVERVIEW OF CHAPTERS ON UNIVERSITY WRITING

The discussion in chapter 3 illustrates the dual social motive of university writing with respect to the writing in very specific courses. The writing elicited in specific, but representative courses is analyzed in detail in order to reveal how students are enabled, through the writing (and as a result of the writing) to take on certain epistemic stances. Textual analyses of the scripts produced open up one kind of window on the nature of this learning; observational analyses of composing activities open another. At the same time, the role of grading and its effect on the writing is also presented.

Chapter 4 focuses especially on the complications inherent in the dual social motive. When genre theory is enriched by Activity Theory (AT), the tensions inherent in the duality are cast in particularly bold relief. Complications exist not only because of the two kinds of motives, but also because, in the larger system of the university, the need to grade is itself juxtaposed against a range of other demands on the instructor's time; hence, the need to grade translates, in most settings, into the need to grade quickly, efficiently, and economically (from a time perspective).

Furthermore, the epistemic goal itself carries within it a series of internal tensions. Whereas the instructor seeks to facilitate the students' learning, some of the very strategies used to "guide" such learning themselves constrain or limit the possibilities of more fertile or wide-ranging inquiry.

Chapter 5 explores the paradoxical situation of writing in architecture. On the one hand, writing itself is not the primary means of semiosis in that field, and consequently written discourse does not have the same kind of privileged position it has elsewhere in academia. On the other, perhaps because attention is diverted from the production of written artifacts as signs of appropriate learning, a very different kind of writing-as-learning takes place incidentally. This typically unremarked and often underground kind of writing is revealed to have remarkable heuristic power. Although it was particularly in architecture courses that this kind of writing was observed, this phenomenon is one that takes place across the curriculum—but sporadically, and rarely as part of the conscious design of courses or curriculum.

3

THE SOCIAL MOTIVE
OF UNIVERSITY WRITING

In this chapter, our intention is to discriminate what Miller (1994) has referred to as the "social motive" of university writing, especially assigned university writing. From time to time, we will call on some data from the world of work to put into bolder relief some of the characteristics of student genres, but our goal here is to discuss what is central to university student discourse: its guiding social motive.

As elaborated in the Introduction to this section our central argument in this chapter is that the social motive of student genres is dual. On the one hand, it is epistemic—in the specialized sense of enabling students, through the discourse production, to learn to use language, "to do things with words," in ways valorized in specific disciplines. Because disciplines differ, disciplinary courses tend to elicit writing that is at once homogeneous (within that class) and also distinctive (as compared to the writing of the same students for other courses). Both these phenomena relate to the underlying epistemic motive.

On the other hand, this epistemic motive is complicated by the existence of another institutional reality: a fundamental activity of the university is the sorting and ranking of students. Another motive for eliciting writing, then, is to allow for such ranking. To be sure, a key criterion for such sorting is the degree to which students have realized the epistemic motive: the degree to which their writing demonstrates their learning (with respect to what the professor has determined that they ought to learn). Nevertheless, the two impulses often exist in uneasy tension.

Many consequences flow from the inextricably entangled dual nature of the social motive—consequences that are realized, for example, in the amount of shared knowledge that is presented in the texts, the rhetorical and social roles of writer and reader, the nature of the rhetorical interaction, and the ultimate role of the text in its context. In the pages that follow, the argument sketched so generally and briefly above will be fleshed out with specifics drawn from the research.

SOCIAL MOTIVE AS EPISTEMIC

The general notion that university student writing is epistemic, or learning-oriented, turned out to be an explicitly acknowledged and widely held view, shared alike by the university teachers and students we interviewed. Thus, when asked during the course of a retrospective interview about the purpose of the writing assigned to her, one student responded (while the others nodded), "He [the professor] wants to see ... that you've understood what the issues are and what the problem is, and that you've used some logical thinking to come up with your solution." As to faculty, we heard various versions of this common refrain. "You learn as you do," as one instructor repeated to his class whenever he elicited written assignments. Implicit in this comment is the belief that writing not only displays learning (which is perhaps a more conventional, but certainly more limited view), but also that it enables such learning.

Of course, to return to a notion that was elaborated in the Introduction to this section, our use of the term "epistemic" is specialized. The goal of student writing is not to produce new knowledge for the reader (as is the goal of academic journal writing, for example), but rather to allow for new learning by the writer.

In the analysis that follows, we show how, in writing the specific genres elicited in their university classes, student-writers came to adopt the intellectual postures (e.g., the modes of argumentation, the constructions of reality) of scholars in that field; in this sense the writing was epistemic—enabling students to see the world, and to categorize reality, in new ways and ways characteristic of specific disciplines. Insights into this learning were provided both through textual analyses of student essays as well as through analyses of taped composing sessions (for assignments that were collaboratively produced).

Textual Analyses: Writing for Law 100

Law 100 is an introductory undergraduate social science course, aimed at generalists rather than intending lawyers; it explores issues in law from a perspective that is intended to be broader than that typical of courses in professional law programs. The course is also compulsory for both public administration and business programs and, for that reason, was selected for investigation.

Law 100 is a year-long course, offered in a lecture and seminar format: 2 hours weekly of lectures, and 1 hour as a seminar. The lectures are given to classes of 250–300 students by the course professor, and the seminars, each consisting of 20–25 students, are led by teaching assistants. As part of their course work, students are expected to write four 800-word essays, each in response to a precisely-worded prompt. In the year that we observed the course, one assignment presented students with a hypothetical statute and asked them to discuss the relevance of this statute to various hypothetical situations, using the principles of statutory interpretation.

For our study, all the lectures were taped and one set of seminars was observed weekly (i.e., a researcher attended and took observational notes of all that took place). All the essays produced for that seminar section were collected and analyzed (including drafts and notes). In addition, six students volunteered to be interviewed individually weekly (for 1 to 2 hours each week over the entire academic year, from September to April) in open-ended interviews focusing broadly on what and how they were learning for the law course. These six students also provided us with their complete academic output for all courses over that same year so that we could compare their writing for the law course to their writing for all other university courses.

Our observations of the lectures and seminars revealed that the students received no explicit directions or guidance as to how to go about writing their essays. Furthermore, the students were exposed to no models of the genres that were being elicited by the assignments. Their textbooks were totally inappropriate as models for their writing, no student papers were circulated as models to the class, and none of the students sought out or read other student papers in law (either those of their peers or good papers from previous years). Indeed, each of our six student informants (and the six represented a range of abilities and composing styles) reported that looking at student models was simply not part of their repertoire as learners.

Despite the fact that the students had no exposure to written models of law writing, our textual analyses revealed that the essays produced for the law course showed a remarkable uniformity in macro- and micro-level structure, tone, lexicon, and syntax. Further, these law essays were clearly distinct from the other academic writing produced *by these same students over the same time period*. A distinctive genre was produced in this class, and by analysing the textual features we learned something about the nature and function of this distinctiveness.

Textual Regularities[9]

One further point. The analyses were primarily based on the Law essays written by the six students we observed in contrast to the other academic prose written by these same students over the same academic year. In order to confirm that the Law essays written by these six students were not, in any way, idiosyncratic, further analyses were performed comparing the Law essays of the six students in our study to all the other Law essays produced in the same seminar section. These analyses corroborated the fact that the students participating in our study produced writing typical of the essays elicited from the seminar section as a whole. In other words, although the following analysis focuses on the work of six students, the description of the Law essays applies to all the writing produced in that seminar section.

Lexicon. From the first assignment, the papers were characterized by the use of the distinctive specialized vocabulary of law. The following recurring instances of specific legal terminology are only exemplary: statute, common law, equity, sovereignty, *eiusdem generis.* Less obvious and perhaps more significant than the use of these legal terms is the use of more general lexical items in a more specialized sense in the law essays. Instances include: precedent, rule, law, common, and civil. The source of these lexical peculiarities is not hard to find: the lectures, the seminar discussions, and the textbook were all characterized by the same language.

Syntax. More startling, because unexpected, are the syntactic differences, whose significance is all the greater because there were no models for such distinctiveness in the prose the students read. One feature of syntax that we looked at was the T-unit—that is, the minimum terminable unit, or the independent clause plus all its attached dependent phrases and clauses. Previous research (see Hunt, 1970; also Hillocks, 1986, for a summary of such research) has shown that the length of the T-unit, especially in written argument, is an index of both complexity and maturity, as is the number of clauses per T-unit.

Our syntactic analyses included counts of the number of words, T-units, finite clauses, and sentences, followed by computations of the number of words

---

[9]The discussion that follows is organized by the categories of analysis. What will be apparent, however, is a difference between Essays 1 and 2 as opposed to Essays 3 and 4. In every instance, Essays 3 and 4 are characterized by all the textual differentiating features to be described below. Essays 1 and 2 display some, but not all, of these features, and as the analysis of syntax suggests, these first two essays seem to represent a mid-point or bridge between the Law essays and other academic prose.

per T-unit, the mean number of T-units per sentence, and finite clauses per T-unit.[10] The analyses revealed that the law papers in general, and papers 3 and 4 in particular, had more words per T-unit, fewer T-units per sentence, and more finite clauses per T-unit than the other academic writing produced by these same students over the same year.

In other words, the law essays as a whole were clearly more syntactically complex than the other academic essays written by these same students at the same time. Furthermore, the syntax became increasingly more complex in the later law assignments.

What makes all this particularly remarkable is that the only conceivable prose model the students were reading was the course text, *Looking at Law* (Fitzgerald, 1985). Two entire chapters of this text were analyzed syntactically, and the same computations were made, revealing that the syntax of this text was considerably closer in complexity to that of the other academic essays written by these students than it was to the syntax of their law essays. The explanation for the greater simplicity of the prose in the law text may lie in the fact that its author (the professor for the course) is a very conscious proponent of the plain English movement in law, and consequently of what he deems to be the plain style. Whatever the reason, though, neither this text, nor anything in the students' reading for this course, provided a model for the increased complexity of their prose.

Rhetorical patterns. In addition to the lexical and syntactic analyses, the papers were compared as to their rhetorical structure. We began broadly with Kinneavy's (1971) classification of aims of discourse. Kinneavy defines six aims, three of which are referential in their primary focus. Writing for law is certainly always referential and furthermore always falls into that specific referential category that Kinneavy names writing "to prove a thesis." In this, the writing for law was similar to most other academic writing. (In contrast, the course text was informative in aim, according to Kinneavy's classification, with the corresponding differences in rhetorical organization.)

Broadly, what characterizes such writing is that the whole is unified by a single thesis, often, though not necessarily, made explicit at both the beginning and end of the piece. The body consists of the proof for this thesis—either in the form of a series of separate points, or one carefully developed train of reasoning, or some combination of both. Sometimes a refutation or counter-argument is included.

---

[10] For a statistical analysis of the law essay, see Freedman (1996).

With this crude scheme as a model, writing for law distinguishes itself from other academic argumentative writing in three ways. First, it differs in degree: that is, it seems to embody the above qualities in their purest possible form. Such writing is almost ruthlessly logical, animated as it is by a precisely expressed thesis to which every specific point is clearly and explicitly linked. There is no room for digressions, and no tolerance of irrelevant or even semirelevant points (no matter how elegant).

Second, writing for law differs in that, far more than any other university assignments, it insists on the inclusion of all possible counter arguments. Consequently, there is a characteristic contrapuntal movement to its development that distinguishes it from the other academic writing produced by the students over the same period. In fact, in all the other essays analyzed, counter arguments were almost never introduced, whereas in the law papers (especially assignments 3 and 4), they were introduced at every juncture.

Third, although all academic writing must be logical in the sense that the conclusions must seem to be connected on a reasonable basis to the premises, the emphasis in writing for law is almost entirely on presenting the reasoning processes themselves. Every logical step must be articulated. In other disciplines, logical leaps are possible: connections are more often accepted as shared knowledge between reader and writer. In writing for law, the whole point of the exercise is to present not so much the logical conclusions but rather the rationale for these inferences. This point is further developed in the following section.

The nature of the argumentation.   Another way of understanding this distinction is through an analysis of the nature of the argumentation in these texts, using a categorization specified by Toulmin, Rieke, and Janik (1979). In this system, the following parts of an argument are distinguished: "the claim"—"the assertion put forward publicly for general acceptance," that is, the thesis; "the grounds"—"the specific facts relied on"; "the warrants"—the "general ways of arguing," that is, the principles for connecting the claims to the grounds; "the backing"—the authority for the warrants; the "modalities," which define the degree of strength of the claim; and "the rebuttals." Toulmin et al. (1979) argue that although all these elements are at least potentially present in every argument, there is considerable variation in the nature of each element as well as the emphasis given it, depending on the audience, the task, and especially the field or discipline.

Using such a frame of reference to illuminate the distinctiveness of the law writing, it was apparent that, whereas for most of the other academic writing undertaken by our students, emphasis was laid on presenting the claim and clarifying its implications by pointing extensively to the grounds (with the warrants often tacit), the primary focus in the law papers (especially the last two assignments) was on specifying the warrants and their backing in detail, and on showing how these warrants applied to the grounds. In the end, it mattered less what claim one made as long as the relationship between the various warrants possible to the grounds, accompanied by the appropriate backing, were all laid out.

Furthermore, the warrants drawn on were far more highly formalized, precise, and exact than those in other academic essays. There are precise rules or principles for statute interpretation and these must be specified in each instance of their use. The following excerpt reveals on the micro level the kind of argumentation that persists through the whole.

> The defense in this case would presumably argue that the wall is not a building by definition. Using *eiusdem generis* (of the same kind) canon of interpretation, it is evident that "building" as seen in section 4 refers to the list in section 3: a house, shed, barn, or other structure, which infers the membership of those structures that can be occupied. Therefore, the exclusion of members of the class, fence and wall, imply that they are not included under the meaning of "building." The elements listed that infer building all imply that one cannot occupy them. Since one cannot occupy (in the sense that one cannot enter into it and take shelter) a wall, Brown's boundary marker is therefore not applicable for prosecution under this statute.

Micro-level rhetorical patterns. Another distinct characteristic of these texts can be seen in a recurring pattern on the micro level. As the previously quoted excerpt shows, there is a characteristic pattern at the level of the conceptual paragraph that involves the following elements ordered in the following way: an elucidation of a central *issue*, the presentation of the appropriate *rule*, its *application*, and a *conclusion*.

Brand and White (1976), in their discussion of the characteristics of legal writing, identify such a pattern and give it the acronym IRAC (issue, rule, application, conclusion). What is intriguing is the degree to which this pattern recurs in the last two law assignments and only in the law essays, although none of the students consulted Brand and White or any similar handbook; nor did the professor or teaching assistant ever make mention of such a pattern in the seminars or classes.

To conclude, these various analyses reveal the degree to which writing for law is distinctive. The lexicon is discipline-specific; the syntax is more complex; the overall rhetorical structure is more purely thesis-oriented, less tolerant of digression, and characterized by a contrapuntal movement; the nature of the argumentation is distinct, focusing on specifying precise warrants, in the context of their backing, and showing their relationship to the grounds; and there are characteristic discourse features at the micro-level, such as the IRAC patterning of conceptual paragraphs.

Furthermore, this distinctiveness is clearly not modeled after any prose the students were reading for this course. Though similar in lexicon, the course text was less syntactically complex. Partly because its aim was primarily informative rather than argumentative, the rhetorical and discourse patterns on both the micro and macro levels differed radically from those discerned in the student papers.

Beyond Textual Regularities

Traditional analyses of genres would have begun and ended with the articulation of such textual regularities. What we will be doing here is to probe the significance of these textual features in terms of the role or perspective consequently taken on by the writer.

In his discussion of how children learn to write, Kress (1982) points to the "world-ordering" and even the "world-creating" function of "textual structures" (p. 97). The textual features described in the preceding section imply something about the way in which their writers approached or interpreted reality—at least during the writing of those texts. In this section, we tease out the implications of the textual features specified above for their writers' stances toward experience, their ways of knowing.

First, however, it is essential to point to the limitations of what can be inferred. The distinction proposed by Toulmin et al. (1979) is illuminating: the form of reasoning presented in these pieces does not replicate "a way of arriving at ideas but rather a way of testing ideas critically" (p. 29), a way of presenting them persuasively to a relevant audience. The steps in the legal arguments do not replicate the mental processes of the writer in determining the solution; instead, they represent the steps by which readers in a certain community can be convinced (or are prepared to be convinced) of the reasonableness of certain claims—claims that have themselves been discovered in as yet ill-understood ways by the writers. In other words, the discovery processes themselves, the internal cognitive operations, cannot be inferred from the products.

What can be inferred, however, is a kind of social action, implied and necessitated by the writing of these specific texts. Thus, the very issues addressed, the phenomena focused on, involve a certain categorization of experience that is different from that of the other academic pieces written by these students (and different from the kinds of categorizations implied in their discussions with us). Specific human situations are addressed, and addressed in a highly specialized way: not from the perspective of the human suffering entailed nor of the social dynamics involved, not from the perspective of universal moral principles, but rather from the point of view of the relevance of certain specialized legal principles.

This highly specialized categorization of experience is implied not only by the subject matter of the essays, but also by their distinctive lexicon. As we have seen, the language of the essays is characterized by a prolific use of legal terminology: law, statute, *eiusdem generis*, precedent. All these items reveal that the specific phenomena examined are being classified and organized according to the classificatory principles involved in the discipline of law studies. The writers not only look at the kind of phenomena typically analyzed by the discipline, they also use the same lenses. Furthermore, both the boundedness of the texts as well as the intolerance for digressions suggest a concentration of focus that excludes other possible perspectives.

The increased complexity of the syntax, the longer T-units and the greater number of clauses per T-unit suggest a more intense interest in the hierarchical interrelationships between propositions: specific propositions are seen in the context of others, and relationships of cause, effect, condition, and concession are highlighted. On the other hand, simple co-ordinate relationship in sentences (as measured by T-units per sentence) are of less interest. In an interview at the beginning of the course, the instructor tried to define what he thought of as distinctive in the writing he was eliciting: he spoke in general terms about the need for students "to see the forest rather than the trees." This search for and focus on hierarchical relationships may provide part of the textual instantiation of what the instructor was trying to suggest.

We can see evidence of this in an illustrative sentence from the assignment on statute interpretation. The task implicit in the assignment was to identify the nature of the relationships among the following: (a) the canons of statute interpretation; (b) the elements of specific statutes; and (c) the specifics of particular situations. Note the second of the following two sentences:

> Is a brick wall a structure? Brown could argue that a court would apply the *eiusdem generis* statute of interpretation and interpret "other structure" to cover only structures of the same kind as a house, shed, and barn, thus excluding "wall" from this classification, and exonerating Brown.

This second sentence has 41 words per T-unit, and an extraordinary range of dependent phrases and clauses, revealing a sophisticated understanding of complex logical interrelationships, involving classification, definition, condition, causation.

The contrapuntal pattern of the later essays is similarly revealing. Each issue or question, at the micro and macro levels, was addressed dialectically: for each point in favor, a corresponding point against was sought. When the array of pros and cons was set out, an attempt was made to arrive at some overarching generalization, taking into account all the arguments on both sides, rising thus to a higher level of abstraction and organizing the specific arguments into a superordinate framework. Here, too, is an example of seeing the forest, of pointing to a pattern that can organize the distinct entities.

This dialectical stance is not unique to law as a discipline: it has important precedents in the history of philosophy, for example. At the same time, it is not the only perspective possible certainly, and not necessarily the best. Coe (1986) has pointed to the degree to which a dialectical approach can be limiting. Without arguing for or against the value of any particular stance, it is important to stress that the dialectical stance evinced in these essays represents only one possible stance toward a question—and interestingly not a stance that was represented in any other essays written by the students whose law essays were analyzed over the year that they were enrolled in the law course. (All their other assignments were analyzed at the same time as the law essays.)

The text analyses also pointed to a distinctive mode of argumentation. In specifying the pros and cons, the writers argued using highly formalized and specialized modes of reasoning. Without suggesting that such modes of reasoning replicated the students' original discovery processes, we are arguing that, at the stage of drafting, the students needed to follow through in writing certain kinds of argumentation: that is, to engage in the application of very specialized methods of inference. In other words, they enacted in writing certain modes of reasoning that differed from the modes enacted for other disciplines.

To sum up, in the course of and as a result of their writing, these students began to look at and interpret reality in certain prescribed ways: they focused on certain kinds of phenomena, categorized them in specified ways, took a dialectical stance, searched for hierarchic relationships, and enacted certain formalized modes of reasoning.

To use Willard's (1982) language, through their writing, these students began "to construe certain phenomena in roughly the same way that other actors in the field construe them" (p. 34). The field in the case we observed was that of law as a disciplinary activity whose goals are epistemic (as opposed to the action-oriented goals of law as an "ordinary" activity). In writing their essays, the students began to share the stance of, and consequently to affiliate with, a certain argument field or discourse community—that of students of law.

To return to the point made earlier, the writing enabled or constrained the students to take on certain ways of construing reality—ways that were similar to those expected in the fields to which they aspired. The social action undertaken in this writing is typical of that undertaken in much school writing, in that its purpose is epistemic—not in the sense of producing knowledge new to the reader, but rather in the specialized sense of enabling its writer to see and interpret reality in new ways; in that these ways are the ways of currently constituted communities of scholars, the purpose of and the action undertaken in such writing is social and cultural as well.

Writing Finance Papers

Textual features of other student papers pointed to other stances. For example, the case studies written by students in a financial analysis course differed from other academic papers in their use of numbers. "It's a numbers course," the professor repeated, but the use of the numbers differed from that in both accounting and economics courses. To quote the professor, the "quantitative stuff" in the course "requires some judgment, whereas in accounting cases, you simply have to consolidate a balance sheet.... Here there is a lot of interpretation." And the interpretation is always expressed verbally. The ability to interpret numeric phenomena verbally is one important course objective. "I find that a lot of finance people know what they're doing but don't know how to *explain* what they're doing.... So one of the pedagogical purposes of the course is to improve on technical finance-type writing." Consider the professor's complaints about a flawed paper:

> Here the problem is he's making statements which have no meaning in finance. For example, well it's more English—"keep the dream alive," "faltering economy," "playing havoc with the economy," "its already fragile credit rating." So, it's not the type of thing a chief financial officer would like to read because he has to almost say, "Tell me, what do you mean by 'faltering.' Show me the ratio which tells me this company's faltering. If you cannot show it, don't say that. If he says something like, "For example, looking at the current ratio (x) and the liquidity ratio (y) and interest calculations (z), it seems as if the company would be unable to continue in its present course." Unless he says that, I wouldn't put any faith in his statement, in his "faltering company," because he hasn't proved to me it's faltering.

Note the invocation of a figure from the relevant discourse community, "a chief financial officer," and the way that the professor slips naturally from what that officer would say to what he, the professor, says. What is at issue in the writing is not only the ways of categorizing experience and construing reality, but also the grounds for persuasion and belief in that community: numbers are persuasive and real; more transparently interpretive phrases such as "faltering economy" are not.

Composing Processes

Analysis of the composing sessions offered another window into the nature of the enculturation suggested by our examination of textual features. Specifically, transcripts of these sessions revealed the degree to which the students' thinking was shaped and enclosed by the ways of knowing and valuing modeled by the professor, although initially this phenomenon was difficult to discern—precisely because the shaping was so pervasive.

Bourdieu and Passeron (1977) provide theoretic analyses of this phenomenon. Specifically, they speak of processes of symbolic violence and structures of symbolic domination, which they describe as "the imposition of systems of symbolism and meaning upon groups or systems or classes *in such a way that they are* experienced *as legitimate*" (emphasis ours; p. 104). Our analysis of student talk in the composing sessions uncovered traces of this process at work. In the following conversation, for example, we saw how naturally the students seemed to assimilate the categorizations of reality implicit in the discipline, especially in their use of nouns.

> Mike: I guess the biggest thing is the debt-to-equity ratio. Notice that? X has way more equity. If you look at Y, their equity compared to their debts is nowhere near, it's not even in the ballpark.
>
> Joe: Which company is it that took a whole bunch of short-term debt?

Note the degree to which such technical terms as "short-term debt," "equity," and "debt-to-equity ratio" are assimilated within the intonational contours of casual conversation.

Furthermore, as suggested by Bourdieu and Passeron, this assimilation takes place without reflection and is experienced as legitimate. There was certainly no questioning in the texts, the composing sessions, or the interviews of the values and warrants presented throughout the course. The assumption or the donning of these values occurred entirely tacitly. On occasion, something in the composing sessions revealed the degree and nature of the enculturation.

Consider the following example, which illustrates the nature of the collaborative inquiry as well as the way in which certain factors are tacitly recognized as irrelevant (the tacitness underlining the degree to which the distinctions were experienced as legitimate). In this excerpt, after a long stretch in which students kept probing at the case-study data, one student initiated a collaborative search for potential causes of the company's current financial plight.

Mike: I think that their problem is that they tried to get too big when they weren't capable of going big. They got screwed. What do you guys think?

    ...

    I think that is one of the biggest problems. They tried to go international and stuff and they didn't have the cash to do it.

Joe: I dunno. I just think that they took on way too much short-term debt.

Mike: Why'd they take on the short-term debt?

Judy: They issued those shares—

Joe: because they were expanding and they needed the cash to fund their expansions and stuff and their share prices were low so they were probably waiting until—

Mike: So, maybe one of the big issues is that they shouldn't have tried to expand. Like, we are looking at what went wrong. They tried to go for something that wasn't there.

Joe: Or maybe the timing was bad.

Judy: Yeah, that too.

Mike: Yeah, a lot of bad things happened

Joe: that they couldn't really control—recessions and exchange rates were killing them.

Judy: The recession.... They had a drought too.

Joe: And when did all those military coups happen?

Judy: (writing) Political problems

    ...

[THE FOLLOWING AS ASIDE]

Joe: Archie McLoughlin screwed them.

Judy: Yeah, peddling—

Joe: Bend over boys, I'm coming to town.
       Laughter

    ...

[Serious tone resumes]

Mike: (reading from text) their stock price from January '76 to July '80 lost 16 7/8 percent.

Note the discussion of Archie McLoughlin, uttered as an aside in a tone reserved primarily for playful banter—as the particular idiom suggests. Archie McLoughlin is the fictional name that we are using here to replace the actual name of the contemporary businessman referred to in the case history that the students were to analyze. His actions played a significant role in the crisis that a specific company was facing in the case history. However, the students had all tacitly intuited that his actions or any responses by individuals were not to be included as part of their written analyses: economic or political forces (political instability, market forces, recession), not the actions or stances of individuals, were understood to be the relevant issues to address in this genre.

At the same time, they all seemed to recognize tacitly that none of the values at issue in McLoughlin's actions—values such as loyalty, charity, adherence to family tradition—would be appropriate as warrants. Consequently, the written case analysis made no mention of him, though talk about him came up more than once in the composing sessions in the same bantering tone, and always as asides.

In short, although there was no explicit consideration given to the fact that the issues surrounding McLoughlin's involvement were not appropriate to the kind of argument they needed to make, the students all seem to have intuited this tacitly; they did not even debate the issue among themselves. They seemed to know that any mention of him would not be appropriate in their written case studies. At the same time, because he is an immensely successful and highly publicized business figure, McLoughlin fascinated them, as their conversation about him suggests.

The writing, more than the talk, revealed a seamless assumption of the values, stance, and ideology of the course. Wertsch (1991), drawing on Bakhtin, talks of the power of dialogism; that is, the degree to which we draw on, echo, or "ventriloquate" (his word) the language and speech genres we have heard in every utterance that we make. The students whom we observed responded ventriloquistically to the readings and classroom discourse, in the tasks set for them. As suggested earlier, they picked up (and transformed in the context of their preexistent conversational patterns) the social language or register they heard. Consider these examples:

A: I figured this is how we should structure it.... First, how did they get there is the first thing.
B: So that's ...
A: Business versus financial risk or operations versus debt. Whatever.... Then ... like we will get it from the bankers' perspective.
B: Yeah, that's pretty much like what I was thinking too.

A: So, right now I have their thing before 78. How do you want it, pre-78 post-78? This is what I did. I went through all

B: Internal comparison and stuff.

In writing their papers, the conversational syntax and lexicon disappeared. In the final draft of a case study, we find the following:

Short-term debt restructuring is a necessity. The 60% ratio must be reduced to be more in line with past trends and with the competition. This will be achieved by extension of debt maturities, conversion of debt to equity, reduction of interest rates, as well as deferral of interest payments.

Through the mediation of and appropriation of the social languages modeled in the course, the students created the new genres expected of them, realizing the roles or subject-positions entailed, and the students produced the written social language designated by their professor as that of a "financial analyst" (see Freedman, Adam & Smart, 1994).

COMPLICATING THE SOCIAL MOTIVE

To suggest, however, that the sole social motive for school genres is epistemic would be grossly misleading. At least as significant is a different intention and often a competing motive. A hint of this is provided in the following discussion by an instructor describing the way he reads student texts.

What I do with these is I read them twice—the entire group. First I order them alphabetically, and then I read them twice—the whole set. I don't do any marking. I don't even think about marking. And the only reason I do that, or one of the main reasons I do that, is I want to get a sense of the quality I'm supposed to expect. So, I read through them all, and that really tells me the quality of a particular group.... And then my second level is when I start marking. But before I do that, while I'm doing this second reading, I'm putting them in piles already. To say, "Hmmm, this has some merit." Or "this is really good." And at the end of this process, I get maybe six or seven piles, and then I start grading them. Because, it's relative, but I do that before I start actually marking them.

The governing purpose of the reading here is evaluation. The need to grade determines when the pieces will be read, how many times, and with what end in view.

Freadman (1987) has pointed to the degree to which a genre can be seen as play and interplay, and the degree to which feedback is part of the genre. The reading practices thus point to another fundamental and illuminating difference between workplace and academic writing. Essential to the institution of schooling is its gatekeeping function and, more specifically, its role in ranking students—that is, assessing them in terms of carefully specified criteria and slotting them into categories according to their relative performance with respect to such criteria. Writing forms the basis for such comparative ranking by externalizing students' ways of construing/constructing reality and thus allowing for the Foucauldian (1979) "normalizing gaze"—the "surveillance that makes it possible to qualify, to classify, to punish" (p.184). To put the matter differently, within the classroom context each paper is graded in comparison to all others, and the institution has a vested interest in ensuring a quality spread. This was not true of the workplace; there, the institutional goal is to elicit the best possible product from each employee each time writing is undertaken.

Bakhtin (1986), Nystrand (1989), and Brandt (1990), among others, have pointed to the role of addressivity and the shaping role of the anticipated reader's response in text production. Similarly, from the perspective of the sociology of language, Bourdieu and Passeron (1977) have commented, "it is the speaker's anticipation of the reception which his/her discourse will receive (its price) which contributes to *what* is said and *how*" (p. 154). The anticipation of such evaluation by the reader affects the writing from its inception. Hence, students' recurrent references to their anticipated grade before and during their writing. Equally revealing is the clearly expressed sense that for the student, for any piece of writing, closure is achieved when a grade has been assigned: only when the grade is assigned (and celebrated or mourned) is the episode experienced as complete.

A physical correlate of this phenomenon is evidenced in the spatial and temporal extension of the texts produced. Student writing has a relatively ephemeral existence. Student papers are often thrown out immediately after the grade is assigned; occasionally they are not even picked up from the grader. Even when they are kept in the student's files, they are rarely consulted again by the writer and almost never by anyone else. In the workplace, however, texts have a continued physical existence (in accessible files within the institution) as well as an ongoing role in the institutional conversation and memory. Smart (1993) quotes one executive officer as follows: "We rely heavily on a history of thought, and the files ... are really important. Questions keep recirculating ... and having the written word is very important, at times, to go back to ... to know what we've done before, and where we've started from." The student writing we observed, in contrast, had no continued existence in terms of intertextual reference.

The concern to rank students affected the reading responses of the professor in other significant ways. Note the following concern expressed by one professor about pieces that were assigned to be written independently: "Sometimes, two or three students would write on the same [topic].... So I put them separately. So I really put them separately for two reasons. One is I want to see how much they have talked to each other and because I had warned them if I ever hear one word the same, excluding the verbs, I'm going to be back to you." A related but slightly different concern expressed was that a particular paper had been written either partly or in full for another course. In the workplace, concerns about originality, about the possible use of others' ideas (except that they must sometimes be attributed) or about one's earlier work are not issues that affected the readers we observed. Workplace writing is characterized by a kind of intertextuality entirely absent from the student writing; workplace writing is resonant with the discourse of colleagues and the ongoing conversation of the institution. The etiquette for citing is complex and political; but the fact of such intertextual borrowing is a reality and a perceived good.

What we are suggesting, then, is that if one goal of university writing is epistemic, from another perspective its purpose is to allow for evaluation. These two are not inconsistent of course: it is through writing epistemically, and as a result of their relative success in so doing, that students are evaluated. This reality shaped the writing in ways both simple and complex: from the differences we have seen and shall see in the relative duration of the texts in space, time, and memory, to different expectations concerning shared knowledge and very different kinds of intertextual practice.

CONCLUSION

Two features characterize recent definitions of genre: social action and recurrence or typification. We should just note here that recurrence in university contexts is typically synchronic rather than diachronic. Thus, as we have noted, there was no attempt to consult models of the target genres by students in university courses as opposed to the practice of professionals in the workplace. That this is so is a stunning fact, and like many linguistic achievements, one that is so naturalized as to be taken for granted.

The recurrence that is characteristic of genres is thus a result of a synchronic mutual construal of the rhetorical exigence. This synchronic mutual construal is possible only because the discursive context is so clearly demarcated and created, and the questions formed in such a way that they point to material somehow earlier cued in the course, as ways of thinking. Furthermore, all this is collaboratively achieved through the complex interaction of all players. Students and teachers negotiate a context, shaped physically, culturally, politically, rhetorically, and ideologically by the discipline, the institution, and society at large, through processes of dialogic interplay and ventriloquation.

4

COMPLICATIONS
AND TENSIONS

In chapter 3, drawing on genre theory, we considered the social motives, the rhetorical exigencies and recurring situations that account for underlying regularities in textual practices and textual form and substance. We identified social motive as key to understanding the nature of potential differences between university and workplace writing. We examined student writing in order to show how the underlying social motive for such writing is epistemic, oriented toward knowledge, as opposed to writing for instrumental or practical purposes, to get things done. However, the epistemic motive is also tangled within the university's function to sort and rank its students, defining a context that shapes student writing in complex ways. That context, as it shapes course design and, specifically, the design of writing assignments, gives rise to contradictions both in teaching practices and in how students interpret their roles and responsibilities.

In this chapter, we examine the fundamental contradictions that emerge because of these conflicting impulses, using the frame of Activity Theory (AT), introduced in chapter 2, to uncover the complications and tensions created by this dual social motive. We look at the design of the assignments that call for the writing, the context of the courses and programs in which these assignments arise, and the social motives that direct their design and how writing is solicited. Cole and Engeström (1993) find it more useful to speak of an activity system rather than activity as the basic unit of analysis: "historically conditioned systems of relations among individuals and their proximal, culturally organized environments" (p. 9). Because AT is so inclusive in its approach—each aspect of an activity is seen and understood as part of the molar whole—it can help us understand what actions, motives, and relationships are actually at play in the activity system called the course within the context of the larger system called the university: its institutional practices, the participants in that system, the design and operation of courses, and disciplinary expectations and practices.

That activity systems function within or in close alliance with other activity systems, as well as the fact that actors in a system are simultaneously participants in other systems, sows the seeds for the contradictions and conflicts mentioned above. Professors move back and forth between classrooms and their academic research with its own set of goals and a different set of perspectives; both systems, classroom teaching and academic research, compete for time and attention. Universities function alongside the workplace for which they must prepare students and with which they remain closely linked and interdependent. At the same time, with increasing appeals for corporate sponsorship, actors within the university are hard pressed to guard their autonomy and retain their identity. It is interesting how workplace management strategies are increasingly advocated for academic governance and met often with resistance if not incomprehension. Students often live on the borders between such activity systems, juggling course demands with social, recreational, and workplace needs. Such complex systems define our roles and afford or deny us certain positions. An interesting account of such conflictual positioning is offered by Bazerman (1988), who traces the development of the multiple and conflicting roles scientists occupy as a scientific article moves toward publication; for example, author, editor, referee, critical reader, user of information. AT helps make salient institutional structures and the complex relationships within them, revealing how individuals' actions within such structures and relationships are far less complementary than they appear, and that students and teachers are bound within certain roles that prescribe actions that conflict or are at least set up some degree of tension among the several goals they ostensibly mean to fulfill. Chapter 6 offers a similarly complex picture of a workplace.

The activity system we call the course reveals two sets of complementary activities. From the perspective of the teacher, we have the activity traditionally called teaching and including actions such as designing courses, assessing, and ranking. From the perspective of students, we may speak of actions traditionally associated with the activity of being a student: attending and participating in classes, completing required readings, preparing and delivering individual and group oral presentations, preparing and submitting individual and group written assignments, and taking tests and examinations. We label these activities teaching and studenting (for want of a better word in order to designate a far more active role than the passive-receptive role traditionally associated with being a student), and we ask how and to what extent the actions that are discerned as part of these activities are congruent with one another. We expect to see, for instance, how the motives directing teaching and the motives directing studenting are not necessarily congruent and reveal on examination some fundamental contradictions. The two activities, teaching and studenting, seemingly complementary and operating in parallel, represent two different perspectives and generate actions whose goals are often at odds with one another. Such dissonances are not obvious, often emerging only on analysis; however, they explain in a large way how writing in university is situated quite differently from the way it is in the workplace.

Our examination of the activity system, the course, within the larger activity system, the university, reveals three fundamental sources of tension: tension between the activity of teaching and the activity of studenting; tension between the instructor's need to teach, guide, and generally ensure that certain concepts are learned and the limits such control places on learning; and tension between the need to grade and the need to do so economically (in terms of time and effort) and therefore limit the amount and kinds of writing that are required, and consequently the opportunity for learning through writing. In the discussion that follows we examine how these tensions are played out in a university course and how they define the place and function of writing in university settings.

WHAT'S GOING ON HERE?

The kind of questions we are asking and the answers we seek are exemplified in a study by Wertsch, Minick, and Arns (1984), who observed the interaction between teachers and young children and parents and their young children as they assisted these children in completing an experimental task. They found that

> [concerned for] the correct and efficient completion of the task at hand, ... mothers viewed the task setting as calling for maximal assistance, whereas the teachers viewed it as calling for maximal independence on the part of the child. (p. 170)

Wertsch et al. (1984) distinguish between formal schooling, where learning is the overriding motive, and household economic activity or work, where the emphasis (for several reasons) is on "error-free performance ... [and] flawless task performance is valued over learning for learning's sake" (p. 155). The AT analysis Wertsch et al. employ allows them to explain how seemingly the same activity (in this case, the experimental task) is defined in two different ways according to the motives of the subjects, and generates a different action in each case. This illustration is particularly effective in explaining some of the differences between writing practices at work and in university discussed in the foregoing chapter. Writing at work as an economic activity justifies the kind of intervention and assistance needed to ensure a flawless performance. Writing at school, because of the focus on learning, allows teachers to discount errors or failures to meet specific demands or expectations, in favor of assessing what has been learned. In fact, such errors or failures may be valued as opportunities to clarify a particular concept or teach a relevant skill. Even though they may set a high value on flawless performance, teachers, including teachers of writing, would question any suggestion that they intervene in a student's writing to ensure a product that meets the specifications they have set. They could see such intervention as contrary to their role and function as teachers, subverting both their goal of promoting learning and their goals of evaluating and ranking students on the basis of what they know and can do.

Such tensions and conflicts arising from contradictory views of roles and goals were amply present in a course we observed over two semesters in a Management Studies program at a Canadian university. Our intention was to discover how writing practices were defined within those two activities, teaching and studenting, and how those definitions complemented or contradicted one another.

Management Strategies is a required course in the second year of a 2-year graduate program. The main thrust of the curriculum has to do with analyzing, evaluating, developing, and implementing appropriate management strategies in the context of solving complex management problems. In the first half of the year-long course, students are introduced to theories and issues in preparation for fieldwork in the second half.

Work Required

Students in this course generally work in groups (6–7 students per group) and generally remain in these groups throughout the semester. Groups are reconstituted for the fieldwork component in the second semester. Most of the work done in the course is planned within groups and presented by groups. Case studies are assigned on a weekly basis, each case-study analysis designed to help students demonstrate their understanding of and apply key theoretical notions. In their groups, students prepare their analyses, using preset guide questions. All groups prepare reports, using overhead transparencies to register the major points of their reports. While only one or two groups are chosen at random to present their analyses to the class, all groups must provide copies of their transparencies and a list of references to the teacher. As these presentations are open to discussion and questions from members of the class, groups that have not presented have an opportunity to raise questions and issues which have arisen from their own group discussions. Four of these case studies will be written up by the groups in the form of one-page position papers to be turned in on the day the case is discussed. Groups also take turns preparing for the class an update on the particular company that is the subject of the case study (what has happened to the company since the case study was prepared), a way of checking their analyses and predictions against actual outcomes.

Evaluation

Grades are calculated on the following basis:

- Participation 25%
- Group case reports 25%
- Four group one-page position papers on selected cases 30%
- Take-home essay examination: an individual case report 20%

As the greater part of work for this course involves planning and presenting in groups, assigning 55% of the final mark to group work is easily justifiable. Individual performance is evaluated primarily on the basis of the take-home essay examination (20%) and on the instructor's assessment of the student's participation (25%).

The second-semester Fieldwork Project presentation, a group project, is graded Pass, Fail, or Excellent. Members of groups that receive a Pass will be assigned the numerical grade they received for their first-semester work. Groups that receive a failing grade are required to write a 30-page report on the project. If the report is acceptable, members receive their first-semester grade for the entire course. If the report is unacceptable, group members fail the whole course. Members of groups that receive an Excellent for the Fieldwork Project have their first-semester grade raised by 5%. Only one of six groups received an Excellent and the extra points. No group presentation was judged Unacceptable.

AN ACTIVITY THEORY (AT) ANALYSIS

We have gone into some detail on the structure and organization of the course in order to situate the actions of students and their teacher, particularly with regard to the place of writing in the course. The following analysis uses the three-tiered scheme from AT (see pages 23–28) to consider how the motive of teaching and the motive of grading and ranking students configure the action of writing in this course. The account is sketched first in terms of the teacher's motive and goals. We go on later to view some of the course events in terms of the students' motives and goals in order to consider whether and how the students' several actions support the teacher's motives and goals.

Using an AT approach, we would identify two conjoint activities: teaching with the motive of promoting the learning of certain concepts and grading/ranking with the motive of both monitoring learning and meeting institutional goals. Toward those ends, the teacher's actions are fairly conventional: lectures and assigned readings with the goal of communicating an understanding of key concepts, and designing and administering a series of tasks with the goal of helping students apply those concepts and at the same time enabling the teacher to monitor their learning and assign grades on the basis of preset and announced criteria. It is when we examine these tasks as a series of actions with their respective goals that we discover several internal contradictions.

From the teacher's perspective, the goals of these presentations are to allow students to develop (during their group discussions primarily) their understandings of the issues involved. Such learning opportunities are further enhanced in that time is set aside after the presentations to "discuss, critique, and elaborate" (course handout) on the presentations. Presenters are expected to respond to questions from the group, and demonstrate their understandings so that they can be assessed.

It is clear from the description of the assignments that the teacher's actions are directed by two major goals:

1. ensuring that several key concepts are learned and applied to real-world problems as simulated by the case studies, and
2. given limited resources, ensuring that such learning occurs efficiently and expediently, and provides at the same time, sufficient and clear evidence for grading and ranking.

Similar goals can be attributed to most if not all university courses; unfortunately, expedience, efficiency, and the need to rank also have unwanted consequences. Expedience requires that oral presentations be promoted at the expense of written analyses, reducing the amount of individual writing that needs to be read in this course to the five-page written case analysis assigned as an examination. These oral reports must be presented on overhead transparencies and include three to five key points (bulleted on overhead transparencies), which allows for a quick and easy assessment of whether the required issues have been identified. According to the teacher, the three- to five-point limit also cultivates a focus on the issues that matter and a judicious exclusion (by negotiation in groups) of issues that can be omitted without misrepresenting the case.

The need to reduce the amount of writing that must be read and assessed leads to a ritual of oral presentations by groups, the one or two groups that present being chosen at random (but all groups come prepared to present), and the opportunity to be publicly accountable, to question and discuss, and to receive peer and teacher feedback. So evaluative criteria are enacted far more publicly (and are potentially more instructive) than they would be if they were relegated to feedback on writing. The working in small groups allows for a process of familiarization with new terminology, the talking through of new concepts, developing oral fluency, sharing of interpretations and relevant experiences—all very much a display of distributed cognition.

Though again there are inherent contradictions. Students are asked to assume important decision-making or advisory roles (product manager, advisor to the CEO of a large corporation, owner's daughter assisting her father, manager of a large steel mill), analyze the situation (as described), and make judgments and predictions. But the situations are spurious; these students as and when they enter the workforce will be at the periphery rather than at the center (to adopt the phrasing of Lave and Wenger, 1991), learning much from observation and the expertise of oldtimers. Despite this worthy intention to involve students in real-world situations, the cases represent an encapsulated reality (to adapt a phrase from Engeström [1991] for how reality is reduced to manageable proportions for the purposes of teaching), and in the sequence in which they are presented, an ordered introduction of key concepts to be mastered. Each case, for instance, calls for and illustrates the application of a specific strategy or theory. Moreover, the problem solutions that students are expected to explore are circumscribed and assured by the five or six questions that the teacher has provided with each case. Those questions focus students' attention on just those issues that are relevant in the planned sequence and also ensure that all groups have addressed a common set of issues rather than strayed in the ways independent groups are wont to. The teaching goal clearly controls the design of the tasks. In the workplace, it cannot be assumed so easily that tasks are as clearly defined and situations unchanging as such simulations imply (Engeström, Engeström, & Kärkkäinen, 1995.)

A brief view of this activity from the students' perspective is also instructive. If we view the activity of studenting as fixed on completing the course with a good grade, we can discern one typical action and its directing goal: attend to and recall the teacher's announced, preferred ways of demonstrating knowledge in order to succeed in this course. Thus as we observe one of the groups working on a case for presentation to the class, one of the members reminds the group to focus on the points the teacher "really emphasized in Tuesday's class" and lists them. Another recalls, "like, these are things she repeated." In another group, a member reminds the group that the professor had said she was looking for certain strategies: "She wants to see that in the paper." It isn't that these are deliberate strategies; rather, a school performance genre has become routinized, what in the three-tiered Activity scheme we would assign to the level of operations: attending to the teacher's expectations becomes second nature in school. The main actions of the group are to follow the list of questions provided by the teacher, report their answers to the group, and then have one or two students use their notes to write up the analysis. In this particular case their analysis must be reduced to a one-page position paper (one of four cases required to be written up in this way). Despite the fact that they are encouraged to go beyond case details to investigate the current situation of the company, use library resources or visit a branch office, for instance, the groups find sufficient detail in the case account itself to be able to answer the guiding questions. The one-page limit for the position papers, the emphasis on oral presentation using overheads (reducing analysis to key points), and the teacher's list of guiding questions ensure that the students will learn what they are meant to learn. The students are in fact reminded early in the semester that they must focus on these questions. And to be fair, there is no time and little room for independent inquiry and fortuitous discovery.

Thus a one-page position paper based on the APE case faithfully follows the discussion questions provided by the teacher (as do the write-ups on other cases we have looked at):

Teacher's Questions	Group's text
Identify 3–4 factors in APE's corporate structure and strategy-making process which led to its decline in the 1980s and 90s.	The main structural contribution to APE's decline in the 80's and 90's was ... Three strategic factors that further pushed the decline were ...
What could APE have done to avoid such a turn of events? What factors helped keep APE afloat after ... ?	To thwart such a turn of events ... The main factor which kept APE afloat after ... Another factor was ...
What are critical factors in turning around an organization?	The critical factors in turning around an organization are ...
Could APE's measures apply in other organizations? Why or or why not?	In order for APE's measures to be effective in other organizations ... APE was fortunate in ... Not every company ...

The teacher's questions function as a template for the writing. The students use the word-processor to specify very narrow margins, both top/bottom and left/right, in order to remain within the one-page limit. The one-page limit was not adhered to in subsequent tasks that specified such a limit. This particular group was aware that other groups had ignored this limit and not been penalized. From an AT perspective it appears that the teacher's action of providing guiding questions is directed by the goal of ensuring that certain key concepts are addressed. The one-page limit, intended to force a narrowing down to the critical issues ("It forces them to summarize the key issues if they only have one page"—teacher interview) acts in the actual discussion as a means of enforcing closure on both the discussion and the writing.

The group position paper is rated an A–, with comments urging elaboration in two places and a reminder to take issues to another level and address them. Such urging to expand and explore, in direct conflict with the teacher's demand for brevity, is a reminder of the teacher's prior concern to promote learning, as is her apparent willingness not to penalize those who exceed the prescribed one-page limit. The teacher's grade of A– confirms to the group that they were right in stretching the page-length limit in order to pursue the teacher's questions more fully. On the other hand, if penalized, they would have in subsequent tasks reverted to the one-page limit, as they (student-wise) did in their first paper, even if it meant they had to forego answering some questions.

But there are other interests at play here in this activity system. With a class size of 50, the teacher needs to ensure from week to week that the key concepts each case exemplifies are recognized by all students. The four or five questions she appends to each case (e.g., How did MENTOR's strategy and organization lead to a loss of momentum? How might Levinson, the new CEO, act to recover lost ground and positive momentum? What long term goals must Levinson establish for MENTOR?) are in addition to questions already appended by the authors of the case. Although we could argue that these questions are likely to forestall ownership of the problem and independent inquiry (as well as the development of analytical skills), the pedagogical imperative prevails. The teacher cannot risk that key concepts will go unrecognized and undiscussed, and that therefore the discussion that follows the presentation of the cases will not focus on the precise agenda those questions set up.

Unlike writers in out-of-school settings, who are expected to provide (or give the appearances of providing) as clear and as full an analysis as would get a job done or enable a decision on the part of those who have commissioned the analysis (the economic imperative), writers in school, while keeping a partial eye on the announced goals of the task, are much more concerned by what it is the teacher really expects of them. This is a serious issue for students when one considers that they must work this out in relation to the expectations of four other instructors with more or less similar demands on their time.

We have examined the activities of teaching and studenting in the context of the actions involved in the case-study presentations. The individual take-home essay examination and the second-semester field-study group report provide, on analysis, additional instances of the ways in which the epistemic motive is compromised by the institutional need to grade and rank.

The Individual Case Analysis

This case analysis, which functions as a take-home examination, requires a five-page report, provides direct evidence of individual learners' progress in the course, and is the only extended individual piece of writing submitted in the course. All other required writing, as we said earlier, is a joint effort: four 1-page position papers and an 8-page analysis ("Use the questions in the course guide to plan your analysis and writing," the course outline advises). Again, this case is written up with four questions to guide analysis. An analysis of practices associated with this task provides a clear message that writing is not seen as a means of informing the reader; it is intended primarily to display knowledge. The teacher knows all reasonably acceptable permutations on how the case ought to be written up, and in fact, provides an answer key to guide the teaching assistant who will grade these papers: "the major points of the analysis," a set of criteria for six grade levels ranging from a grade of "A" to "C", and bench-mark papers. Consistency in grading becomes the ruling criterion. Students who read the situation as a test-taking genre are unlikely to see this case study as an opportunity to pursue innovative solutions.

The teaching assistant reads the papers primarily to establish the extent to which the papers meet the set guidelines, checking off the approved points as they appear ("I'm just trying to underline the relevant points that are given here" - from taped think-aloud during reading). This task is not taken lightly, as the teacher does review the papers and grades to ensure that the teaching assistant has followed the grading scheme.

Writing From a Workplace Situation

During the second semester, each group chooses and studies a company (arrangements to be made by the group; commitments to the firm to be negotiated and met by the group, including a report if required) with the intention of finding an organizational problem with strategic implications within the company, diagnosing the problem, and recommending solutions. Unlike students in co-op programs, these students enter a company as consultants and outsiders. The study involves interviews with members of the company and an analysis of relevant internal and external documents. A similar assignment in a systems analysis course is described in chapter 10.

Each group must present an oral report to the class and invited representatives of the cooperating organization. The presentation is limited to 30 minutes, with a further 30 minutes for questions from the class. Groups must follow certain guidelines for an effective presentation. "Begin with a bottom-line summary, 3–5 subpoints to support central argument, support data for key points, use only data that fits action-oriented recommendations, realistic recommendations" (from course materials). Presenters must use overhead transparencies to highlight the key argument or recommendation(s), the subpoints that bear out the central point, and supporting data.

This project constitutes the entire second-semester portion of this course; however, six preliminary lectures are scheduled that focus on introducing students to issues that relate to their entering an organization, conducting interviews and other forms of data-gathering, and presenting their results in an effective format. Considerable emphasis is given to presentation strategies, focusing primarily on organization of the content in logical fashion. Members of the class have the option of completing and handing in evaluation and ranking forms on each group's performance. The items in the form place a high value on how well the presentation has been structured, preferring a particular order: identify underlying problem, support with clearly-linked subpoints, conclude with summary. These peer evaluations will be used to determine the grade for the group.

This second-semester writing task is intended to help students apply their knowledge to analyzing problems and developing strategies in workplace situations. The faculty, and this program particularly, prides itself on being oriented to teaching skills in context. Because students in a group have to search out and negotiate entry into a company or institution, they have begun to function like professional consultants seeking out clients and with some claim to a special expertise. The report they present in a closing session at the university with company representatives present is intended to simulate a consulting report; however, the guidelines for the task clearly imply the centrality of the teacher's role as intended audience and evaluator.

Because students have to negotiate their own entry into an organization, they are severely constrained in matching the requirements set out for the project with the organization and the problem they eventually identify and study. Specific requirements for the problem they identify and choose to report on are set out in the assignment guidelines, as are the format for the report and oral presentation. The students are used to having a situation spelled out for them in the case study reports, with just those relevant details that help identify a problem situation, which by the way in such situations is always identified after the fact and benefits from hindsight in the writing. They are used to creating a controlled reality from already mediated data many times removed from reality. On site, because they are outsiders, they may or may not have access to all the information they need to identify, describe, analyze, and suggest solutions to a problem. Strategic observations from experienced employees will not necessarily be volunteered. As in the case of the Wertsch et al. (1984) study referred to earlier, these students are quite likely to be regarded by these employees as learners who would benefit most from being allowed to make their own decisions and learn from them. It is less likely, therefore, that these students' reports will be received and treated seriously.

The reports are to be presented orally with the aid of overhead transparencies. These oral reports replace a 30-page written report that was required until the previous year, but was discontinued for reasons discussed below. However, if students fail this oral presentation, they are to write the 30-page report, a requirement that cannot but be read by them as punitive. In AT terms, the activity of writing such a report, which ought to be positively charged, challenging and inventive in orientation, becomes an after-the-fact, course-required and grade-directed (but otherwise inconsequential) activity.

During the presentation the students appeared somewhat uncertain and diffident when guests from their host company were present, compared with when only the teacher and students made up the audience. Clearly, those guests were not the primary audience they were meant to be. Although the guests listened with some degree of interest, none of them took notes. It is quite likely that the students' reading of the situation in the company was not adequate to the complexity and nuances of the actual situation. "Local knowledge" was precisely what was lacking. Although company representatives were free to ask for copies of reports (which would then have to be written), no such requests were actually made. The primary audience was the teacher, whose particular concerns appear to be reflected in students' seemingly inordinate focus on using management terminology. Ostensibly a work activity, the project and its implementation remains in essence a school activity directed both by epistemic motives and the institutional need to rank and grade.

WRITING IN MANAGEMENT

It is not an accident that writing has not been in the forefront of this account. This isn't only because relatively little formal writing is required in this course. The four 1-page position papers were intended originally to be written as individual papers; however, the teacher balked (rightly, it seems, given her workload) at the amount of writing she would have to read. Writing is secondary to oral reporting, the latter being regarded by the teacher as the prime means of reporting in business. The second-semester project confirms this view: the 30-page external report formerly required from the field-work project was discontinued in favor of an oral presentation. The writing, the teacher says, was "superficial," and as for the time and effort saved by not writing, "I would rather have their energy go into analyzing and thinking rather than be … writing up something that's poorly done." What we see here is evidence of a view of writing as an action that is separate from thinking and analyzing, if not actually a hindrance to these processes when one is considered a poor writer. As well, written presentations take up the teacher's scarce reading time. At best, writing is a means of recording information to be reported orally. It is not regarded as a means of exploring or clarifying ideas or shaping knowledge. When it is required, writing provides evidence for assessment purposes; students demonstrate their knowledge, as in the take-home essay examination or in the four 1-page group position papers. All other evidence for grading comes from oral presentations. Because the latter are all products of group work, the take-home examination provides the only clear evidence of individual performance.

Writing within this course is primarily a collaborative activity. Even the one case analysis that is evaluated on an individual basis (as an examination) occurs at a time in the course after students have discussed in groups and in the whole class a total of 10 cases. They have also presented as members of their groups their analyses or heard and discussed the analyses of other groups. (One must recognize though that there is no assurance that written reports are generated by the group as a whole and not the product of a few individual members.) By reading, talking about those readings, writing up their analyses, and collaborating on final reports, they have had ample opportunity to use the language of their field and to apply the concepts they have been introduced to. By the standards of most one-semester courses (13–14 weeks x 3 hour meetings), one might consider this an exemplary course in affording students considerable opportunity to talk through their understandings of and apply the concepts they have been introduced to. It enables appropriation of ways of talking about strategic management, and to borrow from Bakhtin, it affords ventriloquation, the speaking in the language of others, as we have already seen in chapter 3 and as the following extracts demonstrate, as a phase in the passage from speaking into writing.

[At one stage in his group's discussion of the Deacon case, Hans argues:]
I think one of the main things, too, that kept them, that they said was uhm practically keeping alive right after the buyout was the enforcement situation, because you're so highly leveraged that they had to generate cash flow and that's when they said they had to cut inventory and they said it was afterward like … they had to go into JIT [Just In Time] or whatever?
P: It wasn't just…
H: Into the system. But so yeah it, I'd get another computer in their situation and that was part of what kept them going.
S: You mean how they kind of discovered the triad …
T: Yeah, they stumbled on to it almost 'cause they had to cut their inventory. Well, how do you cut your inventory? Well, you go into JIT. Well, what's part of JIT?
L: … triad.
I: That's how it started but then if they weren't, they would have just brought these processes in and …

In their jointly produced one-page written analysis of this case, we get passages like this, passages clearly meant to show their familiarity with the concepts this case is meant to teach:

Deacon's tight cash position after the LBO [leveraged buy out] forced management into a situation where they had to generate cash and the only way they could do this was by cutting costs on inventories and staff; this in itself led to the drive for JIT and eventually the rest of the Productivity Triad …

For the instructor, writing is a means of ensuring and confirming that prescribed readings and analyses have been carried out and that certain theoretical concepts are employed as useful analytic tools. As well it provides the ground for assessing what and how much learning has occurred. In these ways, this course, quite likely, does not differ from most courses in the sciences, humanities, and professions.

Most of the written assignments for this course are the product of group discussion with two of the six to seven members taking turns to write up the case from their notes of the group discussion. This discussion derives entirely from the case notes; so that while students are free to read up on related background material, they find that the case scenario provides all the information they need to carry out the analysis and answer the guiding questions. One can see how the encapsulated reality of the case is even further reduced by the teacher's questions and the predictable answers they inscribe.

In fact, the instructor is concerned to reduce the amount of reading (of their writing) she has to do for several reasons. They write badly, she believes, and she hasn't the time. So they write in groups. The cases are harder; however, she prefers that one person write rather than six people each contribute a piece of that paper. The implication is that writing is a skill that one brings to knowledge in order to provide a shaped, organized version of knowledge. The focus on demonstrating knowledge remains uppermost; and in that case, doing so briefly (one-page reports, bullets on overhead transparencies) is the preferred means. And in fact, it is the oral presentations that represent students' work much more than the writing. According to the teacher, the ability to put together a coherent essay eventually reveals itself in the ability to develop "an overhead presentation or an executive summary" because these forms show whether the key ideas have been realized. In fact, extended writing encourages empty, seemingly impressive verbiage ("bullshit"). So writing is not devalued; rather in its public appearance, it falls far short of the succinct and telling overhead presentation.

What processes are the students involved in as writers? Time constraints and the demands of four other courses would dictate a concern for efficiency and division of labor rather than concerted inquiry. Except for the five-page individual case analysis (a take-home examination), all other writing is done in groups: four one-page position papers, one 8-page analysis with questions to guide the analysis and the write-up, and a field-work report to be presented orally. In fact, oral reports are the principal means of demonstrating learning. The teacher's guidelines for these presentations and written reports put a premium on brevity. Given 50 students, such a tack appears to be an efficient way of ensuring that key course concepts are learned and applied, and that the teacher is in a position to assess such learning efficiently and fairly. In AT terms, assigning writing on the part of the teacher is an action whose goal is two-fold: a means for students to demonstrate their learning and a means for assessing that learning. That, with the exception of the take-home essay examination, all such writing is the product of one or more individuals within groups, may attest to the teacher's commitment to small-group processes as a powerful means of learning. Copies of overhead transparencies submitted by each group (whether they present orally or not) provided a check on whether they have done the necessary work. Oral presentations by one or at most two groups provide occasions for clarification and expansion. Clearly, how writing is assigned and carried out is determined primarily by a concern to obtain evidence of learning within predetermined guidelines and to assess such learning. With one exception (the take-home examination), recorded evidence of individual learning is subsumed under group effort.

From the perspective of students, guidelines for written reports define the goals for the action of writing as one of answering the guide questions and remaining (with some leeway) within the one-page limit (for at least four of the six group writing tasks). Depending on how the groups decide to divide their labor, the task of writing may be assigned to one or more of the group's competent writers, leaving little opportunity for less competent writers to develop their skills as writers in this course. As the teacher argues, "Ideally they'll pool their intelligence ... they'll be smart enough to know that one person should write, rather than ... six people each write a piece."

Our examination of this course as an activity system within the larger activity system, the university, was intended to uncover how the epistemic function of this course and how the writing that might promote that function must contend with complications arising from the goals of assessing and ranking students. A further complication arises from competing demands on the teacher's own time, her other courses and academic research commitments being some of the more obvious constraints. Throughout her interview on this course, the teacher attributes the lack of individual writing assignments to her lack of sufficient time to read them. Similarly, students read the system to determine how they might achieve a high grade in the face of similarly competing demands from other courses as well as from the other activity systems that impinge on their lives.

So one of the clearer patterns that emerges in this analysis is the steady effort to reduce the amount of writing that students must present as evidence of learning and, therefore, for purposes of assessment. Oral presentations, with overhead summaries, replace individual writing as demonstration of work done and learning. The pedagogic imperative, the need to ensure that certain key concepts are learned, prevails in all tasks with the insistence on "key points," which for purposes of assessment are foregrounded in the teacher's lectures, in the appended guiding questions, and the spelled-out grading criteria for the teaching assistant. Students are directed into modes of oral presentation that highlight the display of such points. A strong justification for such presentational modes is business practice, an activity system that impinges powerfully on work in this course. At the same time, such a shift from university discoursal practices provides an expedient means of meeting the teaching and grading objectives of this course, without burdening the teacher with a considerable reading workload. What is difficult to reconcile, however, is the notion that seems endemic to the system: students write badly; so ways must be found around the problem of having to read such bad writing. There are obvious advantages, both instrumental and epistemic, in concentrating much of the writing required in this course into the preparation of overheads, a form of writing researchers on writing have by and large ignored. Clearly the collaborative talking in small groups and the need to be relevant and succinct instigate learning; however, the argument that only a minority of students write well, and therefore time given to such writing by both students and teacher is most likely time wasted, needs to be redirected toward considering how students might be moved from genres they have trouble with to genres at which they might be more successful, for example, writing in the mode of the design notebooks discussed in the following chapter.

It may be a function of teaching institutions that many tasks (in our case, preparing bulleted overhead transparencies to speak to or attending peripherally to the guiding questions the teacher has set) remain at the level of actions with the goal of obtaining a favorable grade, rather than becoming the routinized operations they ought to become. The emphasis on reporting orally, however, can ensure that such actions do become routinized operations, enabling skills that the instructor sees as valued in the workplace. Paradoxically, on a positive note we believe, the action of writing in this course, which is now relegated largely to preparatory work (note-taking and recording group decisions), appears to have become operational in this course, a routinized practice much like talk, and quite likely developing in the same way.

Helping students become better writers, however, is not an object that will direct teaching in this course. Should we be concerned that writing will be displaced in the ways it seems to be in this course, particularly if business practices have been clearly redefined so as to stress graphically enhanced oral presentations, and extended writing is seen as a necessary skill for only a small minority of workers?

5

WRITING AND THE FORMATION OF THE ARCHITECT

In comparing the role of writing in the educational programs of the professional disciplines, we would expect it to make a difference that architecture is, in the end, about nonverbal processes. What finally results from architectural practice is a material structure, a new or modified building. It is true that what ultimately happens as a result of activities in law and government, business management and social work is likewise material and is not confined to the epistemic realm of ideas; the verbal outputs of these professionals will impel or enable people to do things or impede or prevent their doing things. The foreseen outcomes of these practices, however, are mainly quite general and unspecific; although there are exceptions (e.g., a court order requiring an adolescent to be taken into custody), the practitioner, as a rule, is not able to envision as the outcome a particular event or act that will occur in a particular time or place. By contrast, the product of architecture is of unusual specificity and materiality.

As a result, the *semiotic* outputs of the other disciplines and of architecture have different status. The work of public administration and management, at any rate, ends with the production of spoken and written texts. True, these productions are not the final goal of the activity (or of the Activity—see chap. 4); they are only of value in so far as they produce effects in the world of actions. But how people act on these texts is beyond the control and responsibility of the professionals we have studied in those fields; in producing the texts they have done their bit. In other words, their work is simply to write and speak. Social workers are a somewhat different case, in that they sometimes write documents—for instance, treatment plans and presenting reports—that are blueprints for courses of action the implementation of which they will then monitor. Architects, even more typically, oversee the use of their texts (written and graphical) on the site and take responsibility for the accomplishment of the building; their texts are experienced by them as simply mediating means; their goal is a more real and more immediate day-by-day motivation. Writing and drawing are not felt to be final products, the outcomes that mark the limit of their professional domain.

Consequently, a law student writing a paper analyzing a case is being more of a lawyer than an architecture student is being an architect in writing on the origins of Gothic. This is so even though the law student's paper is not framed within a professional genre. She is, nevertheless, exercising forms of discursive thought that will inform the discourse it will later be her core task to produce (see chap. 3). By contrast, generating written discourse is relatively marginal to the core of the professional architect's job. This is not to say that architects do not do plenty of writing. They do, but it is ancillary to their central accomplishment of design, a process achieved through a combination of drawing and writing, with writing in very much the subordinate position.

What is most distinctive about writing in architectural education and that warrants its treatment in a separate chapter is precisely its lack of centrality. It is not just that the main activity of the discipline lies elsewhere, outside language, and in the realm of things and their visual representation. Architecture also, like the other disciplines, has a verbal discourse that embodies essential ways of thinking and seeing, one that would-be practitioners need to learn. But whereas in social work, law, and business, writing is a central means of practicing and displaying mastery of the disciplinary discourse, in architecture it is not. In the work produced over 5 years by the architecture undergraduate one cannot assume there will be a significant body of extended written texts through which progress in the use of architectural discourse may be tracked. In the most significant teaching contexts, the design studio courses, control of the discourse is judged by its assumed fruits in successful design although its main deployment is in speech, both in the seminar-like infrequent gatherings of the class, in the one-on-one "desk crits" —consultations at the student's drafting table—that are the main vehicle of teaching, and in the "crits" in which the work is displayed and orally defended. There is no written test in design studio.

However, although the production of writing in school is relatively tangential to the principal and defining tasks of the job and the discipline, the writing that does get done can be highly significant. Often, moreover, it is very different from anything normally seen in other disciplines, and perhaps hints at alternative ways in which writing might more generally contribute to the formation of a professional.

The phrase "formation of a professional," it is worth reminding ourselves, refers to a function that is entirely absent from workplace writing. The purpose of the latter is either to affect some state of affairs outside the writer or to enable the thinking and recording that underpin action. Educational writing may also, of course, be practically geared to the achievement of an immediate task (e.g., taking notes during a complicated chemistry experiment). But, as we have seen, it may also be motivated very differently, by the need to develop and practice a way of thinking that will remain as a permanent resource for the practitioner. Some writing in the school of architecture appeared to be serving both functions at once.

The uniqueness of the task of architectural education, and also the ambiguous nature of that education's relationship to the profession (see below), are manifested in a distinctive writing profile, although not all the elements of that profile are unfamiliar. The texts produced range in character from the relatively conventional (a reader from another discipline would have no trouble in recognizing what sort of a beast a typical student paper on Palladio was) to the (in academic terms) exotic. A possible broad classification of the variety of genres can be constructed in terms of three relationships of writing to the work of architecture: writing *about* architecture, writing *for* architecture, and writing *as* architecture. In this chapter we take each in turn, concluding with some observations on the relationship between the education and the profession.[11]

WRITING ABOUT ARCHITECTURE

This category accounts for most of the writing produced for course require- ments outside the design studio classes, that is, in courses on the theory and history of architecture, technology, and professional practice. (In the school where we did most of our research there are only one or two of the latter; they do not appear until the 3rd year of a 5-year program and are not regarded by the students as important.) The genre types within which writing for these courses is framed would be immediately recognizable to anyone familiar with the way universities work, despite local peculiarities and the frequent presence of drawn illustrations. It is academic writing, epistemic in function in the sense in which we have been using the term and bearing little relation to writing produced in architects' offices. Indeed, the content of these courses often overlaps with that of other, nonarchitectural disciplines such as literature or art history, as can be seen from Fig. 5.1, a sample page of an undergraduate thesis that will be further discussed below. There is not as a rule any specific or systematic connection between what is learned in these courses and studio practice in design. As we shall see, however, the discourse that writing helps the student to acquire may have powerful effects within the design process.

---

[11]As well as the school of architecture that was our main site, we did some studies in a second university that we here call Cornwall University.

Preface

Although the issue of representation is a fundamental one within architecture, its position within contemporary discourse is uncertain. What does architecture represent? Is its subject architectural, or does it lie outside the realm of architectural concerns? The confusing situation in contemporary practice makes such questions difficult to answer. It seems apparent, however, that the negligence of architectural subjects within the discipline could lead to its further erosion. This being the case, it is clear that the issue of architectural representation presents a problem for contemporary architecture.

The idea of memory is of critical importance to anyone considering the question of architectural representation. For architects, to ask what is being made visible requires speculation on what is worth remembering - what is a proper subject for architecture? What do cities remember? What do buildings remember? When faced with questions such as these, the confusion surrounding the issue becomes evident. Without a subject for architecture, no criteria exists on which design decisions can be based. Design becomes an exclusively subjective activity, and architects are absolved of any responsibility of intention. There is no judgment involved; architecture has forgotten its capacity - indeed its responsibility - to remember. If nothing is remembered, then it follows that no one can be accountable, since there is no 'physical evidence' - nothing has been shown. Without any connection between physical form and intentions or values, there can be no public face to any building or activity, and hence no accountability. Thus, the responsibility for architecture to show the city to itself is denied; one of its fundamental roles has been avoided. Conditions such as these are not encouraging, since they represent the slow suffocation of a discipline through the avoidance of its true subject matter.

One way of addressing this problem is through researching the issue of architectural representation in another context - perhaps one where the issues involved have greater clarity, even if this context seems distant and strange to us. One other context is ancient literature, specifically, the architectural role of the trophy in Homers' Iliad.

As a story, the Iliad contains many examples of ritual acts and mnemonic events which represent the values and desires of a people. These practices have a practical value in that they hold

FIG. 5.1. Page from Preface of Inne's undergraduate thesis.

WRITING FOR ARCHITECTURE

This category refers to writing produced as part of the process of bringing an architectural design into being, in studio courses and in the design thesis that some students undertake in their 5th and final year. It must be said that this use of writing is neither universal nor widely taught or required. Most of our examples are of self-initiated writing undertaken by students because they found it helpful, and often not seen, or at any rate evaluated, by the professor.

Writing contributes to design projects in two different ways, as record keeping in support of the management of the project and as an aid to design thinking. The need for and nature of the first sort is explained by a 3rd-year Cornwall student:

> Writing is more of a tool organizing information and organizing ideas within the development of your idea, within the development of the project. And for me I think it's a most important tool in studio, as a tool to organize, as a tool to record things that you couldn't fit.

The reason for this is the complexity of the project:

> The project starts as a very small seed, but at the end of a term, by your final crit, you cannot fit it all in your head, and you can't think about the building in its entirety at one time. So you have to be very careful to record the original thesis of the proposal, what's motivating it at the beginning, and keep a record of how things are unfolding, and how I see them unfolding, and how I see them projecting, and only then, at the final crit, can I, in retrospect, work it together as a type of thesis. And without writing you couldn't do it. You couldn't do it just in sketches either.... I don't write a lot ... I just write what I need to keep the project going.... when I reach a point in that project, I'm not going to write, you know, four pages about it, I may write a paragraph, I might write three lines.

Such writing particularly records intentions that may get forgotten in meeting the pragmatic imperatives of developing the design. Occasionally it may be required, as Cornwall's Professor Hurlingham explained:

> usually at the conclusion of the first or second [design] exercise, I will require them to distill everything that they have learned in that exercise through design and through experimental investigation. I will ask them to distill it in writing ... I think it is extremely important to be able to verbally articulate it.

and as we heard Professor Schofield explain to his class:

> Now, for next Monday, you should write a page or two identifying the aspect of the subject that you propose to pursue and how you might start.

The following is a sample of this sort of writing, taken from notes for the design of a Canadian war memorial in Normandy:

The thematic structure has to work independently from the actual historical narrative—to avoid the problem of allegorical triviality.

i.e., someone unfamiliar with the actual events would still feel it

i.e., the garden conveys an architectural idea, not a historical one—the two could conceivably be separated, although they are obviously intimately connected

Therefore the focus must be on the *emotional character of the event*, and its many aspects.

- The landscape provides the necessary "canvas" for setting up these conditions. They must initially be reactions to the landscape.

  → Parallel between these decisions and decisions involved in planning a battle—the landscape is always a basic determining factor—sea, beach, cliff, plain.

    → tie together with emotional conditions

But it is not normal for this sort of writing to be required by professors. (In the much bigger professional design projects that are undertaken in offices we occasionally found the same use of writing, and it was similarly brief.)

The other manifestation of writing for architecture, writing as an aid to design thinking, can be illustrated by the design notebook of a 4th-year student, Edith.[12] Professor Schofield had instructed the class to keep journals—"Keep a journal, converse with your own ideas"—but did not formally inspect them. (Nevertheless, he often saw them when students referred to them during individual consultations at the drafting table, the "desk crits" that occupied almost all of the instructor's studio time.) Sample pages are reproduced as Figs. 5.2 and 5.3.

In Fig. 5.2 some of the writing is tightly associated with the drawing, in the form of a label linked by an arrow. Drawing is probably the form of recording we would expect to find in an architecture studio, and indeed there is plenty in evidence, in the students' notebooks as well as in the work for presentation. But we can also see writing inscribing thoughts and ideas that are presumably essential to the design process but that cannot easily be drawn. The preference of most architecture students is, not surprisingly, to sketch, not write, so that when writing is employed it presumably performs some function not attainable through drawing. The notation (it might be misleading to call it the title) at the

---

[12]Whenever the use of writing is discussed in accounts of architectural education, it is usually writing as an aid to design thinking that is referred to, in the range of versions described in this section; for example, Ackerman & Oates (1996), Corbin (1992), Goodman, Fairey, & Paul (1992), Martin (1992), Matthews (1992), McCann (1992), and Upchurch (1993).

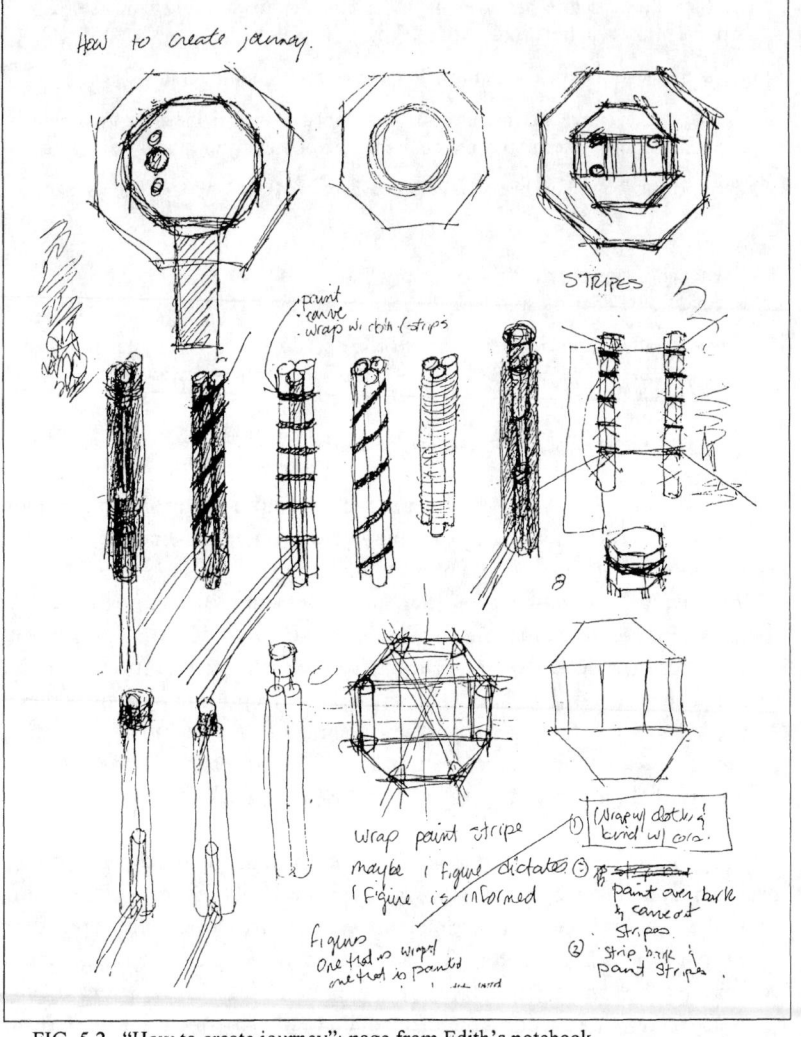

FIG. 5.2. "How to create journey": page from Edith's notebook.

top of the page, "How to create journey," explains how the drawings are to be read, namely as the fulfillment of a particular intention. But if it had been written before the sketch was produced, its function may have been to fix the intention firmly by attaching it to a (verbal) sign, so that it could more easily be adhered to in the face of distractions (cf. Vygotsky, 1978, e.g., pp. 35–36, on the use of words to control attention and overcome the dominance of impulse). The

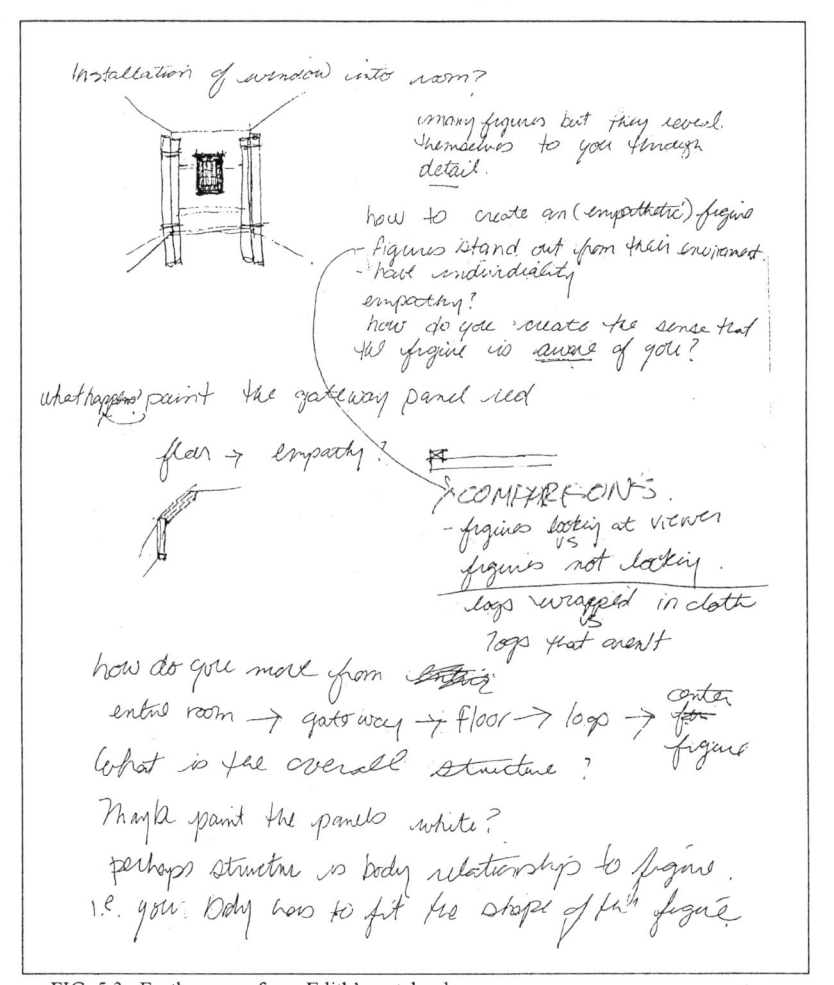

FIG. 5.3. Further page from Edith's notebook.

written intention stands, visibly, as a recurrent reminder to help the student stay on track. Turning to the inscriptions at the bottom of the page, we note that painted-over, carved, and stripped bark can be represented graphically—and they have been, though not with sufficient care as to make the reference entirely clear to an outside viewer. The writing, in contrast, represents not material states but acts—wrap, paint over, strip, carve; these would have been much harder to represent unambiguously in pictures. Also, there is no way of drawing "maybe" (as in "Maybe one figure dictates"). Finally, the two-line text contrasting the

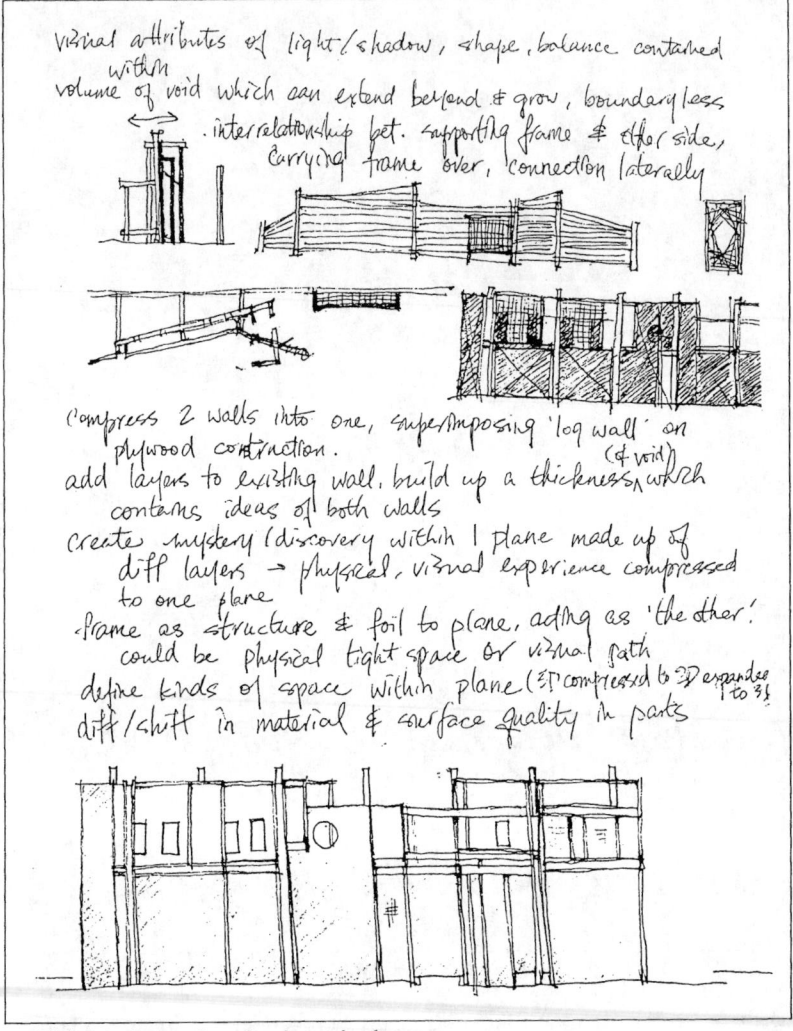

visual attributes of light/shadow, shape, balance contained within
volume of void which can extend beyond & grow, boundaryless
⟷ . interrelationship bet. supporting frame & other side,
         carrying frame over, connection laterally

Compress 2 walls into one, superimposing 'log wall' on
     plywood construction.   (& void)
add layers to existing wall, build up a thickness, which
     contains ideas of both walls
create mystery (discovery within) plane made up of
     diff layers → physical, visual experience compressed
     to one plane
frame as structure & foil to plane, acting as 'the other'
     could be physical tight space or visual path
define kinds of space within plane (2T compressed to 3D expanded
                                               to 3)
diff/shift in material & surface quality in parts

FIG. 5.4. A page from Joan's notebook.

two "figures" (two variously wrapped, stripped, carved etc. logs) does some-thing different again:

1 figure dictates
1 figure is informed *[i.e., receives information from the other figure—our gloss]*

This records the sort of interpretation the viewer is finally to place on the relationship between the two. Dictating and being informed are conditions that can neither be drawn nor *literally* embodied in logs; nevertheless the sight of the figures might evoke that sort of image in us through the operation of our incurably anthropomorphizing vision. Drawing could not have done what those seven words did because what could be drawn could only be a particular instantiation of that intended impression. The drawing could not communicate the intention as a general purpose that has not yet entered into any sort of even provisional commitment to a specific form (Medway, 1996).

Fig. 5.3 has far more writing, and we see further cognitive moves essential to design encoded in written discourse, notably *questions* ("How do you move from entire room to gateway ... ?"), and *oppositions and comparisons*:

> many figures but they reveal themselves to you through detail
> figures looking at viewer
> vs
> figures not looking

Note that in the latter piece of text the resources used are not just linguistic but visual (the central positioning of "vs" on its own line; cf. Kress & van Leeuwen, 1996), and it is generally characteristic of design notebooks that part of the meaning of written text derives from its spatial arrangement on the page. Also characteristic is the use of signs like arrows—used inside sentences and not just to link text to drawings—that derive not from written language but from everyday nonverbal signs or from mathematical or logical symbol systems.

What Cornwall's Professor Hurlingham (quoted above) wants to see writing used for is the specification of qualities.

> I think there's a vagueness, but there's also a kind of precision. Because through writing you may be extraordinarily precise about the kind of quality that you are looking for, right? And so writing can sometimes lead you in a direction....

> I think you have to be as precise about qualities, in qualities of feeling, qualities of emotion, or sentiment, you have to be as precise about that as you do about how you support a roof, if it's going to help, otherwise it's just a kind of free association about everything.

The representation of qualities in these pages of Edith's hardly reaches the "extraordinary precision" he speaks of ("fear," "empathy"), but the written text does achieve something else he says is important:

> ... there's another kind of precision which those drawings *[i.e., ones that use the technical notational codes of architecture]* will never reveal to you. For example if they're ink drawings or pencil drawings on tracing paper, they don't

tell you anything about the *experience* of the building, right? So how does one communicate those to somebody else? Or sometimes even to yourself.... Now some people use drawings to make that clear to themselves, other kinds of drawing.... Or they're writing texts, texts which exist side by the side with the architectural drawing.

In other words, the experiential qualities of a building can be conveyed either through nontechnical drawings (sketches, impressionistic renderings, etc.) or through writing.

The variety found among design notebooks is clearly shown when we add to Edith's the work of three more students. Figure 5.4, for instance (by Joan), displays a clearer separation of text and drawing and an arrangement of text on the page that conforms more closely to the conventions of purely written discourse.

Lisbeth's hard-to-read text in Figs 5.5 and 5.6 reads:

What scale are we talking?
The 1st marker should be small I gather.
I think they should be fairly close—forced.—So forced that they
become uncomfortable.—Maybe that's where the indecision
comes from
The objects a stair (threshold—no—[the object]'s a gravestone
and chair can be spaced out (like me.)
I must create my only language. one that unites the pieces. a
logo—a symbol. —Maybe its a material—a unusual use of a
material—woven twine. no it has to be something fragile
uncertain.
Something distracting—wind operating—Noisy. (maybe a clapper.) —
Yeah—my log book. —each piece can be used to indicate my different
stages.
→ My log is the distraction
[Label on drawing—?Clack Clack]
→ Maybe not noise maker but some sort of marker (visually—after all it is arch.)
→scale worries me

Whereas Joan's writing was firmly referential, representing states, processes and qualities, Lisbeth's is expressive, containing (in addition) declarations of intention ("I must"), explicitly marked internal dialogue ("a, no, b"), and ironic comment on the whole situation of doing this. On another page (see Fig. 5.7) she writes, "This going to be like a 3-D-super big 1st year project."

John's notebook (see Figs. 5.8 and 5.9) comes closer to the precise specification of quality that Professor Hurlingham hoped to find. Clearly, writing is very central to his design process. The project is to design a cafe under a bridge on a canal. He refers, in a careful formulation, to "a more ambiguously dynamic light" that

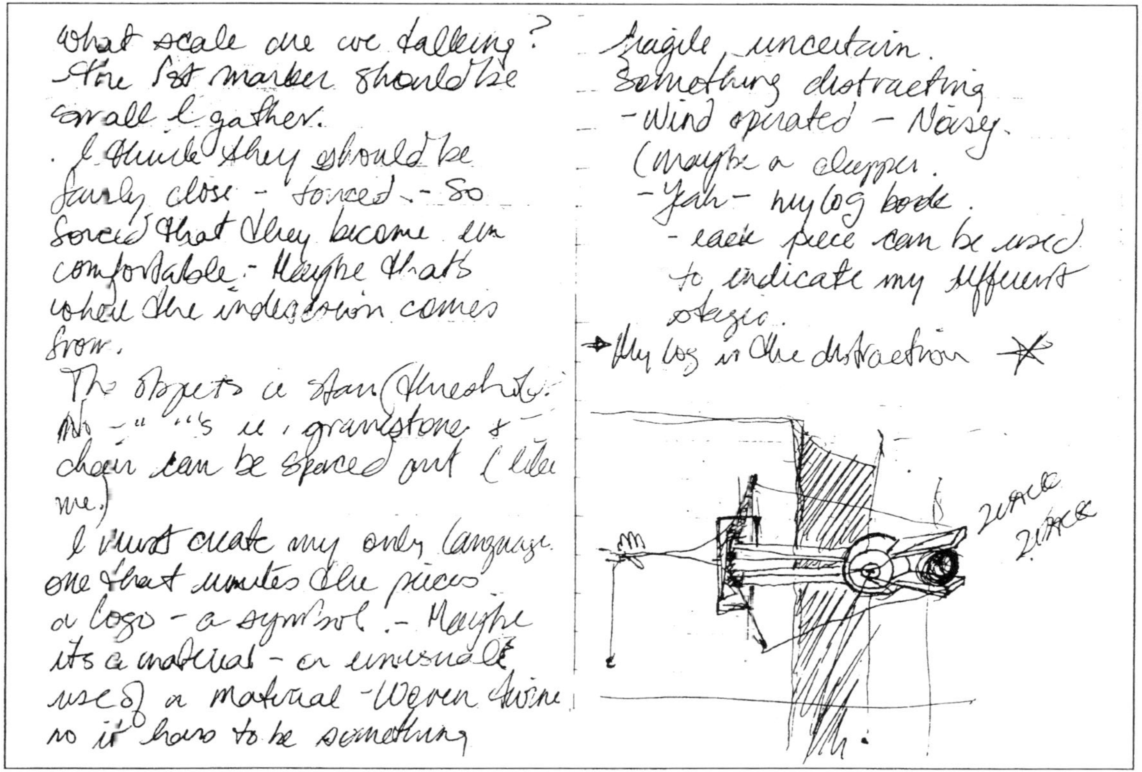

FIG. 5.5. Page from Lisbeth's notebook.

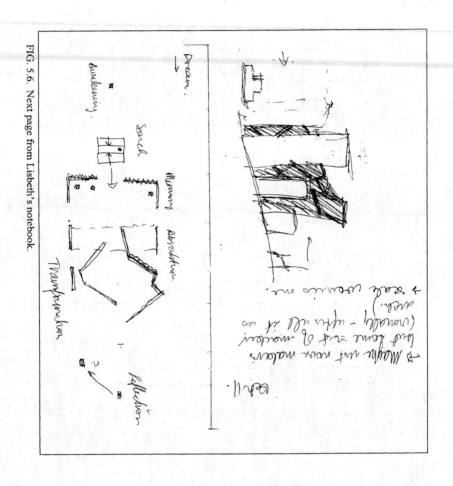

FIG. 5.6. Next page from Lisbeth's notebook.

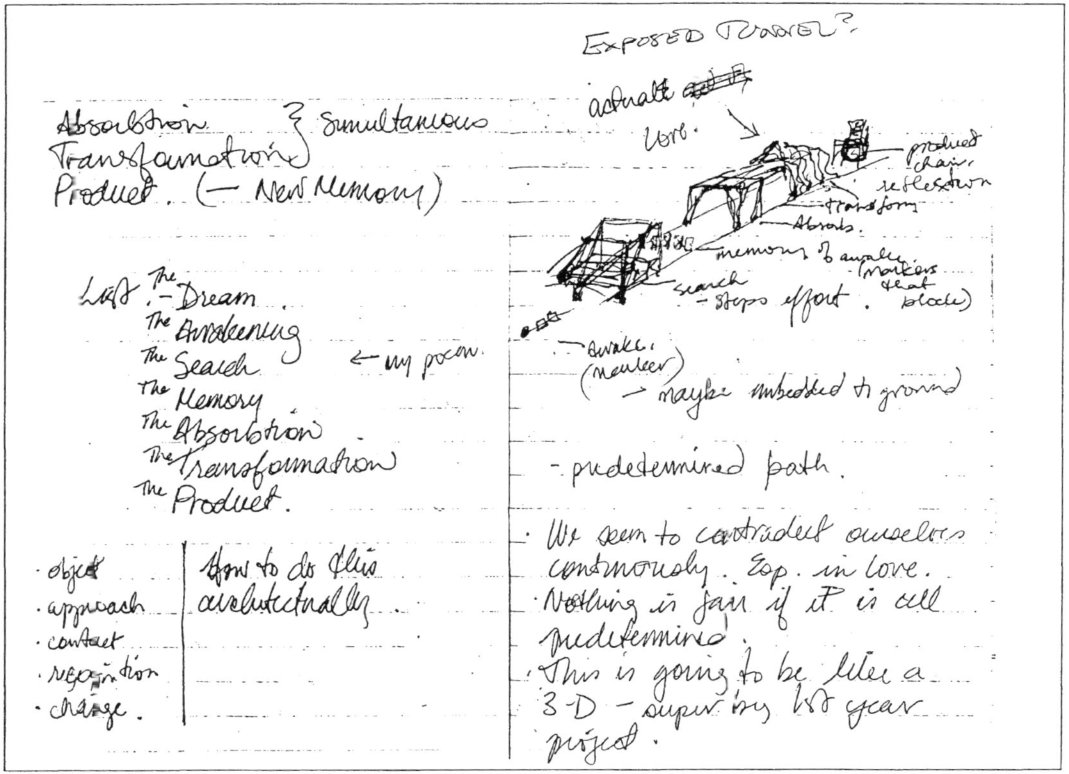

EXPOSED (JOOGL?

Absorbtion   } Simultaneous
Transformation
Product .. (— New Memory)

List   The
— Dream ..
The Embodening
The Search   ← my poem
The Memory .
The Absorbtion .
The Transformation
The Product ..

· object   How to do this
· approach   architecturally ..
· context
· negotiation
· change .

adinate
lore ·

— awake
(nucleus)
— maybe imbedded to ground

— predetermined path .

We seem to controlled ourselves
constantly .. Eg. in love .
Nothing is fair if it is all
predetermined .
This is going to be like a
3-D – superiors 150 year
project .

FIG. 5.7. Further page from Lisbeth's notebook.

95

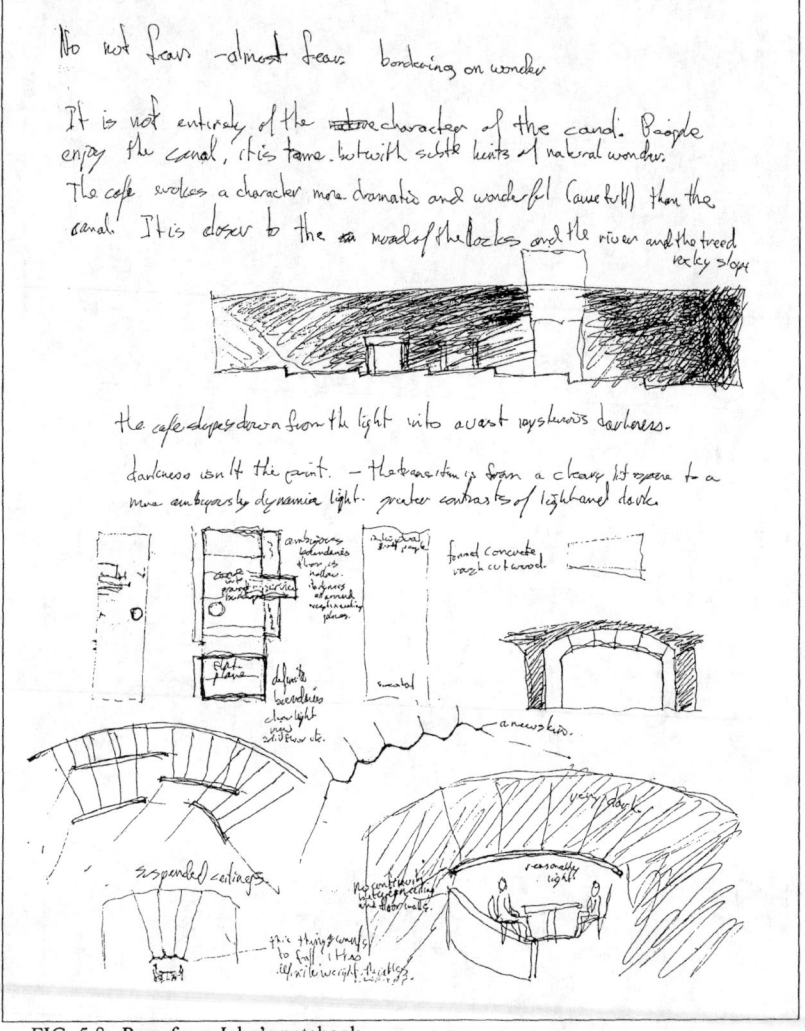

FIG. 5.8. Page from John's notebook.

contrasts with "a vast mysterious darkness." Some of the other things he does we have already seen elsewhere, such as specifying his intention ("I will try to evoke the intimacy between ourselves and an enchanted forest, represented by Emily Carr [Canadian painter]," "The cafe will put visitors in a state of wonder"). But he also does other things we have not seen in the texts already discussed. First, he enunciates relevant guiding principles: "It is impossible to

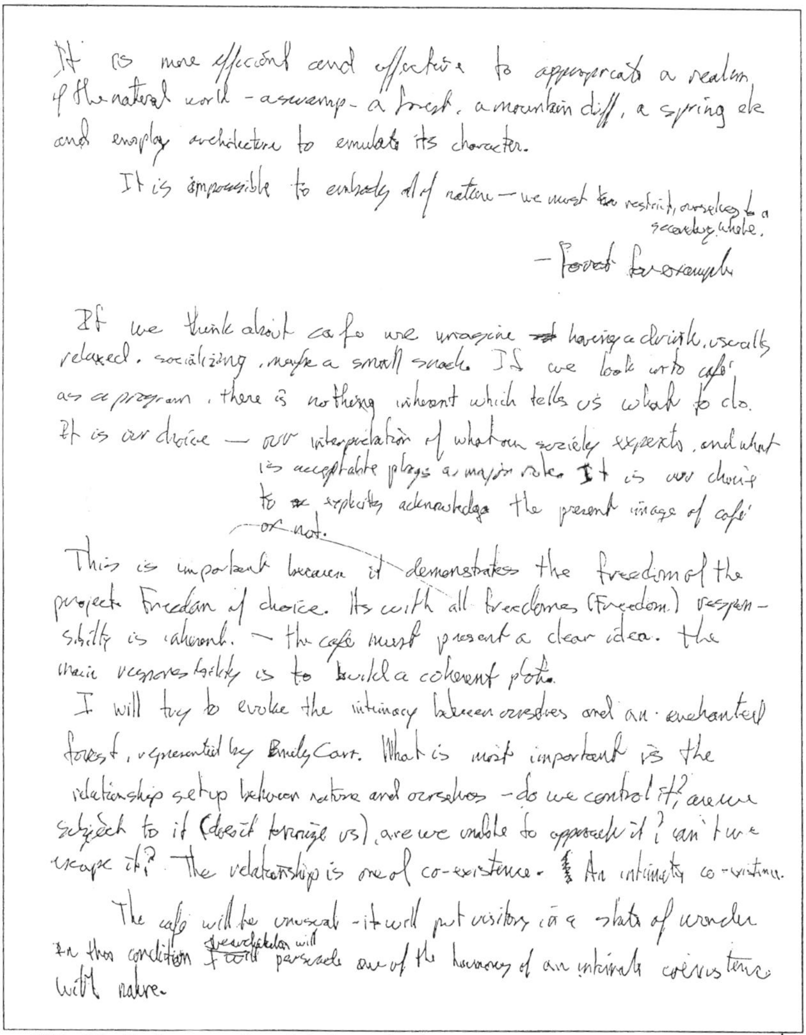

FIG. 5.9. Further page from John's notebook.

embody all of nature—we must restrict ourselves to a secondary whole— forest for example." Second, he articulates the sort of project this is in general terms, by contrast with other architectural projects: it affords unusual freedom (because the built-in requirements of a cafe are fairly minimal and can be met in any number of ways); and "As with all freedoms (freedom) responsibility is inherent—the cafe must present a clear idea. The main responsibility is to build a coherent [?]."

Of course, such word-spinning could be just a form of procrastination, putting off through over-verbalization the tough work of generating forms that will work. But the dilemmas and decisions represented in the text are ones that unavoidably have to be faced in some form in "responsible" design. More experienced designers may deal with them in their heads, but perhaps it helps for a novice to work in overt rather than inner speech.

One of the reasons why writing is valuable at an early stage of design is that, unlike drawing, it can avoid premature specification. Drawing has to opt for specific shapes and positions which writing can leave vague or simply omit, attending instead to more qualitative properties (Medway, 1996). Using language, however, one can use expressions such as "somewhere": for example, "There'll be a fountain somewhere in this area." But, as Professor Hurlingham said, "there isn't a graphical 'somewhere'."

Writing does not have to be extended or elaborate to perform a powerful function; a very brief note can often do the job. The difference between writing even briefly and not writing at all is far more significant than the apparent size and effort of the activity would suggest.

> ... while you're sketching, your mind is racing so quickly, and your hand can't follow that quickly, so you write ... you make a few notations which are verbal, which remind you of a whole ... can remind you of a whole.... You could take the whole history of architecture, in a sense, like a stack of cards and just fold them together, with a few very cryptic written notations. So I think writing is extraordinarily useful. But I'm not talking at this point of doing a kind of dissertation on something, it's ... procedural.

"Procedural" writing might in fact be a useful category for us to adopt from this informant.

Should the design notebook be considered a genre? If so, it is certainly a very flexible one. The proportion of writing to drawing varies from page to page, from 0 to 100%, and between students. One student told us that his "sketchbook has probably about as much writing in it as sketches in it. It's filled with just notes that I write down." The register varies between a speech-like chattiness and gnomic formality, and in degree of syntactical elaboration, from the notation of single words to phrases to complete sentences. It seems equally impossible to define the content of the notebook; alongside the written and graphical design notes, many other forms of notation appear that seem to have been included simply because the writing and drawing surface was ready to hand—lecture notes, domestic shopping lists and reminders, phone numbers, sketches of fellow students, quotations picked up from professors and books. Receipts, business cards, postcards, and letters may be stored between its pages.

Nor is this a genre that is taught, although examples are readily available on the desks of some other students and in the library, in illustrations of the work of architects and designers back to Renaissance times (e.g., Leonardo's notebooks).

But those examples seem, at first sight, hardly necessary, the notebook activity appearing to answer so naturally and obviously to the demands of the designers' situation. That is the sort of assumption, however, that the writing researcher must question.

For us to claim the existence of a distinctive genre of the design notebook, or perhaps more usefully the architecture student design notebook, some degree of institutionalization or conventionalization needs to be observable. In other words, the texts should not be individual *ad hoc* responses to exigence that draw opportunistically and eclectically on the total resources of the language—linguistic, semantic, generic, and rhetorical. The writing should not itself be a totally fresh design job on each occasion. Rather, we should be able to identify the calling-up of some ready-made assemblage: the response to the exigence should be, to some degree, the activation of a standard solution rather than the devising of a fresh one. The evidence that this is occurring will include the consistent absence of certain features that purely functional requirements might suggest could well have been admissible, and the consistent presence of ones that seem no more justifiable than ones that aren't found. (Compare the admitted and unadmitted explications of background knowledge revealed by Giltrow and Valiquette (1994) in their study of certain university student genres.)

There certainly are features that seem conventionalized. In terms of the material instantiation of the genre, design notebooks are perfect-bound in hard covers, are always black, and contain unruled cartridge paper. There are neither lines, as in a notebook I might use, nor square grid ruling such as engineers often prefer. Although much of the content of the notebook is writing, the paper is suitable for delicate pencil drawing or watercolor sketches; the physical notebook could equally become an artist's sketchbook. The writing and drawing, moreover, are almost always in pencil or black ink from a drafting pen—almost never blue ink—almost never ball-point. And the handwriting, even for extended passages of prose, is typically uppercase—a feature that seems actually counter-functional, in that the more usual mix of upper and lower is far more readable.

In terms of content, we soon come to have certain expectations. At least in the particular educational tendency that informs the schools we know, aspects of buildings will be considered phenomenologically—that is, for how they will be experienced—much more than technically. Calculations and topological struggles will not be strongly in evidence (contrast the engineer's notebook). Quite likely to be found are fragments of poetic imagery, shards of metaphoric expression that convey something about a mood that is to be created, unorganized phrases suggestive of parallels and associations and precedents. On the other hand, it would be strange to find more than the occasional sentence of the type that the specification documents for a contract are full of.

It could be said that many of these features simply reflect the distinctive task and perspective of the architect. Given the nature of the way architects conceive of their job, the sorts of text they write and draw in their notebooks can be seen as rational function responses, with no need to invoke notions of convention and standardization; faced with an architectural (as opposed to an engineering) design project, what else would you do? Our initial provisional formulation was that the notebook activity appeared to answer naturally and obviously to the demands of the designers' situation. But "the designers' situation" begs the question, as does "simply reflect" at the beginning of this paragraph. "The designers' situation" is a condition that involves a particular construction of "designer," as an individual who approaches a problem constructed in culturally specific terms, from a particular sensibility and within the frame of a particular discourse. The designer's situation is, in part, objectively given and in part a construct of an architectural view of the world. But a view of the world is a constantly realized *activity* [cf. Vygotsky's (1986, p. 6) insight that the word, as generalization, is activity]: an activity that occurs in different sites, one of which is design notebooks. The genre does not so much reflect the architectural sensibility as constitute one of the sites of its realization. It is not (or is not only) the result of a way of thinking so much as the means for that thinking to happen. At one level, the architectural view of the world exists as its genres, spoken, drawn, and written.

We actually do not know enough, from our own studies or from the literature, to be confident in our appraisal of the design notebook. One speculative hypothesis, however, seems worth putting forward. It relates to the fact the design notebook seems to occur far more among students than among practicing architects. If the exigence is the need to develop a design and the genre is a response to that exigence, we might expect to find instances in both domains equally.

Our hypothesis is that the notebook serves needs and desires beyond the instrumental exigences of design. In performing the genre students may also be "being architects." Certainly the outward accoutrements (such as obligatory black) seem to fulfill this function. Architecture students are exceptionally self-conscious about their actions and are often concerned to accomplish them with style. The notebook is almost inevitably a performance in the theatrical sense as well as a functional means. We sometimes have the sense that students require their notebooks to constitute intriguing evidence of the activity of a lively mind. They are written/drawn/assembled with half an eye to a later re-reading—perhaps years later, perhaps a re-reading by posterity—as the documentation of a curious and fertile intellect and imagination. Hence, what the notebook is not allowed to be is boring; the tediously technical may have a place, but only sufficient to demonstrate the professional competence and seriousness of the designer. The interleaved bus tickets and restaurant receipts may be integral to the genre.

These comments, we repeat, are speculative, offered for their possible heuristic value. An associated hypothesis is that the design notebook is a vehicle primarily of epistemic rather than practical activity. Those parts of the notebook that are about recording intentions and decisions are, of course, directly practical: they help to keep action on track. Those aspects, however, that relate to the conception of the artifact perhaps serve the needs of learning as much as of design. It is significant that the genre, though not widely used by professional architects (as far as we can tell), is not exclusive to students. It is used also by half-academic, half-practitioner architects who teach but also undertake design work. When used by practitioners like Professor Schofield, who is a theoretician, researcher, and teacher more than a practitioner working regularly on design contracts, the design notebook serves the two functions simultaneously of supporting the development of the design, in ways we have seen, and supporting reflexivity: the constant endeavor to bring one's design process into full consciousness and articulation and to make articulate knowledge out of intuition is more an intellectual, even academic, pursuit than a practical one. Thus when Professor Schofield maintains a design notebook, it is *research*, pushing forward the boundaries of understanding and making new knowledge.

When, on the other hand, Edith, Joan, Lisbeth, and John do it as students, it is *education*, not because they do it in the context of a university course but because a major purpose is to practice organizing thought and perception in the terms of a discourse and to achieve fluency in the verbal articulation of intentions and spatial conditions. This may be why the use of the notebook can fall away once this facility has been acquired, unless one wishes to maintain a level of consciousness beyond that required for routine office practice.

Our tentative conclusion, then, is that the exigence addressed by the design notebook in school is less the need to develop a design than the need to learn to think a certain way and to use a certain language—a point that we have already made in relation to the students in the law course in chapter 3. The enterprise can be described as learning a genre only if genre is a very broad category, such that an instance of it can occur in all three modes: writing (mainly students), and speech and inner speech/thought (practitioners). It seems better to say that what is being learned is a discourse, in Foucault's sense (see chap. 10 for a fuller discussion of this issue), although many of the things researchers have said about genre remain true. One of them is Miller's (1994) observation that through genres "we learn ... what ends we may have" (p. 38). The discourse teaches you the sorts of things you could want to do with a building, like making a frame be a "structure and foil to [a] plane," "build[ing] up a thickness (of void) which contains ideas of both walls" (Joan), forcing elements close together so that "they become uncomfortable" (Lisbeth) or "presenting a clear idea" (John). It teaches you, too, ways of seeing the made and natural physical world, such as "tame, but with subtle hints of natural wonder" and "ambiguously dynamic light" (John), flames of a funeral pyre that "play [a] unifying role" in the order of the Homeric funeral (Innes's thesis, see Fig. 5.10). For novice architects, getting reality and possibility to reveal themselves in these terms probably takes conscious thought—and time, which is why acquiring the discourse is facilitated by practice within the slower and more deliberate mode of writing. Once the discourse is learned, however, it no longer has to be consciously "applied"; the world simply presents itself in those terms and speech about it spontaneously adopts the language of architectural vision.

One reason why writing in architectural practice seems to be used more by architects who are both academics and practitioners than by those in full-time practice appears to be the experience of teaching. Professor Hurlingham uses writing to develop his design, but also

> for describing to someone else a process which is described primarily through ... a form of [drawn] notation which we don't necessarily share, unless we're architects or artists. [Writing] enables me to communicate it much more succinctly. And I think that has come about in large part through my experience in teaching, with that constant demand to be able to articulate things that are very difficult to grasp.

The writing can communicate to outsiders, but also serves as a rehearsal for spoken communication.

In the context of the design studio we also find, less commonly but very significantly, a quite different use of writing to generate design. Whereas the written discourse of the design notebooks looked somewhat (though to varying degrees) like dialogic speech or like talking to oneself—one could imagine the they maintain distinct forms. The role of each is specific, and corresponds in both cases to its configuration. The barrow is indirectly described as round, or oval-shaped: Achilles, while mourning, travels 'around' the barrow. He drags the body of Hector 'around' Patroclos' bier; *around* the body of the hero being mourned. This recalls Achilles' pursuit of Hector 'three times' around the walls of Troy. Patroclos' life is finalized in the funeral that Achilles gives him; Achilles' circling of Troy finalizes the fate of the city. The two fundamental events, intimately connected in the story, are given a corresponding architectural metaphor. The pyre, being square, is geometrically distinct from the barrow; it is described in the text as measuring 'a hundred feet each way'. The square configuration of the pyre is also suggested by the image in the vase painting. The pyre's form corresponds to its 'incendiary' role: to burn the body quickly, firewood must be stacked a certain way.

As in these two examples, the overwhelming amount of material and procedure that make up the funeral rites follow a clear organizational structure. In the carrying out of the funeral's various stages, we see strict order and careful planning. The disparate parts fall within this order, but it is clearly the flames which play the greatest unifying role. Every event, every sacrifice, every object is 'consumed' by the glowing evocation that inspired it. The different episodes of the funeral, no matter how enigmatic, are thus channelled towards a higher ideal: the blazing reconstruction of the hero's life and subsequent establishment of his memory.

This desire for architecture is suggested not only in the funeral, but in other episodes of the story as well. One particularly strong example takes place in Book seventeen and describes the horses of Achilles standing over the body of their 'temporary' charioteer, Patroclos. This is one of the first clearly architectural references in the Iliad:

> They were unwilling to go back to the wide passage of Helle
> and the ships, or back into the fighting after the Achaeans,
> but still as stands a grave monument which is set over
> the mounded tomb of a dead man or lady, they stood there
> holding motionless in its place the fair-wrought chariot,
> leaning their heads along the ground, and warm tears were running

FIG. 5.10. Page from Inne's undergraduate thesis.

sentences featuring in a design conversation—this other sort is remote from speech. The discourse tends to do the sort of thing that can only be done in writing.

Lay people like ourselves tend to see design as a matter of finding ingenious solutions to problems—like juggling a lot of awkward shapes to fit them into a particular space. This view is too limited, however, certainly in terms of the perspective that dominates in the schools of architecture we have looked at. What is called for goes beyond technical adeptness in two ways. First, there is often more than one way of fulfilling the brief and dealing with the exigences imposed by site, available materials, financial constraints, and so on; the point is not to arrive at a minimum working solution but to find a solution that is elegant, satisfying, and delightful. Second, the architect's responsibility is not just to the fulfillment of the programmatic requirement but to the enhancement of the culture through contributing a rich addition to the made world. For both these reasons what needs developing in trainee architects is not only the sort of technical ingenuity and spatial vision that might be shared with engineers but also, and distinctively, an ability to generate form prolifically, to come up with new configurations of three-dimensional space. The promotion of this ability is one of the traditional strengths of the school from which we have drawn most of our data. It shows, for instance, in the students' drawings, which are not merely precise and elegant but often stunningly beautiful—for instance those done on 4th-year study terms in Rome, like the one led by Professor Tetreault:

> There were a couple of Italians there, actually, as well who looked very ... they were very curious about what was going on. They looked at the drawings and couldn't believe how beautiful the stuff was, and didn't know where it came from. "How do you do this stuff? Where does this come from?" you know. And [the school] does that a lot, when we go to Rome, almost every year you hear this story, doesn't matter who takes the group. There's a certain energy with this school, that is different than any others. Everybody looks forward to the [school's] show, because it's kind of beautiful. Who knows what that is, where that comes from, which angels are aligned at that point?

Architecture students have to develop a facility in coming up with fresh and varied forms. They must also learn to achieve coherence in a design, so that it is not just a set of relatively unrelated neat ideas. The collocation of elements has to "read" as motivated, not arbitrary. Writing is sometimes used to assist the generation of formal ideas, more in exercises, it must be said, than in simulated design assignments set up as if for actual clients and a real site. Written texts produced by collage and similar techniques involving a random element throw up interesting and provocative collocations that suggest formal spatial possibilities.

One example of this application: what makes the experience of built form a lively one is sometimes the memories and associations the form activates. The experience is particularly engaging if the memories of two different situations or phenomena are simultaneously activated so that the "reading" oscillates between the two. In his own work and his work with students, Professor Tetreault uses writing to help this happen. For instance, he exploited his own bilingualism ("I didn't speak English at all until I was 8 years old") in the following procedure:

> I'd take a piece of text, a given piece of English text and read it as if I was reading French, and so I would use the sound of this text and then transcribe [the sound] and find the closest [French] word to that transcription. So, for an example, the start of one of the examples I have is "From the labyrinth".... It gets translated into *de la birhème*, because there's no *birinthe*, it's not a word. But I looked for the closest word in the dictionary and it was *birhème, de la birhème*, "from the ship, birheme," which is a Greek ship. So "from the ship" replaces "the Labyrinth," it's actually "the Labyrinth" translated to *"de la birhème."* And then I'd keep going ... all kinds of surprises and strange things. And then the rest is all suturing, basically it's actually trying to make sense of the text as it starts evolving.

> I think there is a component of your mind which actually makes connections with the work at hand. I was working on an installation, a construction that had certain intentions, a ship was actually quite a big part of it. It was a Basque ship in this case. I wasn't expecting to find *"birhème"* meaning ship but some strange things started happening. But it was actually quite a beautiful little text in the end and I used it as part of the program for the installation. So ... a fragment of the installation was the Labyrinth, but at the same time some of it was about this ship that it was describing in the second text. So, that was one way that I tackled this gap, sort of playing with the gap.

In a development of this technique, after he had acquired a word processor, he would run English text through the French thesaurus and spell checker and take the closest words that were suggested, and then adjust the text until it made some sense.

> What I'm actually trying to trigger in a sense is kind of a file of memory. If some of these things are actually fluctuating between either one language or another, or two very different conditions from the labyrinth state to the ship, then memory is triggered in order to make parallels between the two. It's like an oscillation between two different conditions. And I think you can do it with objects as well as with sounds or words. So when I'm building something it becomes the same kind of fluctuation, I call it arc-ing. It's almost like a spark existing between two things.

This informant used the word "program" above. In regular office practice the term usually refers to the functional requirements or terms of reference for the design, given by the client or arrived at in consultation between architect and client: it might specify, for instance, the number, type, and size of rooms. But the program may include aspects of meaning or reference, or what is to be achieved more generally. It may set out the range of intentions that will guide the design; thus the connection between labyrinth and ship got embodied in the program. Professor Tetreault's aim is to make the program richer, more "layered," leading to a richer artifact that engages more of the viewer's memories and knowledge and pleasure in speculation.

> There's all kinds of these things that are evolving in the construction from using … the language connection as well as just object connections.

In some projects, including some student projects, the "language connection" is established by writing and becomes part of the program guiding the design. Because both words and objects function semiotically, and because the meanings and associations are similarly various and layered, exploring language can reveal analogously polysemous aspects of the physical objects assembled or alluded to in architectural or artistic constructions.

Developing a rich program that will lead to a dense artifact is one of the abilities Professor Tetreault seeks to teach his students. The program needs to be adequately subtle and complex in the evocations it sets out to activate. It must also be adequately rich and subtle in its conceptions of the needs and habitual practices of users. In professional practice, clients are rarely self-conscious or perceptive enough to be able to supply an adequate description of their own needs or those of other users. It is therefore necessary for the architect to go beyond the provided brief, to research those needs and to construct an account of the life and activity that will go on in the building. This account may not, in the office, be written down, or even spoken, but it *can* be written, and in the school it is pedagogically helpful that it should be. "It's trying to make an architecture that responds to human behavior in space, by framing that space with material." Writing can be a means of researching that human behavior in space. As their first step in a design project set in Rome where they spent a term of their 4th year, Tetreault's students therefore observed people's habits and movements and wrote narratives that might be semi-fictional.

> I think it brought to consciousness some of their experiences, made them think about them at least, enough that if you ask them now to do a bar, a café bar, or a bar as defined by the Romans, for example, it'd be very different than before they went, obviously, because of the experience. But also, if you're sitting there, and you're basically describing what you see, you might soak in a little bit more of what makes it different there, than here. It's not just the fact that it has a counter, four chairs, and a table, that it's a bar—it's the interactions that exist. So quite

often these little narratives have characters in them that are not so strange, that are actually people off the street, or, it might be strange to us, as onlookers, or outsiders. But you realize that this is the clientele for the programs of the architecture, so you're saying, Well, I can't just design for a blank group, right? They do have personalities, and they will respond in certain ways. So if you're thinking of a bar, and you know there are at least four old women who are going to come in at 9:15 every morning to have a coffee, that changes the program of the architectural space. You know that that one table will be occupied by four old ladies. And you ... write that down as a little story. It might seem like an odd little story, but it's actually part of the program. So it's not just the same people as listed in the requirements for the client ... I think [that exercise] changed some people's perception of the relationship between program and architecture. [The program] is not just what's officially given by some bureaucrat.

This is the sort of thing the students write:

Across the street a stranger motions for my attention. Intrigued by the instrument in front of him I moved a little closer. He sat behind a table of amazing craftsmanship which displayed mirrored eye glasses of various shapes and forms. Begging for me to sit with him I obliged making myself comfortable beside the table. He began to adjust his instruments with quick movements of extreme precision—always being careful of what looked like a nickel wound line extending from somewhere above down through the table. I was curious of this character but the sun was shining directly into my face making it difficult to make out any features. All I know (or think I know) is that he wore a hooded jacket to shade himself from the sun and sometimes counted to himself while manipulating objects in a bag. He motioned for me to examine the eyeglasses noticing the quality and beauty of the handmade craft. Several pairs I tried on not being aware of the vendor's lack of interest in what I was doing—busily preoccupied with something under the table.

WRITING AS ARCHITECTURE

In this manifestation, writing is another way of doing architecture, or, perhaps, less provocatively, a way of doing something that is parallel and akin to architecture. The thesis by Innes that we referred to earlier (illustrated in Fig. 5.10) is a case in point. It is significant that the final piece of extended written work from a school of architecture may be a historical study of a work of literature (his title was "The Trophy and Architectural Desire: Aspects of Memory and Representation in Homer's Iliad"). This reflects the fact that "being an architect"—the condition it is hoped the student will arrive at if the education has been successful, rather than formally registered professional status—is thought of less as an occupational practice or qualification than as a state of awareness, sensibility, and capability that may manifest itself in a variety of activities, and not just in designing buildings. What these activities have in common is not easy to define, but there is no doubt that Innes was "being architectural" and exercising a specifically architectural sensibility in his reading of the *Iliad*. The page reproduced as Fig. 5.10 presents part of his case that although there was no architecture in the *Iliad* (e.g., no temples), an essentially architectural impulse was manifested in, for instance, funeral structures. This perspective is the product and expression of a distinctive type of awareness promoted in the school.

A clearer case, however (because Innes's thesis falls within a recognizable academic genre), is Tariq's pilot thesis (a sort of trial run undertaken in the 4th year), which takes fictional form and is entitled "Tales of a Jacker." The fictional commentary, purportedly composed at some unspecified point, that is attached to the fictional tales begins

> 137 years ago there was no history. 136 years and 364 days ago there suddenly was. This was the moment of plague [...] a morning when civilization woke to nothing [...] on that particular morning not one person on record to date woke with any recollection of the events of the past. The entire province of the Allocated Territories retained all mental faculties other than that which controlled, what would best be described as, collective memory [...] many social safeguards were implemented to protect the province from another attack of the feared plague [....] the most effective safeguard became the obsessive recording and subsequent storing of daily events. Within one week the well known Society of Chroniclers was formed [...] One very influential branch of the Society was called the Minor Provincial Ministry of Juxtaposition and Adjacencies. The ministry described itself as one which handled all matters of side-by-sideness. Its wards were usually referred to as Jacks or Jackers (a convenient but less than clever title for one who is involved in *juxtaposition* and *adjacency*) [...]

One of these Jackers apparently left accounts (the tales) of some of the notable disputes and dilemmas he had to deal with. A page of one of them, "Orthogonal Misfortunes," is reproduced as Fig. 5.11. The following extract is illustrative of the way a strongly architectural sense of the world is worked out in descriptions of material states in this fictional world:

> ... each plantation consists of a home for the plantation owner and a water tank in which a particular algae is grown.... Each tank is eight feet by ten feet in rectangular dimensions and four feet deep. The average tank sits submerged in the Aqua waters, only revealing an inch or so above the surface. The tanks are physically separated by thin steel barriers, which have a tendency to move from side to side spanning a small distance between one-quarter and one-half of an inch.

ORTHOGONAL MISFORTUNES

At the western-most edge of the province one will quite easily find the Aqua River. No one knows or, for that matter, cares what exists beyond it as the river itself is so rich a commodity. For many knowns a certain dumb tranquillity has remained here. This would likely have something to do with the method by which property is allocated. Land along the river is available in lots, each of which is the same in dimensions and cost. This is possible because there is only one form of income here: plantation farming. Perhaps farming is an incorrect word as the sort of work that occurs along the riverside is much more like botany.

A view from above reveals a perfect plantation line about the water's edge

Along the edge of the river lie rows of Medicure plantations; each plantation consists of a home for the plantation owner and a water tank in which a particular algae is grown. This algae became a much sought after raw material a number of diminishing knowns ago when scientists discovered that Polcopholin (the most popular and readily used anti-viral drug available) could be extracted from it. The water tanks themselves require the privilege of description as there are important to the events of passing: Each tank is eight feet by ten feet in rectangular dimensions and four feet deep. The average tank sits submerged in the Aqua waters only revealing an inch or so above the surface. The tanks are physically separated by thin sheet steel barriers, which have a tendency to move from side to side spanning a small distance between one-quarter and one-half of an inch

One day the tranquillity of the riverside was disturbed when a startling discovery was made. Knowledge of the known will come with great acceptance on the part of the reader. There are those things perhaps unseen that should be conjured in the mind. Visualise a stillness when water does not move yet something disturbs it by its mere presence. In the cold of the winter there is an old man who walks on the frozen surface of the water contained in the tanks. He steps from one tank to the next as if they were the spaces between railway tracks. For some reason unknown to any, the old man loses consciousness and finds himself in a compromising situation. He has quite conveniently lay himself in a position which placed his right and left on either side of a steel separator. A regularly expected but unusually heavy snowfall buries him for the duration of the winter. As the ice slowly thaws from underneath (which is common for some unknown reason in the west) the old man's body is slowly lowered onto the edge of one of the tank separating walls. In the fall, two neighbouring plantation farmers find that they have received, free without obligation, half of the old man in each of their tanks (a terrible bisecting best described as an Orthogonal Misfortune). Both curse, 'Tank the Fodder!'
This posed a particular problem in the west. The question of responsibility rose. Ignore the fact that half of a severed old man would very likely contaminate the water, who was to accept the burial? It is common practice in the west (out of respect for the dead's last steps) to bury one in the spot where death occurred. Of course neither farmer chose to accept the body. It was then that a very clever compromise was made: Since the man had in fact died on the steel separator it was there that he should be buried. The separator wavers a maximum of one-half inch (a neutral zone between adjacent tanks), therefore a new one could be fashioned with that knowledge. One which was hollow with a one half inch space inside; for rigidity and burial respect the infill for this separator would become the neatly pressed remains of the old man.

not true—but include for effect

FIG. 5.11. "Orthogonal Misfortunes" from Tariq's project.

This encountered condition is an example of the Jacker's discovery

> that the province was not governed by illustrations of side-by-sideness alone; he found that there was a new explanatory dynamic at work—it was that of in-betweenness.

The writing embodies an architect's world view in a more fundamental sense too. The tales as a whole deal at one level with the decline of Toronto within Tariq's lifetime, though he did not realize until afterwards that it was this underlying sense that provided the basis for the writing:

> A lot of it from what I wrote came from, just in the back of my mind, like it never became something that was integrated in the text, but most of it came from impressions I had of the city of Toronto where I grew up and how that city changed and, but, I don't know if I quite realized that till afterwards. I was thinking about that recently. I think that will almost become the base for the thesis. It's trying to talk about how the city of Toronto's changed over, well, probably fifteen years, because there's almost a story attached to Toronto, how we were supposed to be this wonderful city in North America but something has gone wrong in the past few years, it's not really the best place to live any more.

If being an architect, or being architectural, is looking at the world a particular way, clearly that way can find expression in representations of the existing world, whether direct (Professor Tetreault's students' annotations of scenes in Rome) or fictionally metamorphosed, as much as in representations of projected or planned states in design work. The school's view of what it means to be architectural is not exhausted by what professional architects do in firms—a point to which we return in our final chapter.

This chapter has stressed differences rather than similarities between architecture and the other disciplines we have looked at. We, nevertheless, know that other students also engage in some of these practices. Certainly, there is a widespread use of informal and private (or, at least, not-for-the-professor) writing, often utilizing graphical signs and diagrams and spatial as well as syntactic arrangement, as a means of handling and exploring the ideas, establishing relationships between concepts, drafting formulations for use in papers or presentations, noting questions, and the like. Notes made in lectures or on readings are not simply transcriptions and paraphrases but incorporate elements of the student's responses and thoughts; sometimes they are further inscribed after the lecture is over, or they may lead into separate or partly separate abstracts or reformulations. Similarly, surrounding the drafts of a student's paper are often tangential texts of varying length and in different relationships to the paper, anticipatory workings and thinking-throughs, and spin-off thoughts for possible use elsewhere or pursued simply because the diversion is tempting. This range of casual and undeclared written productions may take place in a bound notebook like the ones the architecture students use, in binders, on loose sheets kept in folders, on scraps of paper that are not preserved, or on the computer screen, with or without printout. Our experience is that in these unofficial texts the students are rehearsing both the ideational content and the rhetoric—the terms and argumentative structures—of the discipline.

III

WORKPLACE WRITING

As mentioned in chapter 1, the widening focus of composition studies since the late 1970s and early 1980s has produced a considerable body of research on writing in the workplace. Recently, Cooper (1996) called this work "the most exciting area of research and scholarship in writing" (p. ix); and, she continued, "the most exciting thing about research on nonacademic writing is the way it problematizes the traditional assumptions about writers and texts" (p. x). It is the extreme complexity of workplace writing that challenges those traditional assumptions. Unlike many of the school writing tasks described in the previous section—which typically have discernible beginnings and endings, single authors and readers, and relatively stable, epistemic rhetorical aims—workplace texts are but one strand in an intricate network of events, intentions, other texts, relationships, and readers.

In an early study of workplace writing, Knoblauch (1980) described the rhetorical challenge facing the business executives he observed: "These writers set out to achieve several conflicting purposes simultaneously while responding to the needs of several, quite different, intended readers, each with different expectations of the writing" (p. 155). Anderson (1985), Driskill (1989), and Paradis, Dobrin, and Miller (1985), among others, have specified a range of possible purposes for workplace writing—all of them instrumental or praxis-oriented. This complex picture has been further elaborated in survey research (e.g., Anderson, 1985; Bataille, 1982; Faigley & Miller, 1982) and studies of workplace writers and writing contexts (e.g., Doheny-Farina, 1985; Odell & Goswami, 1982; Selzer, 1983; see also collections by Anderson, Brockmann, & Miller, 1983, Odell & Goswami, 1985). Since that early work, many studies have emerged to further our understanding of the place and function of writers and writing at work (e.g., Bazerman & Paradis, 1991a; Dias & Paré, in press; Duin & Hansen, 1996; Spilka, 1993) .

From this brief tradition of research, we have come to see that rhetorical purpose in workplace settings is in large part institutional rather than individual, plural and contradictory rather than singular and coherent, and ideological rather than merely communicative. Many workplace texts, as Cooper (1996) explains, "are primarily means of restructuring relationships of power and influence in the pursuit of particular goals" (p. xi). Moreover, institutional documentary practices are inseparable, even indistinguishable, from the intricate culture of practices that constitute "activity systems": As Engeström (1993) states, "If we take a closer and prolonged look at any institution, we get a picture of a continuously constructed collective *activity system* that is not reducible to series or sums of individual discrete actions, although the human agency is necessarily realized in the form of actions" (p. 66).

The conflict and difference Knoblauch identifies above are the consequence of complex and overlapping activity systems. In law, government, and various types of negotiation, rhetorical conflict is institutionalized and built into the activity system: courtrooms, committee hearings, parliaments, and other legislative arrangements are structured along partisan lines, with designated roles for advocates, opponents, plaintiffs, prosecutors, judges, and so on. And, as Bazerman (1988) has demonstrated, "the scientific community developed around the engendering and management of conflict" (p. 149). More often, however, the conflicts played out in and through institutional texts are the undesigned, inevitable result of tensions between the discourses of competing workplace interests (Herndl, 1993; Paré, in press). Even when those interests are organized to collaborate rather than compete—as they are in most large collectives— the differences in their motives, perspectives, procedures, topics, arguments, and goals are likely to cause friction. The hierarchical structure of organizations creates economic and political imbalances that work against shared goals, and the continual growth of specialization, including the increased use of technology, rules against any common discourse. Competition for decreasing funds, and consequent concerns for "accountability," further intensify the struggles for power. To complicate matters more, there is in many fields a tendency toward the use of multidisciplinary or multiprofessional teams which become, in Lave and Wenger's (1991) words, "tangential and overlapping communities of practice" (p. 98).

As a result of this complexity, the notion of *audience*—an inheritance from the Classical rhetorical tradition—is inadequate to explain the multiplicity of readers and reader expectations associated with any given workplace text (Ede & Lunsford, 1984; Paré, 1991b; Park, 1982). Any analysis of the reading practices in the workplace is necessarily limited because specification of the full range of potential readers over time is almost impossible. This fact itself suggests a significant difference between academic and workplace writing. The readers of any document in the workplace are both many and indeterminate, in contrast to the students' readers who are clearly identified and generally singular. In the workplace, papers are passed up and down the hierarchy (for collaborative reading/input as well as for action) and potentially consulted at points distant in time and place, by readers with complex, shifting, and often unpredictable agendas.

Even the once-solid image of the author has fragmented in the face of research reports of collaborative authorship, boilerplated texts, and document-cycling practices (Lunsford & Ede, 1990; Paradis, Dobrin, & Miller, 1985; Smart, 1993). Many of the workplace writer's activities would be unlikely, impossible, or illegal in the school context: writing in pairs or teams, claiming authorship for text produced by another, appropriating research without attribution, receiving extensive assistance from colleagues, making multiple submissions of similar or identical texts, and so on. Rhetorical intentions, long considered the author's prerogative, are more accurately located in the workplace community's collective aspirations and goals. As Bazerman and Paradis (1991b) put it, workplace writing is the "textual harnessing of human social energies to support institutional versions of reality" (p. 6). Though individuals may appear to control invention, arrangement, and style, most workplace authors follow a host of implicit and explicit rhetorical rules; successful compliance marks membership, failure may mean career stagnation or job loss.

In large part, the complexity of workplace writing arises from the subtle interplay between various, often competing, social motives. In institutions, there is more than one motive at work, and the motive that becomes prominent—that is, influences all other motives—is the motive of the highest status social group within the institution. In the chapters that follow, we paint a picture of that rhetorical conflict and complexity.

6

THE COMPLEXITY OF SOCIAL MOTIVE IN WORKPLACE WRITING

In this chapter, we provide a glimpse into one complex workplace setting in order to demonstrate the difficulty that newcomers face as they attempt to make the transition into writing on the job. By describing the position of writers and texts within the complicated dynamics of human work, we wish to demonstrate the highly situated, contingent, and ideological nature of writing. The chapter relies primarily on genre studies for its theoretical basis, and offers a picture of the intricate and purposeful organization of genres in an institutional setting. Briefly, our argument is this: workplace genres embody and enact ideology; that is, genres both reflect and create the ideas, interests, and values of those who participate in them and use them for their particular ends. Although the genres of stable, homogenous institutions may display a relatively consistent ideology, most contemporary organizations of any size consist of overlapping communities of practice (COPs) whose genres embody a variety of ideologies, some in concert, some in conflict. Indeed, as we hope to demonstrate below, individual genres may serve as sites of ideological struggle, as different communities within the larger collective seek to advance their own knowledge, values, and beliefs. As individual newcomers enter the workplace and participate in a particular community's genres, they adopt its ideology and join the struggle that is played out through rhetorical practice.

As we have noted in previous chapters, genres spring from a collective or social motive, and that motive is the manifestation of ideology; it is the beliefs, power relations, and aspirations of the community transformed into rhetorical action. We have argued that the social motive of workplace writing is instrumental because its primary aim is to get something done. But because there is more than one ideology at play in complex organizations and more than one thing to do, there is more than one social motive.

The workplace setting that is the basis of our analysis in this chapter is a large, urban hospital for children. In particular, we consider the genres associated with the hospital's social service department. We locate that department within the ideological tensions of the larger institution, tensions created by overlapping, competing COPs, and we consider the multiple social motives that compete for and in the department's genres.

GENRE: ENACTING SOCIAL MOTIVE

Genre theory has helped delineate patterns in the rhetorical complexity of the workplace and allowed us to see how COPs (companies, agencies, institutions, disciplines) organize sociorhetorical rituals in response to socially construed exigences. Bazerman (1994) offers this explanation of that phenomenon:

> Over a period of time individuals perceive homologies in circumstances that encourage them to see these as occasions for similar kinds of utterances. These typified utterances, often developing standardized formal features, appear as ready solutions to similar appearing problems. Eventually the genres sediment into forms so expected that readers are surprised or even uncooperative if a standard perception of the situation is not met by an utterance of the expected form. (p. 82)

Miller (1994) makes a similar point about what Bazerman calls "a standard perception" when she refers to rhetorical exigence as a "form of social knowledge—a mutual construing of objects, events, interests, and purposes that not only links them but also makes them what they are: an objectified social need" (p. 30). It is critical to note that the patterns of similarity that motivate genres are not so much identified as they are constructed: "Sameness is not a quality that can be recognized in things themselves; it is conferred upon elements within a coherent scheme" (Douglas, 1986, p. 59). Genres develop as responses to what is perceived socially or collectively as sameness in situations. The coherent scheme that confers the sameness is ideology. And, because they are conservative forces, genres tend to reify that sameness: they turn the interpretation of similarity into reality. To borrow from Bourdieu's (1972/1977) definition of *habitus*, genres, are "structured structures predisposed to function as structuring structures" (p. 72). Bourdieu's notion of habitus helps explain the dialectic relationship between genres and the collective experience of repeated exigence. According to Herndl (1996), habitus is "the way of thinking we inherit from past experience which then makes sense of our current experience and allows us to act. Furthermore, this *habitus* is itself continuously produced by our ongoing activity" (p. 29). Once communities have developed "a standard perception of the situation," as Bazerman puts it above, a genre is designed or evolves to respond to the situation and to generate the knowledge and ways of knowing the community needs to conduct its business. Participation in these "structuring structures" initiates newcomers into the collective, into its ways of knowing, learning, and doing. A genre, according to Miller (1994), "embodies an aspect of cultural rationality" (p.39), and by participating in a genre, we learn "what ends we may have" (p.38).

Within large COPs, genres produce specific types of knowing and knowledge and are organized as genre sets: relatively stable collections of repeated and related texts. Amy Devitt (1991), discussing tax accounting texts, explains:

> These texts ... interact within the community. They form a complex network of interaction, a structured set of relationships among texts, so that any text is best understood within the context of other texts. No text is single, as texts refer to one another, draw from one another, create the purpose for one another. These texts and their interaction are so integral to the community's work that they essentially constitute and govern the tax accounting community, defining and reflecting that community's epistemology and values. (pp. 336–337)

Within multidisciplinary or multiprofessional COPs, such as hospitals, large corporations, or government departments, genre sets are organized in cross-community patterns so that rhetorical (and therefore cognitive) activity can be distributed across the collective. (See chap. 7 for an analysis of the rhetorical distribution of cognition in a bank.) The genre set of one group is structured and sequenced so that it will (or can) influence another group at some point: the initial management proposal leads to the technical viability report, which leads to a market study, which leads to legal reports and sales brochures, and so on. Bazerman (1994) calls such chained texts "systems of genres" (p. 79); in effect, one group of people think and write in a particular way so as to produce a text that allows another group to think and write a different way. As a result, texts serve as critical points of interaction between and among institutional sub-groups. (And, as we demonstrate in chaps. 9 and 10, it is often in multigroup contexts—hospital rounds, presentations, team meetings—that newcomers begin to learn the organization's discourse conventions and dynamics.)

Fairclough (1995), too, speaks of complex organizational intertextuality, and refers to "the ordered set of discursive practices associated with a particular social domain or institution" (p. 12), which he calls "ideological-discursive formations," or IDFs. He argues that IDFs "are ordered in dominance: it is generally possible to identify a 'dominant' IDF and one or more 'dominated'

IDFs in a social institution" (p.41). Fairclough explains the relationship between ideology and regular discourse practices thus:

> A particular set of discourse conventions (e.g., for conducting medical consultations, or media interviews, or for writing crime reports in newspapers) implicitly embodies certain ideologies—particular knowledge and beliefs, particular "positions" for the types of social subject that participate in that practice (e.g., doctors, patients, interviewees, newspaper readers), and between categories of participants (e.g., between doctors and patients). In so far as conventions become natural and commonsensical, so too do these ideological presuppositions. (p. 94)

Thus, engagement in a genre promotes particular ways of knowing and acting. To participate in a genre is to assist in the production and reproduction of an organization's knowledge, power, and culture. As Coe (1994), following Burke (1957), puts it, "genres embody attitudes. Since those attitudes are built into the generic structures, they are sometimes danced without conscious awareness or intent on the part of the individual using the genre" (p. 183). Thus, genres form a principal means of situating the individual's cognitive activity in the community's overall epistemology and ideology. Genres, Coe says, are "important factors in the social construction of orientations, paradigms, ideologies, worldviews and cultural perspectives" (p. 184).

And though genres do change over time, they are by definition somewhat stable, and their stability promotes a sense of normalcy. Devitt (1991) explains: "The mere existence of an established genre may encourage its continued use, and hence the continuation of the activities and relations associated with that genre" (pp. 340–341). This historical force of repetition creates regularity; sociorhetorical habits become "the way things are done," and the reality they create becomes the ontological norm. In the process, the origins and underlying human agency of genres are obscured. Smith (1974) puts it this way: "Socially organized practices of reporting and recording work upon what actually happens or has happened to create a reality in documentary form, and though they are decisive to its character, their traces are not visible in it" (p. 257). Or, as Fairclough (1995) says, "metaphorically speaking, ideology endeavors to cover its own traces" (p. 44).

A SOCIAL WORK GENRE SET

The complexity of workplace writing and the dynamics of genre are explored in the analysis that follows, an analysis based on interviews with practitioners, textual analysis, and observations of activity in the social service department of a large, children's hospital. During the time at which the data were collected, the department was in the process of modifying its genre set; changes were being made to formats and procedures. This disruption of usual writing practice at the hospital shifted the performance of genre from the workers' subsidiary awareness to their focal awareness, to use Polanyi's (1958) terms: the genres became visible rather than remaining transparent. The social and rhetorical regularities associated with their habitual production of texts were being revised; as a result, the workers became more conscious of the exigences, the social motives, their practice served. In addition, the change made it possible to see some of the attitudes that were being embodied by and embedded in the revised genre set, attitudes that newcomers would "dance" when they joined the community.

Patients are referred to the social service department for a variety of reasons. Sometimes those reasons are relatively benign; for example, parents might need help finding lodging close to the hospital so they can visit their sick child. More difficult cases result when families experience the stress of having severely or terminally ill children, cases sometimes further complicated by cultural differences between families and hospital personnel. A high proportion of referrals are made because of suspected or certain physical and sexual abuse.

The hospital social workers are part of a multiprofessional team that includes nurses, physiotherapists, psychiatrists, medical doctors of all specialties, technicians, volunteers, and so on. The hospital's director of social work says that "80 or 90 different people" might have contact with a patient during hospitalization. Many of those people, as well as the patient's family, would have access to the child's medical chart. The chart is actually a centrally located file kept on the ward for in-patients and in Medical Records for out-patients. It contains a variety of texts or "consults" from the specialized groups that constitute the multiprofessional team. Individual groups maintain their own, separate records as well, but the chart constitutes a collective archive. In theory, each person who deals with a patient reads the chart initially and regularly, because it contains updated medical and psychosocial information. In fact, as suggested by Fairclough above and as demonstrated below, some texts have higher status than others, and may be consulted more frequently or granted greater value. The chart, then, is the physical location at which the hospital's genre sets overlap and the rhetorical location at which those sets become a system: each text in the chart can and should be read by every member of the team, and the collection as a whole represents a unified textual picture of the patient.

According to the director, the "basic rationale" or purpose of social work records in the chart is to document what our professional contribution is to the treatment plan … so that other health care professionals can work in consort with us and carry through the best treatment, the most comprehensive treatment plan possible, for the patient and/or the family. And so the psychosocial is one piece of the bio-psychosocial plan, to use current lingo, that would enable the other health professionals to understand what our contribution is.

In the medical chart, social work texts join other "psychosocial" texts (psychiatric, psychological) and various medical and laboratory texts to form a bio-psychosocial genre system. Before modifications, the genre set that documented social work's contribution was supposed to consist of a referral form that indicated the reason the child had been brought to social work's attention, an assessment report submitted some time after initial contact with the child and family, ongoing assessments or progress reports at regular intervals, and a closing or transfer summary when the case was closed or moved to another institution. In actual practice, however, there was wide variation in individual recording formats and procedures. Records, in the director's words, were

> variations on a theme. Some workers didn't record at all, some workers write in the medical chart [daily notes] and don't write anything else, some workers would take the referral form and just keep on adding other pages…. they never felt that there was a format to do the initial assessment … the complete assessment, and the closing summary. And social workers are notoriously poor about closing cases; they just sort of go on and on and on until you never hear from the family again.

Formats were a mixture of headings and sequences adapted from other institutions or developed idiosyncratically. According to the director, there was widespread agreement among her staff, her management team, and the hospital administration that the genre set needed to be modified, although the arguments used by each of these groups to support changes were not identical, as we shall see below. A consideration of the modifications and their justifications gives some sense of the competing ideologies and the vested interests at play in institutional texts.

A CASE OF GENERIC ENGINEERING

The basic sequence of the genre set remained the same, but formats were standardized and composing and submission procedures were regularized. Each of the four texts was restricted to a single, carbon-backed page and uniform headings were provided. A green stripe was printed down their right-hand margin to make the texts readily identifiable in the chart as social work documents. A blank sheet, also green-edged, was made available in case a text spilled over its allotted space, although this practice was discouraged. Workers were strongly encouraged to submit the referral form to the patient's medical chart immediately and to follow that with the initial assessment as quickly as possible. It became mandatory to submit a progress report on each patient every 3 months, a move designed to make workers reassess cases and, it was hoped, close them more frequently. Regular recording, faster initial assessments, and scheduled progress reports increased the amount of each worker's writing, though it discouraged extensive writing on any one case. The director explained the changes in terms that Aristotle would have approved: "What we've said is, in every situation there's a beginning, a middle, and an end," a referral, an assessment, and a closing summary.

Consistency and uniformity might, on the surface, seem like sufficient reason to revise institutional textual practices and, indeed, most social workers expressed approval for regular record-keeping procedures. The regulation made it more likely that they would do the writing they needed and wanted to do, and updated records made it easier to take on a colleague's case load during holidays or illness. But genre theory encourages us to look more closely, both at the underlying social motives that shape genres, and at the influence those genres have in shaping the life and culture of their institutional settings. And Fairclough's (1995) work in critical discourse analysis alerts us to the "engineering of change in discursive practices" (p. 105), which he calls the "technologization of discourse":

> Technologization of discourse is a process of intervention in the sphere of discourse practices with the objective of constructing a new hegemony in the order of discourse of the institution or organization concerned.... [I]t involves an attempt to shape a new synthesis between discourse practice, sociocultural practice and texts. (p. 102)

Genres are both text and context, and altering the regular features of repeated documents has a ripple effect out to the practices used to create, distribute, and interpret texts, and to the settings within which those documents operate. To borrow terms from Activity Theory: altering mediational means affects the whole activity. Standardizing texts, restricting their length, providing headings, and regulating submission schedules cannot help but affect generic activities associated with the text, such as writing and reading processes and the relationships played out in and through the texts (see Paré & Smart, 1994). Moreover, rhetorical form is heuristic. Form, Coe (1987) argues, is "a motive for generating information. Like any heuristic, it motivates a search for information of a certain type: when the searchers can anticipate what shape of stuff they seek, generation is less free, but much more efficient; by constraining the search, form directs attention" (p. 18). Standardized headings construct the categories under which writers gather and present information. Douglas (1986) writes that "sameness is conferred on the mixed bundle of items that count as members of a category; their sameness is conferred and fixed by institutions" (p. 53). Furthermore, limited space reduces and shapes that which is gathered; hastening text submission times hastens the accompanying practices (interviews, consultation, reflection, interventions, etc.).The director captured this relationship between form and thought succinctly: "We've made headings that require people to focus, and focus briefly." One social worker commented on the influence of headings in the revised text formats:

> I find the headings—okay—I find they've made me structure my thoughts, but I find it difficult at times. I might want to put a lot in one heading, and nothing in the next.... It would have been nice if those headings could be somehow moveable.

Devitt (1991) suggests that the genre sets employed by tax accountants "constitute and govern the ... community, defining and reflecting the community's epistemology and values" (pp. 336–337); it follows that changes to a genre set will influence the community's knowledge and beliefs. The original social motives that inspire genres are often invisible to the newcomer, as are the constraints on knowing (the epistemology and values) that genres embody and enact. Because genres so obviously enable completion of workplace tasks, and because participation in them so clearly marks membership in the community, newcomers may be unable or unwilling to question or criticize them.

"ACCOUNTABILITY" AS SOCIAL MOTIVE;
"FOCUS" AS PRACTICE

The multiple ideologies of the hospital produced multiple social motives, which inspired the genre changes in the hospital. When workers and managers spoke about these complex and sometimes competing motives, they used the term "accountability." Likewise, the many immediate and long-term consequences of the revised genre set were often summarized by the single word "focus": the genre changes were meant to influence—in fact, alter—the workers' practice, to sharpen their "focus" in order to make the department, its individual members, and its genres more "accountable" to their own and others' motives. Four broad areas of accountability were apparent; that is, through their texts, the workers were responsible to four distinct interest groups within the hospital: to themselves and their colleagues, to management (and, through management, to the hospital's administration), to the medical team, and to the clients. In each case, the change in focus imposed by the revised genres changed the workers' motives and practice.

Accountability to Self and Colleagues

Since early in its emergence as a profession, social work has been aware of the epistemic potential of writing: the power that written language has to help the writer make sense of complex information and situations. In the first book on social work record-keeping, Sheffield (1920) said that the social work file is "a body of personal information conserved with a view to ... establishing the case worker herself in critical thinking" (pp. 5–6; see also Bristol, 1936). Similar comments accompany discussions of social work writing up to the present. The director summarized this function of writing: "[The forms] help the worker to focus on what it is their role is, to take a look at their own practice." Here "focus" is self-reflection in the service of improved practice.

In addition, workers wanted greater accountability to each other, and regular recording habits did that by ensuring that documentation was up to date and uniform when holidays, transfers, retirements, or illness made it necessary for one worker to take on some or all of another's case load. As one worker put it, up-to-date recording is helpful "in case you go out and get hit by a truck," because "the person that comes behind you knows what's going on." Inconsistency in recording had meant that some workers had full and detailed records while others had brief notes or none at all. Overall, in this regard, the workers appeared pleased with the ways in which the genre change would guarantee standards in submission and content, but there were some misgivings:

> I am not sure whether—I've tried to put myself in other [social workers'] shoes, and when they pick this [new text] up and read it, do they really know the family? Or do they have a sense of the family struggles? I don't know.

This double motive of accountability to self and colleagues was captured by the director: "[the genre change] is in line with focussing what your intervention is.... if you have to focus it on paper, in the recording, then hopefully you've focused it in your head, and you've focused it in terms of explaining it to the other team members." "Focus" here suggests accountability to self (reflection) and to the team. However, although workers agreed with this intention of the genre change, some were not sure that the new texts and the focus they provided would encourage the necessary reflection:

> [The changes] have taken away a level of dynamic formulation and thinking about the case ... because it's a more superficial assessment. I have to take deliberate time to think in a more sophisticated manner about a case, because the form doesn't demand it.... I have to take the extra time to conceptualize, because the piece of paper [form] doesn't demand it on that level.

> I find this form that we have does not encourage coherent thought from the point of view of really looking at a situation: how it began, what's happening, how it's happening, what's keeping it happening, and how you want to have it changed, and how the proposed changes could impact upon it. It simply doesn't allow for that level of thought.

The motive of accountability to each other and to themselves created a subtle paradox for the workers: regular, brief reporting did produce documentation for others and serve as a heuristic for personal reflection, but some thought the "focus" was too tight to allow for a full sense of the "family struggles" or the "coherent thought" necessary for effective practice. As one worker noted, the changes had "clinical implications, obviously." Two workers expanded on these concerns:

> [The form] doesn't account for a full, dynamic picture. That's completely left out of this form. Because I usually ... get a developmental picture of the child, I get a sense of the family, and where they're coming from. There's nowhere on this [form] really to write that in.

> But if the report doesn't allow you to show the gaps [in your own or others' work with family], then I don't think you learn very much. It's just nice and neat. You want a report that challenges you a little bit. And I find that our system at the moment has not allowed us to appear vulnerable. It's a nice show, it looks good, but it's not meaty enough for me, that's my sense.

Accountability to Management and Administration

A key motive to which the genre changes responded was management's concern with supervision and evaluation. Hospitals are rigidly hierarchical, and social workers are not among the elite. Social service management fulfilled a middle role between workers and administration and a liaison role between the department and other departments. The new genre set provided for ongoing management and monitoring. As one manager put it, "It's like a tool ... for supervision: you sort of go back into the handling of a situation, or you go back into the way in which it's being judged and worked with through the recording." A worker put a slightly different spin on it: "Big Brother is watching." She went on:

> we are naturally much more accountable, okay, because these green [edged] forms go to our supervisors, who bring them to their supervisors, who bring them to the director, who might have to bring them if she's audited ... to the clinical director or the financial administrator, whatever, to explain why a case is left open beyond the 3-month mark.

Another social worker saw the genre change as detrimental: "I don't think it really meets the situation as adequately as the other system, but we have become very conscientious about accountability and every file has to be complete, and people are going to check up on it."

Even when they agreed with the change to the genre set, some workers were rankled by the supervisory implications. One suggested that, "from an administrative point of view, it's a very valuable innovation." Another lamented:

> It worries me, philosophically, this whole thing.... it suggests that things have to be so tight that people left to their own devices will not be conscientious, will not do their work. That's the underlying suggestion: that you won't do the work, if you aren't accountable for it, and if you don't have to write about it all the time.

The pressure to place initial assessments in the chart as soon as possible after a referral had been made, and the required progress reports every 3 months, meant more frequent (though less extensive) writing. A worker complained: "It's physically impossible to do a lot of assessments.... I do a lot of assessments, and I just can't possibly do it. So I downgraded the quality of the assessments." The exigence of accountability to management caused workers to focus on their practice—that is, to practice—differently. Managers needed documentary evidence of worker's efforts for supervisory purposes, of course, but also to appease their own superiors. Paper work, or the version of work that gets documented, is the institution's virtual reality. In effect, no text meant no practice, so managers needed the texts to reflect (and cause) the type of practice the administration required.

Canadian hospitals are state-funded and, like other government controlled institutions, desperate to reduce deficits. This financial motive led to close examination of all hospital units to determine efficiency and effectiveness, as the administration sought arguments to convince their political masters of the need for funds. Failure to meet the administration's standards meant cutbacks. One of the chief advantages of the genre changes for the director, then, was in her dealings with administration: "Well, I think [the workers] feel that there's a lot more accountability because there's a paper to be filled out now. The squeeze is on for many areas ... and I think this is just one of them. I said very clearly to them, if you don't have recording, and you haven't done your statistics, if you get sick, I don't get a replacement for you, because I haven't got the wherewithal to convince administration."

Some sense of the complexity of this accountability to administration and its financial motive is captured in this extensive interview excerpt, in which the director of the social work department explains the link between "productivity" and recording:

> Well, we're constantly being looked at by the administration to justify our establishment, you know? And we do that in a number of ways. Our productivity, and the way we can measure our productivity is by the number of families that we've seen, and you can't pick a number out of a hat. You've got to be able to document who it was that you've seen, and what it is you've done, and try and identify from that what are the major issues that we're dealing with in the department. Because you have nursing, who are into the psychosocial area, you have psychology, psychiatry, pastoral [religious] counseling, all these other hybrids.... We had like the big three here originally, you know: psychiatry, psychology, and social work.... my budget's a million point three, and they're asking what are they getting for that? And if they're going to cut, are they going to cut the operating room schedule or, you know, only operate Tuesdays and Thursdays, or are they going to cut technical staff, lab staff? Are they going to cut psychosocial staff? ... when I came here, we were 43 positions ... and we're now down to 22, and the work is more intense, the problems are more serious, the resources that people have are fewer.... and when administration sees this array of beauty around the table, they'll say, they *did* say, "You've got a lot of workers, and what do you need all those people for?" And it used to be you could just say, well, you know, it's very hard on children coming in to be operated on, or to have these awful procedures. [But they say] "well we're paying others, we have volunteers to do that, we have nurses to do that, and blah, blah, blah." ... we're in a competitive market, and if they want to increase the number of psychologists, they're not going to get a pot of gold to dip into, they're going to have to make some choices. Do they need fewer social workers, or maybe more psychologists?

Social work texts—and, as well, associated activities—must demonstrate cost effectiveness, to use the market's term. They are the visible record and proof of "productivity." Moreover, it is imperative that the social workers produce discourse that distinguishes them from others and that contributes uniquely to the collective enterprise. Institutional documents define cognitive and rhetorical territory and alert others to the group's presence and purpose. If psychosocial discourse can be produced by nurses, psychologists, pastoral animators, or volunteers, why keep a social work department? Social workers must provide textual accounts of themselves and their work, accounts that function as distinctive and essential parts of the hospital's genre system by helping the other disciplines do their work more effectively or by satisfying the needs of higher status groups. Thus, genres are factors in what Bourdieu (1984/1993) calls a "linguistic market":

> There is a linguistic market whenever someone produces an utterance for receivers capable of assessing it, evaluating it and setting a price on it.... [The market] is a particular social situation, more or less official and ritualized, a particular set of interlocutors, situated at a particular level in the social hierarchy—all properties that are perceived and appreciated in an infraconscious way and unconsciously orient linguistic production. (pp. 79–80)

Clearly, one of the social motives operating under the rubric of "accountability" is financial. The hospital is a "competitive market," as the social work director notes, and funding for social services is diminishing. Changes in the genre set were designed, in part, to prove and improve productivity, a move that met with mixed reviews. A psychologist who supervises social workers sees a positive correlation between financial accountability and professional activity:

> there's much more spotlight on all the professions, and that's a good thing: they're not private enclaves, they're funded by public funds, and they have to be open and available and well structured. So [the genre change is] a tightening I think, too, of how we count activity, productivity.

But others are not so sure. Although acknowledging shrinking budgets and the need for professional accountability, some workers worry that a "bottom line" mentality might have negative implications:

> But it isn't the form [genre] that's changing, it's the principle behind the form. Okay, the form itself is a symbol, that's all it is. The reality behind the symbol is more accountability and higher numbers, and greater turnover, and more productivity. Not productivity in terms of quality, but in terms of quantity.... I feel that the sentiment behind the form is to have much more of a turnstile business going ... you know, I keep hearing the slogans, like "Wake up and smell the coffee, this is a new age, we're in a depression, we're in a recession." ... In the financing of social programs ... there is a very short term view.

It was widely accepted that demanding a progress report every 3 months would encourage workers to reevaluate their cases. When workers carry a heavy load of unnecessary or dormant cases, it is difficult to assign new ones. A legislated, regular review of each case would, in theory, result in "closings," or case terminations. As the director said, "the forms will require them, will make it incumbent on them, to rethink ... keeping cases open." The new "focus" would encourage changes in practice. Again, workers were divided on this change in the genre's motive: "If there are malingerers in either the user field or the social work field, then we have to try to get motivated and get through that, because the public isn't as tolerant at spending vast sums of money for little result, you know?" But the same worker saw a darker side: "I hope it doesn't make me more impatient with clients.... this could be a very negative thing where you start ... whipping [your] clients into improving faster."

These multiple, overlapping, and subtle exigences—accountability to themselves and each other, to their managers, to the administration—operated as one constellation of motives and placed writers and texts in a particular network of interests and activities. The changes to generic forms and activities brought the social workers' practice in line with the needs of those above them in the institutional hierarchy. In an institution dedicated solely to social services, with a single genre set, the managerial and administrative network might constitute most of the workers' universe of discourse, but another set of exigences grew from the social workers' collaboration with other members of their multiprofessional team, in particular the medical personnel.

Accountability to Medicine

Social work genres in a hospital must produce activities, including texts, that support the efforts of the medical staff. It was widely agreed that the doctors and nurses were not reading social work records before the genre changes, because they were too long. Narrative is often considered an occupational hazard of social work; when you deal in people's lives, stories are what you get. The changes were designed to correct that situation. As the director said, "we don't want biographical information *ad nauseam*." Nor do doctors or nurses want the "balderdash" or "psychobabble" found in social work's traditional "psychodynamic interpretations," because they are too long and technical and "have no business in a medical chart." She summed up social work's position:

> And I think that's an important thing: this is a medical chart that we're writing in. We're invited to give our opinion. We should give it and thank them.... More than that, I don't think is expected.

As with other areas of accountability, workers were not always in agreement with managers on this question of responding to the social motives of medicine. The speed at which the medical staff worked, and the resulting need for brevity in record-keeping, alarmed some writers: "I find ... that in talking to medical people, especially now when everybody's so pressed, that if I can't give it to them in 25 words or less, then they tune out." Social work discourse, if such an independent discourse can be said to exist, frequently occurs in conjunction with, and at the service of, other more powerful discourses: legal, psychological, medical, bureaucratic (Paré, 1993; in press). For many, this service to medicine represented a conflict of interests, as these workers explain:

> I find the new recording system is useful for a doctor who may be ready to discharge someone. It's useful for the organization. I don't find it useful for social workers. So, so I guess I kind of feel like I do the hospital recording for the hospital; that helps the doctors clear the bed or make appropriate discharge plans.... I feel that my role is much more than that, and I require extra things, and it's almost like the recording doesn't fit into that.

*****

> We have the chart, and that's very much medically-based; and I find for social work purposes, there are things that I like to have a record of that I don't believe should be in the chart. So I do the recording, but it's almost like something I have to do that's not central to my work.

*****

> We have a policy in this hospital that we just have one chart, and it's the medical chart. So it means that if a social worker is careful about what they put in the chart, which they should be, in fact there is nothing there of value to me.

The social motive of accountability to medicine shaped particular texts, texts that were brief and helpful to doctors. As members of a department of social work in a hospital, the workers recognized the inevitability of this focus, but they struggled with the loss of their own discourse and the practice it promoted. The alternative, however, was a form of invisibility and eventual extinction; to coin a phrase, better read than dead.

Accountability to Clients

A fourth broad area of accountability was created by the social workers' responsibility to their clients. Access to information laws have made it possible for clients to read their files, thus creating a considerably altered rhetorical situation. Increasingly, client access to documentation has created pressure in social work to write *to* and *for* clients, rather than just *about* them. The director of social work explained:

> The influence of clients having access to records I think has been good for the profession in terms of making them look again at what they have written, and how other people perceive it.... you can come to a mutual understanding with your client and use it [text] as a tool to have the client say, "Well, where are we at this point?" [And you can say,] "Do you agree with this or not? And how do you want to change it?" There has been a reluctance on social work's part as a profession to do that. I think we're moving into that much more; the people have a right to know what's being written about them.

On the one hand, this move to include clients as readers has clinical justification: recording becomes part of practice, rather than external to or postpractice. Using the text as a clinical tool allows both worker and client to "focus" on interpretations and interventions that previously had remained covert. On the other hand, greater access to records has increased the threat of legal action. The director again:

> At the same time that people have access, there are many more places where they can complain. And so you have to sort of ride a middle ground that you protect yourself as a professional from litigation.

In virtually all social work writing, questions of law create a tension between too much and too little, between the need for rich detail and the fear of legal consequences. Consider the dilemma faced by this worker, who must weigh the value of recording a client's extreme anger against the possible legal ramifications:

> I've had a parent tell me that he wanted to kill his wife he was so mad at her. He didn't mean that, but I can imagine what would have happened if I had put that on the chart, and then this chart was subpoenaed to court. Because some of us have been subpoenaed in family battles, and you have to be so careful.

The imposed brevity of the genre changes made it possible to be "careful" about reporting, and thus avoid legal complications. However, that tighter focus was welcomed by the workers for another reason as well:

> Okay, parents bring a child to the hospital because that child is sick. And so our responsibility is to help them adapt to the situation of the sick child and the impact on their family. Not because they, the parents, want to be fixed up, which in the past there seemed to be a heavy emphasis on. And so I think it helps us focus better, and to respect that family's need for privacy, unless issues impact in the

care of the child.... there's absolutely no question in my mind that it keeps us better focused.

*****

I think also, many times, that we misjudge parents because we're seeing them in situations of crisis, where ... nothing is right with the world, their world is upside down, and their behavior sometimes is a response to what's happening to their child. And I think that this [form] helps you focus on that.

Here the "focus" is determined by confidentiality, by how and how much one needs to write (and think) about the child and family in order for the collective to do its work effectively. The rich and detailed narrative of previous recording, so helpful to the self as a heuristic and to others as "a full, dynamic picture" of the family, becomes here an intrusion into the clients' private lives, and the genre changes imposed a limit to that intrusion; in effect, the changes constrained practice.

However, as with all of the other social motives that shaped the new genres, there were subtle contextual variations in this exigence of accountability to clients. One worker, whose specific area of concern was the Inuit in Canada's far north, offered a compelling argument for abundant information:

I've made decisions that have been, you know, placing a child in the south is a major, major thing.... I tend to overwrite, usually, and I make sure I send [records] up north; every step of the way I let the north know about it. Partly to protect myself, because the decision making is made up north, partly to reinforce that it's their responsibility to make decisions. It's also to train the Inuit workers, show them how I'm thinking.... And they have requested that, too, that they want to see what, what we think, what we write. And then I guess some of these kids one day may wonder, "Well, why did that happen to me?" And I want there to be records. And I want them to see where we were all headed and what the arguments were.

Like many statements made by the social workers, this last one points to the rhetorical complexity of these genres and to the competing social motives that struggle in and through them. It also indicates the rhetorical sophistication of participants in the genres. This worker resisted the administrative, financial, legal, and medical interests that sought brief accountability, in favor of a more detailed account that exposed her own thinking and the institutional forces that created an individual's life story. But the conflict between social work's professional social motives and the bureaucratic, medical, and other social motives at play in this workplace creates a tension that a newcomer would find hard to resist (or even to recognize as such).

In this chapter, we have offered a picture of the complexity of workplace writing, of the intricate sociorhetorical activity in human endeavor. The situatedness of workplace texts—their inextricable relationship to particular ideologies, settings, times, people, other texts, and activities—renders arhetorical (or under-rhetorical) any academic attempt to replicate them, no matter how sophisticated or elaborate the simulation, case study, or role play. Genre theory predicts, and our research confirms, the presence of highly structured textual rituals and patterns in the workplace, but those genres are inseparable from their context. So, although it might well be possible and even desirable to show students copies of workplace texts, and to have practitioners talk to students about their participation in those texts, the lived experience of texts is impossible outside of their enactment.

7

DISTRIBUTED COGNITION AT WORK

As we have seen in chapter 2, distributed cognition is one term that is used in that nexus of notions arising from the literature on situated cognition, activity theory, and socially-shared cognition. These are overlapping notions emerging from the same paradigm; however, at this point it is useful to separate out the notion of distributed cognition, and to probe it as a way of differentiating what happens in the classroom from what happens in the workplace. Specifically, this term highlights the degree to which, within specific activities, knowing and/or learning and/or thinking are often distributed among co-participants, as well as mediated through the cultural artifacts available—artifacts which include semiotic, technological, and organizational structures: the process is dynamic and interactive, within a delicate, subtle, constant interplay among participants and means as they operate in tandem (although often with friction) toward the object of the activity.

DISTRIBUTED COGNITION DEFINED

As Salomon (1993) points out, the notion of distributed cognition is distinct from the sense in which cognition is conceived in conventional cognitive theories:

> Traditionally, the study of cognitive processes, cognitive development, and the cultivation of educationally desirable skills and competencies has treated every-thing cognitive as being *possessed* and *residing in the heads* of individuals: social, cultural and technological factors have been relegated to the role of backdrops or external sources of stimulation. (p. xii)

In contrast, theorists and researchers working within the paradigm of situated learning and practical cognition recognized that "people appear *to think in conjunction or partnership* with others and with the help of culturally provided tools and implements" (p. xiii). Salomon points out that, in this more recent work, "the social and artifactual surrounds alleged to be 'outside' the individuals' heads [are understood to be] not only sources of stimulation and guidance but ... actually *vehicles of thought*" (p. xiii). Furthermore, as he explains, "the arrangements, functions, and structures of these surrounds change in the process to become genuine *parts of the learning* that results from the cognitive partnerships with them" (p. xiii, all emphases in original).

Salomon stresses the fact that distributed cognition is not the same as division of labor; nor is it the same as "mutual stimulation" (p. xv). Instead, as Cole and Engeström (1993) argue, distributed cognition takes socially mediated activity in cultural contexts as the appropriate psychological unit of analysis. In their words: "The combination of goals, tools, and setting (or perhaps 'arena,' in Lave's, 1988, terminology) constitutes simultaneously the context of behavior and the ways in which cognition can be said to be distributed in that context" (p. 13).

The activity, the distribution, and the interplay are dynamic: "the continuously negotiated distribution of tasks, powers, and responsibilities among the participants of the activity system" (Cole & Engeström, 1993, p. 7).

DISTRIBUTED COGNITION AT THE UNIVERSITY

In this chapter we focus on one particular workplace, a governmental financial agency, the Bank of Canada (BOC), and use the notion of distributed cognition to frame and understand our observations; however, we preface our analysis of the BOC with a brief account of how distributed cognition applies to the university. We hope thereby not only to define the concept in a familiar context, but also to discover from this particular perspective how the university and workplace compare as sites for writing.

If we perceive the university's primary purpose as to accredit or to rank students, it is clear that the cognition involved in such functions is distributed throughout the university. Each instructor's role is to know (inspect, rank) their students according to the culturally mediated systems available (e.g., A, B, C, D, FNS, INC, DEF). The final grade is based on the professor's and/or grader's inspection of the students from this perspective on the basis of class performance, exams, and papers.

The grade for each course is reviewed and signed by the appropriate authorities (which vary by institutions), and then the grades for each student are amassed at some central registrarial office, where the student's performance as a whole is monitored, and assessed according to institutional regulations concerning progress: for example, number of courses required for specific degrees, grades required for honors, et cetera.

Finally, as a result of a review of the records—typically performed in departments by faculty as well as in registration offices (often monitored by grievance and appeal committees), the president of the university officially gives the student the diploma accrediting a certain kind of performance.

Different players all contribute to this analysis of the students' performance over the school years. Note that there is a complex interplay among actors, technology, and recording systems; that there can be variation by institution; that grievances are possible; and that subversion too is possible—for example when a professor decides to grant a *de facto* deferral (in contexts where that is not allowed) by handing in an estimated grade and then allowing a student to hand in a paper late and submitting a change of grade form if there is a discrepancy between the estimate and the actual grade. All of this is maintained through genres of records and documents, which establish and maintain certain kinds of social interrelations and define the ways in which students are to be classified and "known."

However, the distribution of cognition throughout the educational institution of the university as a whole is of a very different kind from that which occurs in the classroom where the term *distributed cognition* is better replaced by the term *socially shared knowledge*. In the classroom, the teacher possesses knowledge—some of which she intends to "share" with the students, in the sense of enabling them to hold it in common with her. In fact, a goal of the class is precisely the sharing of this knowledge; and the inspection and ranking of the students takes place with respect to their ability to display their acquisition of this knowledge. (Of course, this is not to deny that, as in most communities of practice, teachers may learn as well—especially with respect to their craft of teaching—and that learners may learn something else that is not known by the teacher and incidental to the purported objective of the classroom.)

DISTRIBUTED COGNITION
IN THE WORLD OF WORK

As described earlier (chap. 2), Hutchins (1993) uses the notion of distributed cognition to describe and explain the management of the navigation of a ship. This analogy, in its concreteness, provides a powerful way of understanding and explaining what happened in the various institutions we observed. We begin our discussion by pointing to the comparison between the concrete activity of navigation and institutional activities in the Bank of Canada (BOC).

Navigating a Ship and Managing Economic Policy

Just as in the ship that Hutchins (1993) described, the activity undertaken in the BOC draws on the efforts of many participants—with different tasks assigned to each, but all involved in and focused on the single objective of moving forward toward a clearly defined goal. On the ship, the focus is on reaching a specific geographic, physical location. In the BOC, the goal is the achievement of national economic well-being through price stability. (See specifics below.)

In both cases, there are one or two people at the helm who take direct and final responsibility for decision making. At the same time, though, and this is a point we wish to stress, all kinds of important judgments are constantly being made at lower levels of the hierarchy, and these judgments are funneled up through intermediate layers to the person(s) at the top. At the BOC, the person at the helm is the Governor; aboard the ship, it is the captain.

In both cases, there are constant calculations being made at all levels to answer the questions specified by Hutchins (1993): "Where are we? and If we proceed in a certain way for a specified time, where will we be?" (p.39). Both the ship and the financial agency map their progress using charts and graphs. Hutchins points out that the maps used in navigation look more like coordinate charts in geometry rather than like maps in an atlas; this is true as well of the mathematical models and graphs guiding the progress of the BOC.

As suggested above, in both instances there is a clear movement forward toward a goal. For the ship, the goal is its physical destination. At the BOC, that goal has been defined very specifically in recent years as price stability or low inflation.[13] In reaching their respective goals, both the ship and the BOC must pay constant attention to a host of external variables, many of them outside their control: winds, currents, other ships on the one hand; world financial markets, political uncertainties, market interpretations, on the other.

In both situations, there is considerable "overlap" (Hutchins, 1993) in the knowledge among the players—partly because players often move up the hierarchy, and partly because internal structures are established in such a way

---

[13]This policy is not without its critics. Indeed, the BOC's focus on controlling inflation as the primary goal of monetary policy has been questioned by some academics and financial journalists. In fact, the initial formulation of the policy came about as a result of considerable internal discussion (conducted extensively through writing, as is suggested later), and justification of the policy recurs in many of the externally oriented genres, as our analysis of BOC speeches will suggest.

that information is interpreted and reinterpreted by different groups. Errors are more easily caught because of this overlap: more senior people often have an intuition that something does not feel quite right in the analysis of data that is being given to them—on the basis of their own work in the area earlier in their careers. ("The management of the Bank is composed largely of professional economists, most of whom have a long Bank history" [Duguay & Longworth, 1997, p. 1].) The overlap in knowledge and the possibility of reflexiveness contribute to the robustness of the decision making.

Contrast with Ship Navigation

Of course, the situations also differ in some basic ways, and the differences too are instructive. Navigating a ship, for example, is largely based on interpreting physical realities, whereas, to a large extent, the world navigated by the BOC is socially constructed in particularly complex ways. For example, central bankers must continually monitor external market developments, which are themselves being interpreted and constructed by traders and investors in the light of hunches or instincts—that is, interpretative strategies that are not necessarily consistent with those of, or even fully understood by, central bankers.

Although it is true that the decisions of the BOC have material outcomes, as the public and the media are quick to point out, nonetheless, the world in which the BOC operates is far more textually constructed than that of ship navigation. It can be argued that the very notion of an economy is an intersubjective reality established through discursive practices, as Brown (1993) contends: "The 'real economy' is not knowable as a direct or brute fact of existence independently of its discursive construction. The 'economy' is represented as an object of analysis by a set of discourses which constitute it as such" (p. 70).

In the end, the destination of a ship is fixed: the port of Montreal can be counted on to remain at a certain fixed longitudinal and latitudinal position. In contrast, whereas the overall aim of the BOC—to guide monetary policy—remains the same, the precise specification of that objective is socially constructed. Indeed, the issue of price stability has been subject to considerable debate within a range of discursive venues the press, Parliament, and the BOC itself.

In addition, unlike navigation, where most of the operations are fairly routinized so that the cognitive load for each individual is quite minimal, the economists at the BOC, from the most junior level, engage in sophisticated acts of interpretation. At each juncture, they must—either jointly or severally—produce extended pieces of reasoning. They do not simply record, for example, navigation points, but instead analyze in considerable depth, using complicated instruments of analysis, the significance of data transmitted to them. These analyses, as we shall see, are presented textually according to the expectations of genres specific to the BOC (which are themselves part of interlinking chains of other genres in the larger sphere of public policy), and involve complex extended trains of reasoning expressed in mathematical and verbal symbolic systems.

Indeed, the traditions of navigation that Hutchins refers to in his analysis are nearly all embodied for the BOC in the form of genres (primarily verbal, often accompanied by tables sometimes involving numbers within their verbal syntax, and in the most technical pieces, equations); it is such genres that newcomers to the BOC must learn to acquire as an essential part of the enculturation, even as they learn that new and changing circumstances will inevitably entail adjustments to these genres.

Distributed Cognition at the BOC

The following paragraphs flesh out more fully the nature of the distributed cognition that takes place at the BOC, pointing especially to an important difference between navigating a ship and conducting financial affairs: that is, the place of writing in the BOC, as the prime site for the distribution of cognition, where knowledge is both shared in the sense of communicated and collaboratively created. It is through complex webs of discursive interactions and, in particular, genres, that the cognition of the BOC is accomplished distributively.

The activity of the BOC is shaped by its primary role. This function has traditionally been described broadly as one of conducting the country's monetary policy. The Governor of the BOC, Gordon Thiessen, described the BOC's goal to a radio audience as follows: the Bank's main purpose is to "make [everyone's economic] life better *through getting inflation down*" (April 1995, interview with Peter Gzowski, *Morningside*, CBC).

In order to achieve this larger purpose, that is, "the gradual elimination of inflation" (Duguay & Poloz, 1994, p. 196), the BOC has developed a highly regularized and carefully orchestrated sequence of communal actions over the course of the year, each enacted through cycles of genre production. These communal actions include forecasting and projecting future trends; analyzing incoming economic data; monitoring the projections regularly in the light of incoming data; and, on these bases, determining short-term and long-term policy. Here is how the annual cycle is described in a public document:

The Bank staff prepares economic projections of varying levels of detail through an annual cycle. The cycle consists of semi-annual medium-term projections, which focus on a 6–7 year horizon; two quarterly short-term updates between medium-term exercises with a horizon of 7–9 quarters, mid-quarter reassessments between each of the formal projection exercises, with a near-term focus of 2–3 quarters, and weekly updates based on newly-released data. (Duguay & Poloz, 1994, pp. 192–193)

Significantly, each communal exercise described above involves the collaborative production of specific and distinctive genres, that are so recognized and identified by all the participants. These include formal and public documents, such as *The Annual Report* and *The Monetary Policy Report*; formal and elaborately produced internal documents, involving projections[14] for the future (for example, the *Staff Economic Projection* commonly referred to as the *White Book*, along with the mid-quarter reassessments, *The Inter-Quarter Information Package*); and the genres entailed in the monitoring necessary for the Tuesday and Friday morning meetings (analytic notes and briefings). Table 7.1 sets out these different genres, their social actions, and readerships.

In turn, these genres are linked to related generic meetings, often with designated names. For example, the following generic meetings are associated with the projection exercise: "The Issues Meeting"; "The Starting-Point Meeting"; "The Projection Round Meeting"; and so on. (See Smart, 1998.) Written genres thus co-ordinate much of the work of the BOC's economists and the nature of their interactions over extended periods of time.

At the same time, the collaboration involved in the production of these genres is a collaboration that extends outside the BOC to include the community of central bankers, in general, and of contemporary economic thinkers. Interpretations at the Bank are tacitly shaped by what Fleck (1935/1979; see also Douglas, 1986) called thought styles: hence, the recurrence of certain lexical phrases (which represent categories of experience) and argumentative warrants. There is an emphasis on productivity and growth; the underlying paradigm is one in which general well-being is equated with economic well-being, and where the individual is understood to act in terms of rational self-interest.

There are also other characteristic modes of argumentation. The presentation of alternative scenarios, for example, so common in many documents (for example, the *Staff Economic Projections*), reveals another facet of the thought

---

[14]A projection in the BOC, as on a ship, is more than a prediction or forecast. It includes some forecasting of outside events, but it also specifies the actions that the BOC will have to undertake, in the light of the outside constraints, to achieve its monetary goals.

TABLE 7.1

Bank of Canada Genres*

Genres	Social Action	Readership
Annual Report & Monetary Policy Report	both account for policy decisions in context of world & national economic events	external or public
White Book	both "enable" and record "projection exercise"	internal
Analytic Notes, Briefings	both monitor economic events & projections on weekly basis	internal

*These are only some of the genres observed at the Bank of Canada, specifically those that are referred to in this chapter.

style shared by economists. Here we see an instantiation of the paradoxical commitment of economists to scientific modeling, on the one hand, along with an awareness of the indeterminate world of human actions and market forces, on the other. As a result, there is everywhere evidence of a mode of thinking that continually considers alternative eventualities. (Hence Truman's famous plea for a one-handed economist.) *The White Book* almost always includes alternative scenarios in its projections. And indeed, even when a specific scenario is being presented, a negotiation between conflicting perspectives is often presented. Here is an example: "X has happened. This may reflect ... ; Alternatively, it may reflect ... The Staff chose an intermediate stance in that...."

Modes of thinking, approaches to data, and categorizations of experience are reified and institutionalized within the genres of the BOC. The genres function consequently as repositories of communal knowledge, devices for generating new knowledge, sites for enculturation, and forces to be resisted if and when change becomes necessary.

Decision Making:
From Data to Policy Through Interweaving Genres

Overall, decision making at the BOC entails a complex, highly interactive process of distributed cognition, in which many layers of analysts and analysis are involved. One way of showing how the complicated process of policy making is enacted and communicated is by starting with the most basic regular analyses and tracking the weekly process. Of course, as suggested in the preceding section, the weekly actions take place in the context of the annual cycle (as described above by Duguay & Poloz, 1994)—a process that involves long-term goal setting, regular projections, and constant monitoring with respect to those projections. Nevertheless, there is a weekly process, and tracing it is instructive.

As cited above, a major goal of the BOC is to keep inflation low; its tool in doing so, as the Governor explained, is raising and lowering interest rates. Every week then, analysts in each of the main divisions of the BOC, each with its own specialty, look at the economic data provided largely by Statistics Canada with respect to their area. The data themselves are neither collected by the BOC, nor held in secrecy for the BOC. When asked in a radio interview, "Do you have sources of information that are not available to the rest of us," the Governor replied: "No. What I probably have in the Bank is a lot of very good analysts who can judge ... how things are going to turn out."

This is crucial. What the Governor, and the BOC, depend on is the interpretation and analysis of junior-level economists, whose interpretations and analyses are filtered through to the top—through various layers of further interpretation, synthesis, and evaluation by more senior analysts. (This is reminiscent of Latour & Woolgar's, 1986 notion of inscription.) The whole process will be described below, but a digression is necessary to describe the BOC's major instrument of analysis: the Quarterly Projection Model (QPM).

QPM, as it is commonly referred to at the BOC, consists of a series of equations intended to represent the economy. The model was developed within the BOC over an extended period of time (based, of course, on standard econometric techniques and widely accepted economic notions), and represents consequently a repository of the staff's cumulative understanding of the workings of the economy.

QPM is computer-run and was collectively produced. (See Duguay & Longworth, 1997, for a discussion of the internal development of this model.) As such, it is a classic example of the meshing of tool and symbolic system that Engeström (1997) points to in his pun on collective "instrumentality." Especially interesting is the degree to which this "mentality" was and continues to be achieved and expressed through interweaving genres. Thus, the development of QPM, to replace an earlier model, was achieved through a series of genres, each appropriate to the different stages of development, occasions, and audiences: first, explanatory notes distributed among the model-builders; then, persuasive internal memos to the senior executives; and finally informative external papers, each at differing levels of technical sophistication.

Furthermore, the model continues to be subject to constant monitoring and revision as necessitated by changing circumstances—with the same kinds of explanatory, persuasive, and informative genres at work, geared both to communicating and to reshaping the model. (Many of our BOC informants attested to the creative and constructive power of formulating notions in written language.) On the basis of QPM, overlaid by the judgments of specialists, an overall projection of the major economic variables is made quarterly in the *White Books* referred to earlier, and the components are updated periodically within the quarter (in the *Inter-Projection Information Packages*) on the basis of incoming information.

To return to the weekly process, what happens, from the perspective of an outside observer, is the following. As the Governor pointed out, information is conveyed to the BOC regularly from Statistics Canada (the government's data-gathering bureau) and other sources, with the data organized in tabular form. Table 7.2 shows a typical example of a text from Statistics Canada

Although everyone at the BOC has access to this newly released data (sometimes by electronic mail for new daily bits of information and, at regular periods, in hard-copy volumes for more global and comprehensive statistics), it is the staff economists responsible for each sector of the economy (e.g., housing, investment, consumption, government spending, etc.) who read it and analyze it. Their analysis consists of interpreting the data and especially of comparing the actual incoming data (the numbers, in this case) with the projections that had been made earlier by staff economists, based on the quarterly projection exercise described above. In other words, the data are compared to what would have been the case had the projection been correct in its forecasting. This analysis takes the form of "analytic notes."

TABLE 7.2

Consumer Price Index

	Jan–Feb	Feb–Feb
	unadjusted	
	% change	
All-items	0.1	2.2
1. Food	0.2	2.4
2. Shelter	−0.1	0.3
3. Household Operations, Furnishings	0.0	1.6
4. Clothing	1.1	−0.3
5. Transportation	−0.1	5.3
6. Health & personal care	0.4	1.5

Note. **This is a truncated version of the actual table.**

These analytic notes involve comparisons that are frequently presented in tabular form, but always with an accompanying prose explanation, pointing to and interpreting any changes and especially disparities between the actual and projected figures. Such disparities occur with regularity, and a major function of the analytic notes is to identify them, to contextualize them, and to suggest possible revisions to the projections on their basis.

These explanations accompany whatever tables are presented and always appear in prose form: there may be numbers, but the numbers are subsumed in a verbal syntax. Here are some sentences taken from an analytic note (our explanations are presented in square brackets):

- According to X, total Y rose 10.3% in March to attain a level of ____ units ... This represents the highest level of monthly sales since.... [Here, the data is being interpreted in the light of other data sources.]
- Final Y estimates for February from Statscan [Statistics Canada] were roughly in line with preliminary X estimates with a very small downward revision [i.e., to the projection].
- This strong growth in which sales (first indicated in Z) represents a positive surprise ["surprise" is a heavily laden word at the BOC, suggesting that results are inconsistent with QPM predictions]. As a result, the monitoring for consumption growth for ____ has been revised up to x% from y%....

In the BOC's parlance, these interpretations are "stories" (see Smart, 1985). It is a commonplace in the BOC that what is expected in writing (and in oral presentations based on written analyses) is more than elevator economics: that is, this went up and this went down. There must always be interpretation, analysis, comparison with forecasts, and possibly suggestions for revision to these forecasts. This first layer of interpretation is enacted by staff economists, who are sometimes technically more expert than members of the executive staff and certainly more conversant with the data in their specifically designated sectors of the economy. These interpretations of fairly specific fields, the genres of the staff economists (the analytic notes), however, are reanalyzed by middle-level executives, the department chiefs, in weekly briefings to senior executives (i.e., members of the management committee). The genre of the briefing involves verbal discourse and charts, and entails BOC "storytelling" at higher levels of generalization. At this level, what is expected is an interpretation of all the incoming economic data, particularly in the light of the most recent projection exercise.

For their part, executive members of the management committee examine the sifted and interpreted data that are reported to them in the briefings, reinterpreting what they receive in the light of the following:

- their understanding of, and experience with, the projection exercise;
- their own economic intuitions based on past experience: sometimes they sense that interpretations of certain data cannot be right, based on their own extensive experience;
- their own independent knowledge of information that is unavailable to the staff economists.

The staff economists may make certain assumptions, for example, about another country's current financial policies, while the executive committee may have more recent information that might cast these interpretations into doubt. "It should be noted that staff projections are only one input into the policy discussions of senior management. Other inputs would include independent private-sector forecasts, views obtained directly from outside contacts, and conditions in financial and foreign exchange markets" (Duguay & Poloz 1994, pp. 195–196).

Finally, a judgment is made by the management committee as to policy with respect to the short-term interest rates, on the basis of a discussion following the briefings made by different department chiefs. Until recently, this outcome was delivered in a standardized press format (which was presented orally on radio and TV, and in written form, in the press).

All in all, then, the BOC thinks and distributes its cognition through sets of genres, each with its expected form. The original bases of analysis are the data sets distributed by Statistics Canada and other data-gathering sources. These are interpreted, sometimes individually and sometimes collaboratively, by specialists in the particular area of interest in the first instance (as mediated by the internally produced artifact, QPM), and the analyses are expressed in familiar forms: analytic notes, which involve comparative tables plus brief prose interpretations. These notes are collected, compared, and reinterpreted by department chiefs, with the knowing similarly enacted through the genre of the briefing. Each layer of interpretation involves fewer tables, and more prose; the final genre, the press release, is almost entirely prose, with the exception of the actual figure announced.

In addition, there are other genres, more public in character, which are closely connected to these genres and this work. An example is the "Bank speech." Speeches are written documents that are read aloud—after going through several iterative rounds of writing and revising, involving economists and managers at all levels of the hierarchy. The revising is extensive, and there is extreme sensitivity to the potential import of every possible nuance in the phrasing.

Ultimately, the speeches draw on the primary interpretations of the most junior staff economists as well as the weekly briefings and policy recommendations of department chiefs, but the material is presented at a much higher level of generality, and with far less reliance on technical language or mathematical evidence. Numbers are introduced sparingly, and tables disappear.

An important feature of the typical speech is its opening, which inevitably involves a few paragraphs outlining the basic goal of BOC: price stability. Indeed, part of the social action implicit in each speech is to persuade the public at large of the continued value of a policy oriented towards low inflation. Such discussions of course rarely appear in internal documents, because the values of low inflation and price stability have become, at least for the moment, shared norms in the institution.

The goal of the speeches is to explain monetary policy in a way accessible to lay people, with little technical knowledge. As suggested above, the "story" is presented at a much higher level of generalization, but is consistent with all the information and analysis that has been passed on. Most speeches review past economic trends (especially interest rates and exchange rates) and recent economic developments, then look forward to general trends in the economy especially with respect to inflation. Speeches never project or forecast interest rates and exchange rates, and there is great sensitivity to and concern about possible "entrail-readings," the fact that public pronouncements by the BOC are inevitably probed for possible hints as to the BOC's future actions—probed both by those reporting on, and especially by those acting in, the markets. (Note that this is in contrast to internal briefing notes and the *Staff Economic Projection* or *White Book*, where there is a great deal of what is called "forward looking" in the BOC; that is, an attempt to forecast what might happen if the BOC were to act in specific ways.)

To sum up, we have here an activity that involves the interaction of many players, in which each plays a slightly different role. The activity is mediated through a socially constructed tool of analysis (the QPM), which is itself always being readjusted in the dynamic process of interpreting and reinterpreting incoming data. The people at the helm make final decisions based on some knowledge that they are privy to themselves, as well as on intuitions formed within the traditions of central banking, but also initially framed through the

various interpretation and reinterpretations offered by the set of genres constituting the staff projections. Of particular interest to our work is the role of verbal
discourse in the distribution of cognition—especially in the form of sets of
interweaving genres that are not just the media and shaping agents for the
interpretation but also, as we shall see, the sites both for social sharing and
communal creation as well as the sites for identifying and negotiating internal
contradictions.

From the perspective of distributed cognition, then, how close or far apart
are the worlds of university and of work?

DISTRIBUTED COGNITION AT UNIVERSITY
AND AT WORK COMPARED

The convention, the tacit assumption of schooling, is that the teacher "knows"
and that what she "knows" will be "learned" by the student—just as the
convention of, say, therapeutic work is that the therapist "understands" and that,
as a result of her interaction with the therapist, the client will gain some of this
understanding.

But note that we are now talking about a different kind of social sharing than
that which is at play in the institutions analyzed before. To encourage students
to take on the same stance—to share some of the same knowledge—as the
instructor is not the same as having them contribute to the work of the institution
in the way that employees at the various institutions do. To put it simply, the
captain needs the information provided by his most subordinate navigator. The
Governor of the BOC needs the lowliest analyst's report. The professor,
however, does not need any specific student's essay in the same way. A student
who does not hand in his work does not impede the operation of the university.
(In fact, he eases the instructor's task of grading.)[15]

In pointing to these distinctions, we begin to get a sense of the radical
difference in the nature of the interactions between student and teacher—as
opposed to that among employees in even hierarchical structures. Certainly,
until the highest levels of schooling, and in most classes, there is little expec-

---

[15]Of course, if there were no students or if none of the students handed in their essays, this
would indeed disrupt the activity of the institution—in much the same way as if there were no
incoming data from Statistics Canada for the BOC or if there were no incoming data, because of
instrumental breakdown and/or meteorological calamities, for the ship's navigators.

tation that students will contribute to the ongoing activity of the classroom in the way that fellow workers do.[16]

Even the notion of shared knowledge differs in the two contrasting kinds of setting: the classroom and the workplace. In institutions such as government agencies (or universities *qua* degree-granting institutions), there is overlapping or shared knowledge, a kind of necessary redundancy without which the whole operation is in danger. At the same time, however, there is also a parceling out, a division of knowing such that some people know (a notion that includes both mastery or ownership of facts as well as interpretive power over them) that which others do not. Furthermore, the latter need to rely on the knowing and interpreting of the former. Finally, for the good of the institution, there is a reciprocity so those higher up in the hierarchy depend on the knowing and interpreting of those lower down at the same time that those lower down depend on the summarizing and interpreting of those higher up for the maintenance of the organization and for the achievement of its goals. In all these institutions, a relationship of mutual need is established among all participants. All this contrasts with the classroom, where any particular student can usually drop out without doing damage to the workings of the class.

Finally, it is important to recognize that, in certain settings in some institutions, the relations among individuals do not involve distributed cognition. For example, it is often the case that the goal of the institution is such that one category of individuals is operated on, or inspected or known by another. In the workplace, such evaluation and inspection procedures are employed not only for hiring, firing, and promotion, but also on occasions involving guidance, entrusting, or task assignment. The difference is one of degree and of the relative dominance of the function. Thus, patients in hospitals as their name implies are acted on; so too are clients in social work agencies, as are applicants who wish to be hired by personnel officers in most institutions. Students at university are like patients and clients in this respect. The focus of the institution, and of those representing the institution, is to know and inspect them.

This reality is sometimes occluded because, as teachers, we focus on the fact that the role of the student is to learn—as opposed to that of the patient, which is to get better, or the data, to be interpreted. But, if we recognize that in each

---

[16]Some instructors are currently trying to organize their classes in such a way, that is, by making them into communities of practice, so that cognition is distributed among students. Insofar as this is a successful pedagogic or epistemic strategy—that is, insofar as it helps students learn more effectively—it is desirable. In the end, however, such practices will be limited by the underlying and dominant institutional imperative of schooling that insists on measuring the relative performance of each individual.

institution there are actors, an activity, and objects of the activity, it is clear that at the university, the actors are the teachers and the administrators, and the objects of the institutional activity is the knowing and the inspecting of the students. The "knowing" of the students, and their "learning" is measured—just as automobile sales are at the BOC.

CONCLUSION

In other words, the relationship between students and teachers is radically different from that among fellow employees (even when there is a different status). For this reason, making the transition to the workplace, students need to take on very different kinds of responsibility, with respect to cognition, from that to which they have been accustomed in their classroom settings. It is this transition that we wish to focus on in chapters to come.

8

FROM WORDS TO BRICKS: WRITING IN AN ARCHITECTURAL PRACTICE

When we think of what architects do, drawing, not writing, is the activity that first springs to mind. Because drawing is its primary semiotic medium, architecture raises most strikingly the issue of what is distinctively and uniquely left for writing to contribute, after everything that can be done through other more (to architects) accessible means has been done. Speech (and its attendant technologies of telephone and voice mail) are, of course, available to the practitioners of all the professions we have studied in the research, but architecture is distinctive in the extensive use it makes of drawing. Here, uniquely, writing is up against not just the ephemeral modes of speech and gesture but another permanent, trace-leaving, record-creating inscriptional medium. When writing is used, therefore, it has a particular significance that derives from the constantly present alternative possibility of graphical representation.

In fact, writing in architectural practices is extensive and important, and exists in varying relationships to drawing, relationships that are of interest in themselves. As we saw in chapter 5, writing in the school of architecture presented the phenomenon of implicatedness in bimodal or multimodal productions in which the meaning communicated was a product of writing and other semiotic modes (notably drawing and photography) working together in relationships of interdependence. Such relationships characterize some of the work in the office also. However, it is for those characteristics that differentiate it from school practice that writing in the architectural office is of most relevance for this study. In our introduction to this section we singled out three features that we identify as distinguishing workplace writing generally from student writing in the university: complexity, multifunctionality, and implicatedness in power relations. Writing in architectural practices demonstrates both further variants within that description and also certain features not shared with writing in the other professional contexts we have studied. One function of this, the final chapter in our workplace section, will be to demonstrate how diverse are the practices of different professions. While the main import of the book has been to leave beyond doubt the distinction between educational and workplace writing, that emphasis should not be taken as implying that there is any such thing as "workplace writing" as an identifiable and describable species; there are only a plethora of widely varying activities.

In this chapter we describe architects' writing as we observed it in one office.[17] We begin with an overview of the kinds of writing architects perform in the course of their work on a building, and then proceed to a more analytic account in terms of function, genre, relations between participants, the place of standardization and other issues that have concerned us throughout the book. An illustrative case then follows, illustrating how a particular short text was able to be effective in the context of its deployment. And finally we draw together some of the salient differences that have emerged between workplace and university writing in architecture.

THE STAGES OF AN ARCHITECTURAL PROJECT AND THEIR ASSOCIATED GENRES

We begin by describing the range of what architects write—or, rather, of the writing to which architects put their signature, because the architectural work of a practice is performed in Canada by practitioners of 2 professions or specialisms, architects and architectural technologists. The latter are trained in the technical aspects of construction, the building code, the preparation of contract documents and the coordination of the tasks of construction, and not in design. In this firm, the status of the senior technologist, Dudley, was not inferior to that of the architects; in fact he would allocate work to them and was an associate in the firm, second in status only to the three partners.[18] In some offices the work of architects and technologists is strictly separated, but here boundaries were fluid and relationships nonhierarchical; on some aspects of the job the project

---

[17]Our thanks are due to the firms who have allowed us such free and ready access to their work, and to all those, architects and technologists, who let us observe and/or interview them. We are grateful also to Scott Weir for assisting in the interviews, and to Scott and to Graham Smart for some preliminary analysis.

[18]The firm included eight architects of whom three were the partners, two senior technologists and a number of technologists. It had a reputation in the city as the leader in terms of design quality. Most of the office's work was public buildings such as schools, fire stations, transport depots, community and leisure centers, and apartment blocks.

architect would say what was to happen, on others the senior technologist. And, most relevantly for this account, the latter produced a considerable share of the practice's written output and spent most of his time writing.

A project, as architects call the set of activities that center on the design and construction of a building, goes through typical stages which in Canada are broadly as follows. Each stage has its characteristic written genres:

Securing the contract, or getting the job: The firm usually has to work to get work; few clients approach an architect directly with a commission.

Once the firm has been appointed as architects for the job, the work typically falls into three stages weighted, in terms of workload, in the following proportions:

Conceptual design (25%): This term refers to the development in broad outline of a design that satisfies the client as a basis on which to proceed toward construction. The end point of this stage is the client's approval of the design and go-ahead to proceed to the working drawings and specifications that will enable a builder (contractor) to be appointed and the building to be built.

Working drawings and specifications (contract documents) (50%): This set of documents comprises the complete instructions for building the building, and are the basis on which a contractor will be appointed and the fee for construction agreed.

Construction (25%): The architects have a continuing role right through construction, supervising the work and authorizing any changes that circumstances or the client's wishes necessitate.

We now describe these stages in more detail.

Securing the Contract

This stage has characteristic documents for the different types of bidding procedure in operation. The firm may be invited to submit a proposal, or it may respond to an advertisement in a newspaper inviting an *Expression of Interest.*

Public building contracts tend to involve extensive and tightly prescribed documentation, sometimes in more than one phase. Typically, the first phase (the expression of interest) comprises a written proposal that includes a corporate CV giving an account of the firm and its work and specifying who would be working on the project. The second phase is the design proposal; public authorities typically lay down precise rules about how this will be written, specifying such aspects as length, the inclusion of a table of contents, whether single- or double-sided, and manner of stapling; the criteria by which the proposal will be judged are also given. Some 50% of the document will be standard boilerplate or pre-cast text, and the rest will be adapted boilerplate together with perhaps 30% of text specifically written for the purpose. The hard work in putting this together is less the composition of the text than obtaining and coordinating input from a number of consultants, whose contribution amounts to up to half of the document.

Competition entries call for rather different sorts of document, which will be referred to in the following.

Conceptual Design

This stage, the first in which the firm is acting in its role as appointed architects, is also likely to be subdivided. A prerequisite for the physical design is a *program* or *brief* that sets out what the building is required to provide and the requirements it must meet. Clients with extensive experience of procuring buildings may present the firm with a brief that they have drawn up themselves or commissioned from a specialist consultant. Otherwise it falls to the architect to write the program or brief in consultation with the client. Either way there is likely to be considerable communication with the client to clarify or develop the description of the job, involving successions of drawings accompanied by a lot of writing. The outcome of this phase is the *program document* that sets out functions, rooms, space per room, et cetera, and that comprises schematic drawings with text in list and tabular form.

Once the program or brief has been established, the architects proceed to design, typically presenting their developing ideas in a series of face-to-face meetings with the client. The main work at this stage is drawing. What writing there is includes letters to the authorities (fire, city, etc.) to clarify what is possible and permitted, and invitations to consultants to associate themselves with the project.

There are great variations within this overall pattern. On one current job, for instance, the firm had been appointed to design only the specialized high-tech control room in a new building over which, as a whole, a different firm of architects was in charge. The client had presented our firm with a *design intent manual* on the basis of which the firm had made an oral presentation and, after negotiations, secured the contract. The client then supplied a *brief* and the architects developed and presented their design (orally, with drawings) in two main stages, *schematic* and *resolved.*

Working Drawings and Specifications (contract documents)

This documentation, half drawings and half written specifications, constitutes a complete description of and instructions for constructing the finished building. There are typically four sets of drawings: architectural, structural, mechanical and electrical, with on occasion an additional set related to the demolition of existing structures. Two sorts of writing are involved: *drawing notes* written on the drawings and *specification notes* in a separate document and referenced on the drawings. Thus in one set of documents the phrase "patch and make good" appeared as

> a note on the drawings, but "patch and make good" in a written specification has a two page description of what is acceptable as a patch and what is acceptable as a make good. So these notes give a visual indication of the scope of the work, the specifications give a very precise description of the nature of the materials, the level of finish, the quality of the workmanship and the products that we use. (Greg)

In any legal dispute, the written word will prevail over the drawings (see below). The specifications are considered to be "technical writing," in contrast with genres that need to be more evocatively descriptive or persuasive. They are divided into a general section and subsections; in one current job there were 16 of the latter relating to the individual trades involved in construction.

The contract documents have to be submitted to the authorities for approval, often with accompanying letters that explain, for instance, why a particular zoning regulation has not been observed; for example, because the occupants of a low-cost housing apartment block were expected to own fewer cars than usual, application was being made for a waiver of the regulations on parking provision.

An *invitation to tender* is next put out to contractors who will propose a price for the job on the basis of the contract documents. The negotiations with contractors will involve the architects in considerable correspondence both with them and with the client, leading to changes in the design that all need to be recorded in writing. As the culmination of this process, the architects will write a *letter of recommendation* to the client concerning the appointment of the contractor, after which the contract for construction is awarded.

Construction

In this stage the architect spends 80 or 90% of the day writing: "it's all paperwork, nonstop." Visits to the site to inspect construction in progress, and reports from the contractor and consultants throw up queries and reveal problems that are addressed through a variety of relatively standardized written genres such as *Contemplated Change Notices, Change Orders,* and *Site Instructions.* All changes have cost implications, and the preservation of these documents is essential in settling whether additional costs are to be met by the client, the contractor, or the architect.

Renovation of Old Buildings

The stages and types of documentation detailed above apply to new buildings, but architects are often called on to restore or modify existing buildings. This task calls for different types of document. On a current project involving a heritage building the firm had first produced a *building study* or *condition report* describing the state of the building and establishing the scope of the work needed to restore it, and then a *design report* specifying the action that the firm proposed. According to Dan, a junior architect, the subsequent full working drawings differ from those produced for new buildings in carrying far more writing, reflecting the need for extensive procedural description:

> If you want to make a single room where there were former washrooms and other rooms, you may have exposed brick for a while, and you might have a little bit of tile and you might have some drywall, and how it meets the ceiling changes.... So you have to describe to the contractor, "Remove this tile, keep this tile, paint this brick, expose this brick, match that"—that's what we're trying to do now.

More will be said about this below.

Other document types occur throughout the process, most notably the *agendas* and *minutes* that the architects must draw up in connection with the various meetings they have to attend.

WHO WRITES WHAT?
THE DIVISION OF LABOR IN THE OFFICE

The *division of labor* between architects and technologists affects writing. Dudley, the senior technologist in the office we observed, spent most of his time writing. He was the one who knew the correct wording for specifications. For this reason and because the work is too much for the project architect, the technologist often comes in and takes the lead after the design has been done to translate the drawings into written specifications (a switch that can lead to problems, as we describe below). At the same time, some architects do much more writing than others so that Greg, who was seen as writing easily and well, had ended up doing the lion's share of the firm's proposal writing.

FUNCTIONS AND MODES OF COMMUNICATION

We now proceed to a more analytic account that seeks to identify the nature of architectural writing in terms that relate to the theories we use and enable comparisons to be made both with the other professions discussed in the book and with educational writing in the school of architecture.

Functions

Halliday (1985) describes all texts and utterances as performing three metafunctions: the text performs, first, an ideational (we could substitute the term referential) metafunction in that it is inevitably about something and represents some entity, process or state of affairs; second, an interpersonal metafunction in enacting relations between communicating subjects and expressing the speaker's stance in relation to the ideational content; and third, a textual metafunction, about achieving a coherent verbal construct. Whereas Halliday does not speak of the relative weighting of the three metafunctions within a text as variable, it is in fact illuminating to describe texts in terms of their *dominant* metafunction, adopting Jakobson's (1987) notion of numerous coexisting functions of which one is always dominant. In particular we find it useful to identify certain texts as carrying a more ideational and others a more interpersonal emphasis. (The textual metafunction is less relevant for our purposes here.) We noted earlier that the documents written to secure a contract tended to be clearly persuasive, which is to say that their metafunctional weighting was interpersonal, although the presence of an ideational component representing the design idea and the firm's reputation was also, of course, unavoidable. Later in the process, after the job has been secured, we find many texts that are more obviously oriented toward accurate representation than effect on audience, although the ultimate concern, not currently foregrounded, is still to affect the documents' users so that they will build the building correctly.

In talking in such terms we acknowledge that we are taking liberties with Halliday's system. His metafunctions are specifically related to linguistics and the grammar of sentences, and not to utterances and social processes. A speaker's or writer's communicative intentions and social purposes are quite a different matter from the function-meanings encoded by a system of grammar. We, nevertheless, find it useful to purloin Halliday's terms for discussing the former.

We can now approach the diversity of office writing with those two functional emphases, distinguishing texts in which the dominant functional orientation is interpersonal on the one hand and ideational on the other. Underneath those broad categories we can then group a number of more specific functions. Thus, in texts with an interpersonal emphasis we can identify communications that order or instruct and those that seek to persuade, in contexts where a response of non-cooperation is a contemplated possibility. Examples of the former are the spoken and written requests and instructions to the contractor to diverge from the design in some respect. An example of the latter is the note already referred to that sought to get the planning authority to agree to a waiver of a zoning regulation. Also interpersonal in their dominant orientation, though not primarily persuasive, are communications that seek to elicit information, advice, or response from parties who are not subordinates but from whom cooperation can be expected in the normal way of professional relations.

Ideational demands are clearly dominant in two sorts of communication that need to be inscribed on paper rather than uttered by word of mouth. The first is the precise graphical and written indication of the work that is to be done by the contractor in order to bring the building or alteration into being; these representations fall into two parts, working drawings and (written) specifications, which together constitute the *contract documents* and define the precise job for which the price is to be agreed. Two sorts of ideational content have to be unambiguously represented: the physical reality of the building to be achieved and the processes to be performed to achieve it. Any subsequent work required that departs from these descriptions will have be paid extra for by somebody, depending whether the change is the result of an error made by the architect in design or the contractor in construction, or of a change of mind by the client. Any such change has to be authorized by the architect and placed on record, the adequacy of the record (for subsequent accounting procedures or for the determination of responsibility) being assisted by the use of a standardized genre (such as the Contemplated Change Notice, Change Order, or Site Instruction mentioned earlier), often generated with a software package that ensures the later accessibility of the information and keeps track of the allocation of costs.

The second main manifestation of the ideational concern is the creation of a *paper trail*. Documents produced for this purpose do not have much obvious addressivity;[19] their effectiveness resides in their existence, their demonstrated authenticity (e.g., as having been written at the time when they claim to have been) and their preservation. Their record-keeping function may be fulfilled in two ways. The first is through the production of writing within a dedicated record-keeping genre such as a log (which actually does have an addressivity related to a currently unknown future reader who might have need of the information within it).

The other form of record keeping does not involve a dedicated genre. Ostensibly, the documents enact rather than record a transaction, as when a Change Order instructs a specific other that

> You are hereby directed to include this work below in the contract.... 1.0 Floor call in elevator car system to be Key Controlled @ the following 3 floors only: Parking Level, 2nd Floor, 3rd Floor (not Ground Floor and Floor 1A).

The record-keeping function appears to be achieved not by the writing, which was done to effect a change at the time of writing, but by the keeping and filing of a copy. In reality, however, most such documents are written primarily as records, despite appearances; if there were not the need for a trace the transaction would be carried out orally, as it often used to be in less litigious times. Putting it another way, contractors, because they need the physical trace, will not nowadays carry out an order without written instruction. Although the contractor's staff may already know from oral communications both what the

---

[19]The Bakhtinian concept of addressivity is perhaps best explained in *Marxism and the Philosophy of Language:* "Utterance, as we know, is constructed between two socially organized persons, and in the absence of a real addressee, an addressee is presupposed in the person, so to speak, of a normal representative of the social group to which the speaker belongs. The word is oriented toward an addressee, toward who that addressee might be: a fellow-member of the same social group, of higher or lower standing (the addressee's hierarchical status), someone connected with the speaker by close social ties (father, brother, husband, and so on) or not" (Voloshinov, 1986, p.85, emphasis in original).

architect wants done (the propositional content) and that they are to carry it out (i.e., that a jussive, or ordering-and-complying, situation is in force), the "felicity conditions" (Austin, 1962) for a valid order include the requirement that it be written. Therefore, "everything stated verbally on site must be put into writing." The essential record-keeping function is then fulfilled by placing copies of the document on file. (We discuss a particular instance of this sort of transaction, involving a Site Instruction, below.)

Interpersonal and ideational do not, in the event, exhaust the functional emphases discernible in the communications of the office. Another purpose that may motivate communication is the one we have called epistemic, that of arriving at rather than communicating ideas or understandings. (There is no equivalent in Halliday's formal system because such a function is not reflected in the grammar of sentences, though the "mathetic" category that he proposes to cover young children's heuristic or discovery-related uses of language is relevant; Halliday, 1975.) It is a significant fact about the office that the epistemic purpose, while clearly dominating preliminary sketch processes and design discussions over the drafting table, hardly appears in the writing, a point we will comment on when we later compare office and school writing within architecture.

The Available Modes of Communication

For the realization of the purposes we have just defined, a variety of semiotic means are available. The choice between drawing, writing, and speech is determined partly by convention, partly by the representational strengths and inadequacies of each, partly by considerations of convenience and time, and partly by the attitudes and dispositions of the participants. Where the ultimate motive—the Activity—is a general wish to communicate or record X, then there may be an effective free choice between the media. In the more thoroughly institutionalized aspects of practice, however, what often happens is that an utterly familiar exigence is registered and an utterly specific medium-and-genre response automatically activated. In such situations we may say that the experienced need is a need for, specifically, a set of working drawings or an Expression of Interest letter, and is not the more general need for the communication or recording of X. (There is no point in distinguishing such general and unspecific needs unless alternative means of fulfilling them are effectively available possibilities.) In situations where established conventional practices rule, the Activity is, quite directly, "meeting the need for a set of working drawings" or "meeting the need for an Expression of Interest letter"; and the *action* that realizes the activity is, in turn, producing the drawings or writing the letter.

Sometimes habit and what comes easily and sometimes practicality lead the architect to have recourse to writing. There are things that only writing can do, or that it does more conveniently. Writing's distinctive contribution is particularly apparent in the labels and notes that are often added to drawings, where they may describe the material or give an instruction. As Michael explained,

> Say I want to make a change in a construction process, I want to eliminate a door from a room. I could do a drawing that shows, "This is what we had," and another drawing showing the room without that door. But really it's a lot easier to say "Get rid of that door."

Conversely, of course, there are things that only drawing can do. Words are "almost completely useless" in communicating complicated three-dimensional configurations. But not all of the parties involved can read drawings. Sarah, a junior architect, had found that not only some clients but some older tradesmen have never acquired the skill:

> I think it's just the way things were done in the past—everything was much more hands on. You would come to the site and say "Do this" and "Do that" and you know, you'd never really refer to drawings.... Like I've worked with ... Italian tile layers "Just tell me what you want," like they don't really understand the drawing.

One of the most powerful pressures to write derives from the fact that in law writing overrules drawing. But there are a variety of other reasons why writing may, on occasion, be preferred to speech. In communications between, for instance, architect and consultant, a written request for information can be consulted repeatedly and the data needed for the answer collected piecemeal. Similarly, if the architect is accumulating a number of questions it is easier to write them down and fax them in one batch than to phone them. The availability of the fax has led to a shift from speech to writing in some types of communication. Tom, one of the partners, told us:

> Generally, however, speech is preferred to writing because it is quicker. We *could* write that, but there's no need to do it, and there's so many reasons to fill your time doing other things that anything which is at all extraneous is not done.

And when persuasion is the purpose, in those situations in which spoken communication is not ruled out (as it is in proposals to public bodies), speech (in combination with drawings and models) scores by being more expressive. In "architectural project getting":

the written response will determine your success, but not necessarily in implementing, because once you've got the job you're drawing and talking and really seducing your client into the idea that your ideas are worthwhile. It's not usually to do with writing, it's usually to do with sitting and talking about the job and saying, "I think this is better," or saying in this case, "What we want to do is feature X because Y."

Alan, one of the other partners, explained the typical situation, in which the feel and appeal of a design have to be communicated as expressively as possible:

So you're relying on pointing to this with a client and saying, "What I am proposing, you can't really understand what it's going to look like, because—." Anybody at an early stage looking at that is going to have to believe a lot of what you're saying. Just look at it, it's just a nice little sketch, I don't really know what that means. So the communication is very important with words.... the client has to be excited about what we're doing. That's a very big part of being an architect.

The preference for speech is reinforced by the architects' attitudes; they tend to feel comfortable with drawing and speech and less comfortable with writing. Sarah explained:

We're so used to expressing ourselves in drawing terms that when you want to express yourself in written words, I find I'm not necessarily comfortable all the time that what I'm saying is what someone is going to interpret correctly.... I think that everyone feels a bit uneasy when it comes down to trying to write something. You know, you always feel a bit, is it right, am I expressing myself right. If it's something really important I always refer to [one of the partners].

Our informants frequently represented writing and the management of written documents as alien to the architect's sensibility: "Architects are not bureaucratically meticulous."

THE IMPORTANCE AND RHETORICAL DEMANDS OF WRITING

Architects may not like writing but much depends on their doing it well. Getting it wrong—interpersonally or ideationally, in persuading, instructing, or recording—can cause big problems. For that reason, not only care but often considerable rhetorical skill are demanded of a writer like Sarah in architectural practice.

A large part of the writing architects do is simply to cover themselves: everything has to be [written down] because there's always this thing, "Well, I didn't know that's what you wanted," and so if you have to go back and say, "No, what I wanted was this and this is what I said"—well, how can you make someone do and redo unless you have actually proof of that in writing?

But writing is also fraught with dangers, as when a second practitioner—often the senior technologist—is brought in to write the specifications after the working drawings have been completed: "A lot of times we tend to do the specs at the last minute and someone else might be helping you out doing the spec."

Well, I find a lot of errors can be made between the spec and the drawings.... that's one thing that actually tends to happen a lot is the discrepancy between the drawings and the spec. I mean you put something on the drawing and someone else is doing the spec and the two don't really go hand in hand. The spec [prevails] which is the unfortunate thing.... If you're not that familiar with the job [you, the writer, are likely to make] certain errors around there, [like] getting the wrong materials, so a lot of mistakes like that end up costing money because you want to go with what's on the drawings but the spec overrides it.

Misunderstandings can and do lead to legal disputes. Contractors make their profit by exploiting loopholes and ambiguities in the specifications and substituting cheaper solutions. There are many ways the specs can go wrong, as Michael had discovered:

If you have completely screwed up a section of the specifications, it has all sorts of potentially very serious ramifications, particularly in what's called the front end which relates to contractual relationships.... There was an instance where the salient point was that, because of some ambiguity in whether a certain item was in or out of the contract, if item A was in the contract, then this contractor, if it wasn't, then the other person was actually lower [in price], so there was a lot of confusion, the lawyers got involved ... because obviously there's a lot riding on something like that. The contractor's invested hundreds of hours in time and it could mean, in this economy, the difference between the firm surviving or not. So it gets hairy.... Or it might happen because you do something dumb like take a spec section from another job and just throw it in because you thought it was the same thing but it wasn't really. That can happen.

The problem can thus be compounded when boilerplate from other jobs is used inappropriately.

Disaster can also follow from failure in filing—an aspect of literate practice that, incidentally, has no equivalent in the world of the student. Every important document is copied to a chronological file and a project file, and a computer record is kept. Bureaucratic fastidiousness is a vital insurance policy for firms, as Greg (junior architect) was able to exemplify:

We received a call over the summer for a project that we carried out in 1987. It was carried out by someone who is no longer with the office and it was a survey to go around various branches of a trust company and to do a quick survey ... looking for the presence of asbestos.... We got a call back in the summer saying, "We've sold this branch and the purchaser has found asbestos in the building, and is demanding a rebate of X number of dollars, and he says you are liable for that." So we went looking for the file and the file doesn't exist. We didn't even have accurate dates for when it was completed, so we went through the chronological files which has all of the correspondence in chronological order, starting back a year prior to when we thought it was going to be, going through every piece of correspondence, looking for documentation, and after half a day we found one letter that says, "We have visited these branches, la, la, la, and the survey in this branch, we saw obvious traces of asbestos, and in conversation with yourself, you have decided to undertake further studies of your own, blah, blah, blah," signed off. So it's clearly says we found asbestos, and there's evidence of it, we spoke to you, you have agreed to carry out further required studies, and that was the end of our project. We said, "Do you want us to fax you this letter?" and he says, "No that's ok, just keep it," (laugh) and that was the last we heard of it. So that's how important a paper trail is.

Architectural writing is perhaps most demanding in its persuasive function. Proposals invited by public bodies normally have to be in writing, so that the persuasive arts of speech are not able to be employed. One recent failure to be awarded a contract was attributed to a wording that had evidently failed to convince. The need for persuasion arises not only with the client but also with the authorities, with whom communications are mainly required to be on paper. In their proposals for the renovation of a 100-year-old building (referred to earlier) Dan and his colleagues had depended on their written and drawn submissions to get the approval of the heritage authority:

> What we try to do is work hand in hand with them, so we would explain to them that we have to do the floors. Of course they come from the point of view that, "Well, do you really have to do the floors because you're damaging or potentially you could alter the structure?" So we have to convince them that the changes are necessary to keep the building maintainable, that [the building] won't be abandoned if it continues to be usable by the client, that it will last, and also persuade them that the infringes that we are doing are sensitive enough to the building.

Although to the outsider much of the writing in the architects' office seems formulaic and the genres standardized, a more active rhetorical alertness is often called for than may be apparent. The senior technologist, Dudley, was able to attest that persuasion was regularly required:

> There's several issues that it comes down to approvals with authorities and getting things through out of the city of Ottawa or Ontario fire marshall's office.

You have to write letters to persuade them about the approach you're taking is correct ... and also getting back to the client and telling the client, "Well, it doesn't matter what you've done in the past, this is what you have to do now because somebody's asking for it."

Dudley insisted that tact was often critical, and that persuasive strategies using logic and reason had to be tailored to what one knew of the different authorities in, for instance, arguing for a particular interpretation of a building code.

You have this building code which is that thick (*demonstrates thickness with fingers*), the Ontario building code, and then you have a national building code which is also that thick (*demonstrates*) and then you have the Ontario fire code which is that thick (*demonstrates*) and then you have the plumbing code and the electrical code and all these codes, and you say, well that's the code, I mean, you just follow what it says. But it's not like that at all. I mean, I'll read the sentence and I'll say, "Well, that means this." Well, somebody in the city of Ottawa will read the sentence and he'll say, "No, that's not what that means, that means this." And somebody in Gloucester will say, "No, no, no, it means this." And then you go down to Toronto, and you can call down to Toronto and get an interpretation from the head office of the Ministry of Housing who writes the building codes, and they'll research and say, "Well what we really meant to say is this".... but the final authority would rest with the city that you're dealing with.... If you can't convince them that your interpretation is right, or Toronto's interpretation is right, then the only next way to go would be to take it to a hearing, and that takes a long time, 3 or 4 months.... you have to use logic and reason in order to read between the lines ... and argue for your reading, about why that's—[*Interviewer:* Sort of like biblical scholarship?] (*laughs*) Well, it is. And then trying to convince a client of that is another step....

Even the writing of the specifications called for careful judgment. On a renovation, particularly, where the condition is not exactly known before work begins, one must beware of assuming what is not known while at the same time being as specific as possible; the trick, for Dan, is to make the contractor responsible for checking the dimensions.

"Plus or minus" is a godsend.... If this is a new room, we can make this twenty four hundred long, twenty four hundred millimeters. In existing conditions, if you want something to fit in, these are existing walls so you have to describe it as, well, it could be twenty four one hundred or twenty four ten, twenty, or—Anyway, it goes back to the writing in the contract documents. You try to be as specific as possible, and at the same time you don't want to tell them it's twenty four hundred, because you'll be wrong, and you'll be [writing] Change Order number five hundred and ninety nine. [So you write "plus or minus."] You try to delegate responsibility so that you can't assume responsibility for certain items and that it is up to the contractor to be responsible....

The construction phase, too, requires tactful writing and "delicate phrasing," as when Dudley has to tell a client that he needs to pay extra because some item was missed in the specifications:

> When you get into construction, that's when you're writing letters to the client explaining why he's got to pay an additional $10,000 on a job [because of some] omission on the contract documents or something has developed on site that wasn't anticipated, so you have to revise things. "It's going to cost you even more," so you have to explain to him why.... So there you have to get into a bit more delicate way of phrasing your information.

Writing is a demanding challenge for architects in part because of the complexity and extensiveness of the social relations in which their work is implicated. Architects have to deal not only with each other and the technologists within the parameters of seniority (partner, associate, other) and the permanent and ad hoc (i.e., project-specific) division of labor, but also with outsiders, the numbers and roles of whom vary with the type and size of job, and transactions with whom vary according to the party's relative status in the project. Thus clients and public authorities who call the tune and have to be dealt with tactfully and persuasively constitute one category. A second is co-participating professional colleagues such as other architectural firms, engineering consultants and lawyers, and independent actors such as materials suppliers who provide information and advice. A third group comprises parties who are under the architects' authority, such as contractors and their subcontractors. The speech acts, spoken and written, that issue from the architect reflect these relationships and vary from delicate solicitation and artful persuasion of those with power, through businesslike consultation and negotiation with equals, to the direct instructing of subordinates. The contrasts are most stark in the written documents; in spoken exchanges between, say, the architect and the contractor's supervisor on the site, the peremptoriness of the written instruction (as we shall see later in the chapter) is considerably softened; tact and courtesy need to oil the wheels even when formally the architect is in a position simply to give orders.

Although architects generally do a surprising amount of writing, some jobs involve far more writing than others. What makes the difference is not just the size but also the complexity of the job. In this office the most complex jobs were modifications of existing buildings. Unlike a new building, of which only the final aimed-at state need be represented in the documents, modifications involve drawing and writing to show both the current and the final intended state of the building and the procedures that will lead from the one to the other.

The exceptional complexity of the heritage building job already referred to, a 19th century drill hall still used by the military, was reflected in the quantity of documentation that Dan and the other architects expected to generate:

> I would say that this job ... is more complex because you have so many existing pieces of the fabric of the building, and you're doing all these interventions. The interventions range—normally a building has a program, say it's a hospital, so you know you have operating rooms, and it's sort of the same genre if you will, there's still sterilization procedures and things like that has to be involved in a hospital. In this project it was very diverse. We had rifle range, which is a shooting range, weapons vault, which is high security, storage of weapons, quartermaster stores, which is a large military storage area, we had heritage messes which are officers' messes which are bars, there was five of those. We had office areas, we have a museum space ... and a large acoustic band room, so you can see there that you're not doing an opera house, you're not doing a museum, you're not doing a shooting range, they are all involved in the building. On top of that you have the heritage concerns and what exactly you're doing to the existing fabric, and then the things that must be done like the structural reinforcement of the building. So to bring all of those pieces together in an existing fabric, I found it was quite difficult.

The renovation, recently completed, of a similar building next door had involved 600 Change Orders instead of the usual 100. There were 4 separate clients and instead of the usual 5 consultants there were 14, together with a range of supervisory bodies. All these factors increased the paperwork:

> If you look at any typical file [for a complete project], [it would be] perhaps the length of this page *(about 3.5 feet)*, and in that is the construction phase, working drawings, design, the client files and disciplines. On this job we probably have about this amount *(about 3 feet)*, and we haven't gone to construction yet, so we'll have double the amount if not more.

Most of his 3 years on the job had been spent by the project architect in writing "fat reports in which every word is new," old buildings being unique and the firm's resource of boilerplate descriptions thus being unusable.

Complexity also arises when the architects are in charge of only one part of a job. For Michael, designing the high-tech control room in a public service building (referred to above) involved working with a great many professionals who were not under the architects' control, as well as with middlemen for the various agencies.

> It's a control center in the new [public corporation] headquarters.... It's a job that we have on the second floor of the building, so we're not the architects of the building, we're not the architects for any of the interior design in any of the other areas except this one part of one floor, because of our experience having

done something like that before for them. So there's interior designers, we worked with someone whose title was "interior design manager" who was responsible for coordinating the design professionals, there's a project manager, there's the developer, the client ... there's the contractor, anyway there's a lot of parties involved.

A major problem for the architects in such a situation is keeping everyone informed about and happy with what is being proposed, "resulting in copies to everyone":

> There's nothing to be gained by cutting someone out, so you might as well tell everyone all the time, it's in your own best interests, and people like to be informed as well. Even if they don't talk to you for 6 weeks, they like to find out that things are actually happening here, you get a sense of the problems.... Sometimes you feel like you might be wasting people's time by copying things to them and then other times they probably up and ask you why they didn't get a copy, so it tends to just be simpler just to spread it around. It's a protection mechanism too, no one can say that you didn't tell them something. You know, if you have a problem with this why didn't you respond to it 3 weeks ago when I told you about it?

ARCHITECTS' EXPERIENCE OF THE WRITING PROCESS

Writing in an architectural practice seems to afford a strangely mixed experience that includes both tedious routine and scope for creative flair. Representative of the former is the use of boilerplate, an essential element in the firm's writing activities. Its careless use can lead to problems not only, as we saw, in specifications but also in other documents. According to Alan:

> You often find in documents ... certificates of payment and letters and things like that, if it's come out of your computer, I don't know, there's a certain tendency not to necessarily read it at all.

Technology has thus rendered widespread the strange phenomenon of a writing process in which writers may not exactly know the content or wording of the text they are writing, because they can avoid engaging with the individual words and even sentences that they write, manipulating nothing smaller than entire blocks of text. Without boilerplate, however, document production on the scale required could simply not be achieved. To illustrate that scale, this small firm puts out 300 proposals a year. Greg, who writes most of them, showed us the typical breakdown:

So this is what they've asked for, a description of the firm, a description of who we're going to put in charge of the project ... a proposed work schedule, and then a list of our related experience, and we were asked to limit this to only 10 pages. Everything here tends to be collegial, I would write the base text, it would be edited by a partner. Any of these descriptions have been written over the course of time. Whenever it was appropriate to describe a project, I would generate written text for that and store it on the computer, then I would assemble an explicit list for the job. So this was assembled for this job from existing text, and I would go in and slant some of these descriptions to be appropriate for the project.

Likewise, the use of standardized formats, made easy by the computer, affects letters, Change Orders, Change Notices, certificates of payment and various legal documents as well as proposals. Specification writing, according to Dudley, is particularly unexciting:

There's specification writing, it's a set format that you take, issued by the government, it's all government standard numbers, and you're basically taking a spec that you did from one job and editing it for the requirements of the new job.... There's a set guideline of rules that you have to follow and technical phrases, particular words that are repeated over and over and over again, so there's not really a lot of thought goes into the writing. It's more, the thought goes into the actual information that has to be imparted.

At the other extreme we have noted writing tasks that require the architect to be rhetorically sensitive and adaptive. Such tasks presumably afford a degree of satisfaction to writers who possess, or are acquiring, the necessary literate resources. One satisfaction that is rarely available, however, is that of writing the sort of critical and theoretical text (more "abstract and intellectual") that the architects had experienced in some school courses, though some competitions may call for it. When the submission is successful, excerpts from the architects' own description may find their way into reports in the professional press.

HISTORICAL INCREASE IN WRITING

Architects currently spend a lot more of their time writing than in the past. The original specification documents for the 1879 drill hall, for which the firm was proposing renovations, comprised six pages. The contrast with even 50 years ago had struck Sarah; the increase affects documentation in general, both drawing and writing:

We tend to really detail our drawings here, especially the working drawings, because now everyone's trying to undercut someone and it's very important to get exactly what you want in a drawing so that you don't have to come back and say that it wasn't on the drawings.... If you look at a set of drawings from 40, 50 years ago, you'd open a set and you know, like, 4 or 5 drawings for a whole school where they have a plan, 4 elevations and maybe one typical wall section, and a few notes, and very little dimensions because a lot of that kind of stuff was established once the job started construction. Whereas now if you want something it's got to be on the drawing, so now we have schools that have 25 or 30 drawings to a set. So you know you've got to go through the building and detail everything, or else everything is going to be an extra once it goes out for construction, so you're always trying not to have any extras which cost us and it may cost our client, and it doesn't look very good for us, because it looks like we haven't done our job.... The specs are getting thicker and thicker and thicker all the time too.

One of our informants, Joe, had noticed an increase in writing even during his professional life of some 10 years, ascribing it to an increase in litigation (and hence a greater awareness of liability issues) and changes in technology (particularly the photocopier and fax machine). Another reason, Tom told us, is changed procedures for obtaining contracts:

The way work is allocated has changed. In the sixties there was a lot of work going on but if you were a client and you wanted a building built, you might inquire around and say "Well, I know that five firms have a reputation. Let's interview them," and then we'd perhaps go along and be interviewed and show you examples of our work and you'd choose one. What happens now much more frequently is that the client will advertise saying, for example, "We are considering the construction of a headquarters office building for so and so and so and so. Expressions of interest are invited from suitably qualified architects." And they may advertise that nationally. In one case they did recently, for a building on ... Avenue, and they had over 90 replies, all written in books about this to this thick (*demonstrates*) saying this is our experience, this is how we approach it. They then short-listed, I think, 30 and called for more information, so there's more writing, more intents. We got down to the last five who were then called for an interview, so we need preparation material for an interview, and then after that they chose an architect from Toronto, so we say "Well, that's gone." That wouldn't have happened 5 or 10 years ago. It might have happened for something like the National Gallery, but now it's happening for all kinds of tiny jobs.

In Greg's view, this obsession with documentation is excessive; so much time and effort have to be spent on preparing the proposal that chances of making a profit are drastically reduced.

This increase in writing has not been welcome to architects. They feel it has not enhanced their ability to produce good buildings, and they experience it not as contributing to a central and satisfying aspect of the architectural process but as a tedious distraction. Their dissatisfaction recalls the responses to a similar increase among the social workers reported in chapter 6, though the latter group felt the demands for writing more as an oppressive imposition that was fraught with dangers for themselves. As a result of these historical changes, architects are now experiencing certain writing processes that are alienating. It is true that architects by their own account don't much like writing anyway; but it seemed to us that some of this work really was depressingly mechanical, an impression forcefully communicated by Greg, the young architect who does nearly all the proposal writing for the firm. First, the usual rewards of reader response are often lacking; it is common for a text produced with care and long effort to receive no reply. Second, the process is extremely laborious; Greg gathers the information he needs by discussion with the project manager and consultants, collates the material and then spends the weekend at the cottage writing the proposal. Finally, the writing is not of a kind that one can take pleasure or pride in:

> This is lowest common denominator writing. It's really, really dry writing.... You want me to read some of it? I'll just read you a paragraph, you'll appreciate this one. "[Person's name], professor of urban design at [university], is the senior urban designer for [government department]. [Person's name] will advise the team on urban design issues.... " You know, some of these go on half a page, but they all read the same, "So-and-so is this, has this experience and has done this in the past." It's really dry stuff.

Perhaps 2 pages of a 100-page document allow Greg to write in something like the way he had learned in school and that he values. This writer feels distaste for the writing he produces, and told us that he needs, when away from the office, to compensate by writing for himself in more poetic vein, to keep alive the sense of what writing can do.

LEARNING TO WRITE FOR THE OFFICE

None of the architects considered that they had been trained in the school of architecture for the writing demands they were now meeting at work. (The technologists, on the other hand, had taken at least one community college course in technical writing, as had the three junior architects who had been technologists before taking their architecture degree.) While the senior architects in the firm regret that their young employees generally do not always write well and may produce texts that need editing for grammar, usage, and jargon, they do not consider that schools of architecture should teach the specialist professional genres of specifications, Change Orders, and the like; these skills can be picked up on the job, whereas design skills, the correct focus of the school, need to be established during education.

Correspondingly, all our subjects confirmed that the special skills of professional architectural writing were indeed acquired at work. Greg had been steered into proposal writing because of his general writing skills (which he attributed to the fact that his grandmother had been a grammar teacher and he had been a great reader) but had learned the specialist genres since joining the practice. Both the layout and relationships of this office were identified by Sarah as facilitating the learning that novices needed to go through:

> The good thing about this office is that it's an open concept. I think you learn through watching other people also. You're doing your own work but you [pick up] conversations or something that's happening out of sight, and you hear other people's experiences. Even though you're doing two things at the same time you always tend to learn from other people and I think that's the way that this office is. We all tend to learn from each other … we always have conversations and talk about things that have happened and so I think you know we tend to learn, I think all of us have learned a lot just from each other. There's some offices where you go and it's falling into a [groove] and everyone does their own thing.… Here you tend to get lots of opportunity to touch on all areas of the profession, which is good.

Learning is promoted through "attenuated authentic participation" (see chap. 9 below) with its opportunities for practice coupled with supportive supervision procedures; one of the partners is responsible for each job and provides whatever guidance and correction is necessary to the junior architects and technologists. Dudley, the senior technologist, explained how he had learned the necessary genres from the revisions made to his work by the partners—a procedure which, far from being ego-bruising, he had found comforting:

> I don't mind it at all. It's actually a bit more comforting (laughs), you know, when it does come back it says, well, you had your shot at it too. No, it's fine, I don't have any problem with that at all. Their comments are all welcome and very valid, and actually it helps your writing in the future, I mean you learn. Alan and Tony and Steve have so much experience amongst them to handle different situations, and they're also very in tune with the client—for the most part they know the client much better than you will ever know him because they've done other work with him in the past … and they know how that person is from a personality point of view, so they know what will work and what won't work and how best to explain things, so you just learn from their experience. They each have their different way of writing and their different way of explaining things, so you tend to borrow from each of them as far as you know, and developing your own writing and how you handle the situations.

One of the things we found most impressive about this office, as Sarah mentioned earlier, is the opportunity it affords for learning new skills. Dudley, though trained in technical writing, finds himself on occasion engaging with the demands of proposal writing—and enjoying the challenge:

> You want to sell [the client] on a job, so there's quite a bit of liberty taken as to the writing. It's a descriptive thing but it has to be very positive, so you're taking your own thoughts and your own ideas and any ideas from Tom, who's the partner in charge, of what he was trying to get, and trying to describe that in the most delicate, elegant way you can, to sell them on the job. So there, there's quite a bit of artistic nature to the writing ... which I generally don't get into but there are occasions when it's required. [*Interviewer:* Do you welcome those occasions?] Oh yes, I'm getting more familiar with it. Writing has actually never been one of my strong suits. So just through experience, getting more and more experience into it, becoming more and more accustomed, and more, I don't know, confident or able to do that sort of writing, because, I don't know, formal education [e.g., in specification writing] is more like filling in slots.

What has to be learned by the novice is not exclusively formats and conventions. Nothing about school writing, for instance, teaches the need that Michael had found for reticence (in both speech and writing) within certain transactions:

> Particularly when you're dealing with people who aren't familiar with the building process generally or the normal sequence of decisions, it's not always useful to raise issues that they're not really normally going to be concerned with anyway. If you raise it then somebody has to deal with it. They shouldn't be concerned with that. You only ask them questions that you need to know an answer ... because if you ask them what kind of doorknob they want, they'll think they have to respond to that, and they'll say "Well, show me what I can get," so all of a sudden you're up to your neck in looking for doorknobs when really there was only one that you had in mind anyway....

> There's definitely a technique to it, but someone like Alan would be—because it's definitely a skill and it has to do with a whole series of intangible variables, just the personality of the person you're dealing with. Some people like to be involved in a project in all the detail, and you try to keep them out of it and they get irritated and wonder why you're blocking them out. So a lot of it's by feel, intuition, and experience.

Once a design has been extensively developed, the natural impulse is to communicate it to the client in its entirety, converting the contents of one's own notes into public form, but the architect soon has to learn that the imparting of information must be carefully phased, with as much emphasis on holding back as on giving out:

The difficult thing for me was learning to do the steps in sequence. It seemed more natural to do everything all at once, but you tell the client only as much of the story as they need to know at one time.

A striking difference between school and work is in the degree of emphasis placed on the verbal articulation of the ideas and principles that underlie a design. Tom, who, like the other partners, regularly teaches and sits on juries in the school, explained that in commercial practice there is neither need nor time for making ideas explicit:

We seldom do that. I know they do it at the school of architecture.... the professors have formulated an approach which gets the students to establish a theoretical base for their solution.... We start at another place and solve the problem in terms of all the constraints which come to bear on the problem. We very seldom write a theoretical approach to our building.... There's no doubt about it that ideas are in the buildings, the buildings don't grow without ideas and ideas are what they are. But whether we articulate those ideas is something else.... We very seldom sit around and talk about them as groups.... I wrote a series of design ideas which were built into that school *(discussed earlier in the conversation)*, and I dashed them off only because [local architectural journalist] was writing an article on the school.... I had intended to write a piece on the design of the school and to put it—we provided 3 time capsules for the school which are supposed to be refilled every 50 years, and the first one [was to contain] 7 drawings and the philosophy of the design of the school.... I never did that, didn't have time to do it, I just didn't get around to doing it. Partly because there [are] always other things cooking, partly because I'm a bit lazy.

What does have to be made absolutely explicit is "the physical reality of the building." As Alan, one of the partners, put it:

If you spoke as per one might write an article on, say, high-minded issues about where a project is standing in the historical framework of architecture, whether it's impressionist modernism or associated with post-modernism or aspects to do with where it is stylistically, what it's doing as a form of critical debate to do with function.... Well, I haven't met a client who says "I want to hear all about it." They don't want to hear all that. Because they don't understand they get really frightened by it. What they want to understand, is simple, clear, direct language. At times you might touch on the fact that you understand a certain set of complexities that you're working with, but in my experience don't try to describe it to them, you're going to lose the project (laughs). So there's two sort of things you're doing. One is working how you work with the client, and then in turn how you work with consultants and authorities, to get approval and so on, which is the majority or ninety per cent of practices' work. And it's only because you get cases like Tom, Steve and I are doing a bit of stuff up at [the university] and things of that nature, whereby the critical discussion can in any way become part of our language. So other than that, you're reading it in magazines that you buy

and you're maintaining this life from your period of time when you were a student
and you hit the high road, and you're trying to maintain this when only a tiny,
tiny percent of it is ever going to be used ... because people aren't interested in
that stuff, generally.

Complexity and Multifunctionality

Because the above account was mostly somewhat generalized, a closer look at
one written transaction may allow a more concrete sense to emerge of the
complex ways writing affects the situation. These could in no way be guessed
at by a simple inspection of the text. The following is an example of writing
that was successful in that it worked in its context—or, at least, it had worked
so far at the point when our study took place; for some texts the real proof of
the pudding comes years later when they are pulled from a filing cabinet in the
investigation of some issue of dispute.

> Lower ceiling @ corridor 327 as per attached sketch SK 26-01 and revise to
> acoustical lay-in tile as shown.

This Site Instruction was sent by Joe to the contractor's site supervisor, Luc. It
conforms to generic type in its omission of the definite article, its simple
imperative form, and its reliance on an accompanying graphical representation
to convey the detail of what is required. The text looks like a fairly straightforward accomplishment; and, indeed, every project architect in the practice
routinely issues considerable numbers of similar Site Instructions. But there are
a number of ways in which this act of written communication could have been
wrongly enacted, and the way the text needed to affect the situation was quite
complex.

In the first place, the architect, Joe, a junior in the firm despite his several
years experience, would have been wrong to issue this instruction without
consulting his senior, Steve, the partner in charge of the job. This is not because
Joe does not have the authority to issue Site Instructions. He had been quite in
order, without asking Steve, to write an instruction to "revise location of
mechanical diffusers to be centered between light fixtures on undulated wood
ceiling." The difference is that the first instruction had substantial design
implications. A stretch of ceiling was to be lowered along a corridor to
accommodate unexpectedly bulky ductwork. This modification, unlike the
relocation of the diffusers, would have a highly noticeable effect on the
appearance of that part of the building; the ceiling would visibly change levels
in different parts of the corridor, dropping 100 mm at one point and resuming

its original level at another. It was the firm's policy that in design decisions affecting appearance the seniors must be consulted. Had Joe written the Site Instruction without asking Steve, although legally valid, it would have been unfortunate in lacking the partner's blessing.

Secondly, the instruction could have resulted in a damaging disruption of good relations with the contractor if the instruction really had been what it appears to be, the peremptory issuing of an order without justification or warning. To avoid such an effect, the communication needed at one level to be, as it was, almost redundant, Joe having already asked Luc and Luc having agreed, in their conversation on the site, to effect the modification in question:

Joe: First of all what we're going to have to do, we're going to have to lower 3 inches anyway.
Luc: On the west side, the [inaudible].
Joe: Yes.
Luc: You'll let me know the elevations.
Joe: Yes, I'll let you know the elevations.

The instruction does not, therefore, communicate new information to Luc; what is to be done—the "propositional content" of the communication—is already known, apart from the exact dimensions of the alteration (the elevations). Converting the instruction into writing meets the "felicity conditions" for the successful performance of the speech act of Site Instruction. What the writing provides for Luc is essentially a piece of paper that he can produce to others, as evidence, if it is needed, that he has the authority to proceed and that the decision is the architect's and that the cost of the work can be allocated accordingly. Joe is in a sense writing not to Luc but past him to an array of future and possible readers, some of them faceless: the contractor's head office, the client, the auditors, and potentially lawyers and judges in the event of a dispute over responsibility. This text, then, appears to "work" within the complex nexus of relationships inside and outside the firm only in so far as its content is not original expression but something like quotation. The decision needs to have been gone over with Steve, the senior colleague, and some formulation like the one in the text already arrived at; similarly with Luc, the site supervisor. These two parties will be happy with the instruction in so far as they recognize it as what they have already agreed. Steve is part of the audience, even though he is not addressed. So is the consultant, whose original error in advising on the space his ductwork would require had created the problem in the first place, and who can now breathe more easily—although he was expecting this relief, having, like Luc, been in on the site conversation. For him also the Site Instruction works less by conveying its meaning in clear and unambiguous terms than by its intertextual reference—identifiable only to insiders within this situation—to that earlier conversation, the text of which it recognizably quotes and reaccentuates, in Bakhtin's term.

ARCHITECTURAL ACTIVITY
IN SCHOOL AND WORK

As we saw above, nobody in the office claimed that university taught them how to write at work; all stressed the learning they had needed to do on the job. At the same time, a minor note we picked up in some of our discussions was regret at not being able to make much use at work of the habits of critical and theoretical writing that had been acquired in school. In this section we want to focus on this lack of crossover, and seek to understand the reasons for it.

First, in line with our general stress in this volume, writing in the two contexts of the architectural education exercise and the commercial architectural project must be understood in terms of the overriding activities (using that term with its full Activity Theory associations—see chap. 2) that are being pursued in each, because from them follow many differences in the more specific needs for which writing gets used. Architectural education as we described it in chapter 5 is about the inculcation and assessment of individual capabilities, the most important of which is design. Design is evaluated by specimens of design work, architectural works realized spatially and visually, and not verbally; assessment is based primarily on drawings, photographs, and models, with writing (and speech) in supplementary roles only. It is true that designs are expected to be rational and principled, and that the rationales and principles may be essentially propositional in form and capable of verbal explication—an explication that may have been extensively developed in written notes and discussion during the work and that may be elicited orally in the final review. The presence of this thinking is principally judged, however, not through its verbal elaborations but through the coherence and intelligibility of the proposed building or other structure. Thus any writing that occurs in the process is mainly in aid of the writer's own epistemic purposes of clarifying intention and constructing a publicly sustainable account; little of it is seen by anyone else.

Architectural education, in relation to the competencies required in the profession is partial and selective. The price of an emphasis on design ability is the relative neglect of other skills that are held to be best developed in the office context, such as procuring buildings within particular cost limits, observing codes, avoiding legal and financial traps, and managing contractors. What the student stands to secure by his or her design efforts is a university degree, and not a professional ticket that has to be worked at over the first years of office practice and that will be assessed by further examinations conducted by a professional body. As we have seen, the architects in this office tend to feel that the school's emphasis is right in that design needs formal education whereas technical and communicative skills can be acquired in practice.

Because the development of design ability, and therefore its assessment, are seen in the school as an individual matter, school design projects tend to be individual and not group tasks. This feature, too, is in contrast with—and even appears perversely to contradict—workplace practice, to which collaboration is central, providing another instance in which it is only in a partial and indirect sense that the school can be said to provide professional preparation. It further reinforces our sense of disjunction between the overarching activities of the school, which we have described, and those of the architectural workplace, namely securing contracts and bringing about completed buildings. In the securing of contracts, it is true, some convergence with the school project may be discerned, because the task for both student and architect may be seen as persuasive. The student's purpose is to convince a jury of his or her abilities; the architect's, to convince a client of the firm's competence to produce the design and manage the construction of a building or renovation, and of the desirability and value for money of the building that would be the result.

What is involved in achieving such conviction is, however, very different in the two situations. The student's case rests primarily on the visible artifact that is essentially supposed to speak for itself, to be immediately accessible to visiting critics who know nothing of the student's background and to constitute evidence, through its physical configuration, use of materials, and anticipated user experience, of the student's intelligence, vision, and knowledge. The team of architects have, likewise, to produce a design that convinces as a sound and pleasing physical structure and as an environment for activities, and present their ideas by similar visual means. But they have to convince on many other grounds, too, which require different sorts of presentation. The claimed cost must be justified by the presentation of itemized pricing and calculations, and the time line for completion by the presentation of evidently realistic estimates of the time needed for the stages of the process. Ability to manage the project must be demonstrated by a display of knowledge of what is involved. The professional team, therefore, need to deploy different sorts of warrants (Toulmin, Reike, & Janik, 1979—see chap. 3) in support of their case for being awarded the contract; in Aristotelian terms, the nature of their *proof* needs to be different, and this implies the production of different sorts of manifestations for presentation: figures, lists, and schedules, for instance, as well as drawings. They also do what the student neither could nor would be allowed to do, namely make a strong appeal on the basis of *ethos* (in rhetoric, the speaker's own character) by creating a sense of their credibility, reliability, and trustworthiness. They do this by various means, including the professionalism and, where appropriate, visible expensiveness of their presentation, but principally by appeal to track record. A great deal of work typically goes into a document, mainly written but often illustrated, that enumerates the firm's successful past contracts, competition successes, awards and so on, and seeks to establish a proven ability to deliver buildings that are pleasing and that meet the three key criteria: "on time, on price, no leaks."

Of the two main branches of professional activity, therefore, the securing of contracts and the bringing about of buildings, the one which appears to share with school activity an ultimately persuasive purpose is actually very different in the means deployed. The student's presented "proof" has to stand or fall by its internal character, without much chance of deriving advantage from appeals to his or her character and experience or from artfully speaking to the known emotional disposition of the critical audience (Aristotle's *pathos*). The professionals typically make both those appeals; their activity might accordingly be said to be more comprehensively rhetorical than that of the student. To put that more generally, the professional activity is more social, not because the school project is not embedded in social relations but because in making their case the professionals address their persuasive task by working on a wide range of interpersonal motivations and histories, rather than relying solely on the ideational content of their proposal.

A greater degree of sociality is, thus, evident in the professional activity, securing the contract, which most resembles student work. It is inescapably and pervasively evident in the other main activities that take place after the contract has been obtained, namely the designing of buildings or modifications and the management of construction. This work is social mainly in requiring the contributions of many individuals and institutions for its accomplishment. The activity also enacts a different mode of the practical. If securing the contract is a practical pursuit in the sense that rhetoric is always practical (in seeking to affect a social state of affairs), designing and constructing the building are practical in the sense of bringing about physical rather than social and personal states. The collaboration involved in that achievement is still dependent, however, on skilled rhetorical action on the part of the architect, both within and outside the practice and through both spoken and written means.

CONCLUSION

Unlike students and unlike writers in the government financial institution, architects have considerable formal power, exercised through language: for them, "saying makes it so," at least at certain critical points. Much of their interpersonally oriented writing has performativity, bringing about the states of affairs it names; architects "hereby" advise, recommend, and order. But language with this sort of legitimate effectuality does not inherently have to be written, and not so long ago often was not; the architect would go on the site and simply say what needed to be done—if the builders did not already know from their craft knowledge and experience. Writing has reached its present inflated scale largely as a result of the relentless progress of bureaucracy as the dominant mode of organization in modern times, and comes at times to resemble the "iron cage" that Weber[20] described in this connection. Hence the proliferation of systems of genres, the whole days spent writing and the rows of filing cabinets full of preserved papers that will mainly never be looked at again.

If anything, however, despite the mindlessness of much of the writing they have to do, the architects we observed seemed to be less oppressed by their writing tasks than do many students in their university courses. We attribute this to certain qualities that the participants pointed out in this particular office; we have little idea how widely they are found in other practices too. Role definitions here are fluid and personnel move between a variety of responsibilities. Formal qualifications and titles (such as "technologist") seem minimally constraining. Thus, somebody trained in specification writing as a technologist finds himself or herself engaged in the delicate work of "architectural description" in proposal writing. Consequently, we think that all the players in the office have a wide knowledge of and considerable commitment to the overall project of "the firm's work." We can put this in Activity Theory terms. Working in this office seems to mean, to the participants, getting good buildings made, whereas in more alienating environments the activity may be more narrowly defined as, for instance, plowing through this pile of specs. In the sort of office we studied, intrinsically uninteresting writing doesn't get more interesting but may become more tolerable when the writer identifies with some larger purpose.

If the office seems a good environment for motivated and productive work, it is also, and by the same token, a good place to learn; and the opportunity to

---

[20]"Feeling, spirituality, and moral values would shrink in importance as societies constructed an increasingly restrictive 'iron cage' of BUREAUCRACY in every area of social life, from religion to education to work to the law." From the entry on Max Weber in Johnson (1995).

learn in turn enhances motivation and commitment. The junior architects universally mentioned access to the diverse skills and experience of the three partners as a great advantage for their own professional development, not least in writing. None of the younger practitioners seemed to have had an education that seriously attempted to prepare them for the range of writing they would have to do at work; but this did not matter because the office was a good school. Novices learned by practice, by eavesdropping, and by having their drafts reviewed by more experienced writers. Principles of writing were, it seems, rarely made explicit, and what the junior would learn in an exchange about his or her text with one of the partners would be as much about the personalities and sensitivities of clients and other addressees as about getting the genre right; but from these experiences of collaboratively adjusting texts to the acutely observed characteristics of the various recipients, the younger writers would at the same time be absorbing more general lessons about the rhetorical fine-tuning of documents for audiences, things that it would probably be impossible to extract and teach in propositional form.

The role and forms of writing in the architectural workplace could hardly be more different from writing in the school of architecture, or indeed in the university in general. For the students whose activities were reported in chap. 5, writing was the vehicle of the epistemic work of thinking through design problems and learning to think within an architectural discourse. Much of the work in the office is necessarily epistemic also; a great deal of thought goes into the production of a design. The difference is that in the office this work, in so far as it involves language as well as sketching, is done either in the head or in conversation, and hardly ever in writing. And whereas students have to work out and present their theoretical ideas in more formal papers, the practitioners, although their work no doubt draws tacitly on theory and critical argument, rarely have the time or the pretext to write their thinking down *in extenso*.

The scale and range of architects' writing, however, impress us as far more significant in their contrast with school. Students get little experience of collaboratively writing long documents of great complexity (often through collaboration with other parties outside the office, such as consultants based in different firms around the city), of writing that impacts on a situation in multifunctional ways, saying different things to different readers, or of writing that is implicated in power relations, either as the vehicle of the exercise of power or as the hostage to fortune that draws financial and legal retribution from others in power. Students do not give orders to others, go on record as making recommendations, sign certificates of payment for thousands of dollars, adjust their writing in the light of the known backgrounds and foibles of a whole cast of important other players, put documents meticulously away for indefinite storage, or get out of trouble by retrieving 5-year-old documents from dusty files. They do not have to insert their writing into the middle of tangled intertextual webs and chains of speech, writing, and drawing, nor, above all, do they see writing, fed into a situation, instigating massive financial flows and titanic physical operations with cranes, trucks, earthmovers, tons of materials and armies of differentiated workers. The writing done in the architects' office, tedious and fiddling though much of it is, always seems to absorb meaning and dignity from the grandeur and buzz of the whole enterprise, those characteristics that keep the junior practitioners turning up and working late night after night for little pay. Architecture finally seems satisfying because it is felt to be "real work," an evaluation that works it way down into all its contributory activities, including writing.

IV

TRANSITIONS

How, then, can students move successfully from the academic writing described in Part II of this book to the complex rhetorical environments of the workplace portrayed in Part III? What school-based or on-the-job experiences might help students make the transition?

Many students, of course, appear to have no bridging experience; they move from term papers, essays, book reviews, examinations, and lab reports to professional writing without benefit of much explicit or formal instruction. Their rhetorical acumen allows them to relearn writing when they switch from the epistemic social motives of academia to the instrumental social motives of the workplace. They learn, it seems, by jumping into the rhetorical pool and swimming.

A veteran social worker and current faculty member in a school of social work offers this succinct view of how students learn to write workplace texts:

> I think the way they learn to do it is in their field of practice, because they learn what they need to write for whatever they need to write wherever they are.... Certainly, I learned my writing skills in practice. I mean, I had to. I've had to do case reports, I've had to do briefs to the government, I've had to analyze policy, I've had to apply for grants. You know, you look at your audience, and look at how one presents to that audience, and then you learn how to write for that audience. You learn from experience, I think that's the way you learn it. I don't know how much of that can be taught.

On the other hand, we have often heard complaints about this tacit process of instruction by immersion or osmosis. Many practitioners seem to feel that students should already know about professional writing, and frequently decry the lack of attention to workplace writing in professional training programs, and complain about the time it takes to teach newcomers how to write on the job. Students, too, criticize universities for failing to prepare them for the demands of workplace literacy. For their part, many academics, unfamiliar with nonacademic texts and contexts, argue that it is the responsibility of the workplace to provide the appropriate setting for learning about professional documentation. Yet others recommend the use of case studies to introduce students to the rhetorical demands of the workplace.

In our research, we have observed several university-based writing experiences that helped bridge the gap between school and work. We have also observed workplace-based writing experiences that allowed newcomers to develop quickly and effectively the professional literacy required on the job. In the chapters that follow, we consider a number of such experiences, in which students moved toward workplace realities by experiencing approximations of professional practice. These experiences may be seen as points on a continuum of situated learning that describes a movement away from school and into the workplace. Though all learning is situated, the examples we present demonstrate the profound and varied ways in which context influences the activity and outcomes of learning. In chapter 9 we present in finer detail those theoretic notions alluded to in chapter 2 that are relevant to understanding the contextualized learning of new genres, and in chapter 10 we describe in some detail a range of transitional experiences between academic and professional life, experiences shared by many who take a traditional route through school to the workplace.

9

STUDENTS AND WORKERS LEARNING

As described in chapter 2, a new field in psychology has emerged in the past decade, variously called situated learning, socially shared cognition, everyday cognition, or situated experience. A primary focus of this new field has been on knowing and learning, but these terms have been redefined so that they carry very different meanings from those held within traditional studies of cognition. In fact, this new field is not so much cognitive science as a response to cognitive science as currently conceived. Fundamental to this work is the notion that knowing is social, not in the sense that one mind transmits knowledge to another, but rather in the Vygotskian (1978) sense that the source of intrapersonal cognitive functioning is the interpersonal.

The field of situated learning, however, is not unitary. Although the importance of both social and collaborative performances in learning is commonly recognized, scholars and researchers understand many of the key notions differently. The commonalities underlying this field are these: learning and knowing are context-specific, learning is accomplished through processes of coparticipation, and cognition is socially shared. Given these commonalities, however, there are different streams within the literature. Lave (1991) has specified three different theories of "situated experience." In the first, the "cognition plus view," researchers simply "extend the scope of their intraindividual theory to include everyday activity and social interaction.... Social factors become conditions whose effects on individual cognition are then explored" (p. 66).

The second, the "interpretive view," "locates situatedness in the use of language and/or social interaction" (p. 63). Furthermore, "language use and, thus, meaning are situated in *interested*, intersubjectively negotiated social interaction" (p. 67, emphasis added). Individuals work together hermeneutically, through (largely verbal) interactions, toward a shared understanding, within contexts where they are each or all actively engaged.

Both the first and second theories are limited, according to Lave, in that they "bracket off the social world" and thus "negate the possibility that subjects are fundamentally *constituted in* their relations with and activities in that world" (p. 67). The third theory, "situated social practice" or, where appropriate, "situated learning," includes the interpretive perspective along with an insistence that "learning, thinking, and knowing are relations among people engaged in activity *in, with, and arising from the socially and culturally structured world*" (p. 67). A qualified version of this latter perspective informs our analysis.

Fundamental to that perspective is the recognition of the degree to which human activity is mediated through tools, especially that most powerful semiotic tool, language. In his discussions, Wertsch (1991) emphasizes the need to complement situated learning with Bakhtinian notions. Wertsch emphasizes in particular the way in which speakers ventriloquate portions or aspects of their ambient social languages in attempting to realize their own speech plans. All our words are filled with, and are echoes of and responses to, others' words. (To quote Bakhtin, 1986, "No-one breaks the eternal silence of the universe" [p. 69].) Our utterances are dialogic responses to earlier utterances as well as anticipations of our listeners' responses. The relations are multiple, complex, shifting, and dynamic. They demand and reward engagement and attention. They involve notions of complex interplay between an individual's free speech plans and the speech genres available, between an individual's own utterances and the ambient social languages.

The literature on situated learning has produced (at least) two analytic perspectives from which such learning can be viewed: Rogoff's (1990, 1991) "guided participation," and Lave and Wenger's (1991) "legitimate peripheral participation." Although these two perspectives have not been developed as alternatives to each other, they do in fact foreground different aspects of the learning process. In our analysis of instances of situated learning, the two perspectives mark the beginning and ending of a continuum of learning that plots a movement out from the home to the school and into the workplace.

Rogoff (1990) uses the term *guided participation* to describe the learning process or cognitive apprenticeship that primarily middle-class children experience in their homes. (Elsewhere, Rogoff (1993) contrasts guided participation with aspects of child rearing in non-middle-class homes ["Guided"; see also Heath's 1983 *Ways with Words*].) In Rogoff's (1990) view:

> Guided participation involves adults or children challenging, constraining, and supporting children in the process of posing and solving problems through material arrangements of children's activities and responsibilities as well as

through interpersonal communication, with children observing and participating at a comfortable but slightly challenging level. The processes of communication and shared participation in activities inherently engage children and their caregivers and companions in stretching children's understanding and skill.... [and in the] structuring of children's participation so that they handle manageable but comfortably challenging subgoals of the activity that increase in complexity with children's developing understanding. (1990, p. 18)

This perspective echoes notions like *scaffolding* and Lev Vygotsky's (1978) "zone of proximal development" (pp. 84–91): that space where a learner can perform an action (cognitive or rhetorical) *along with* a skilled practitioner but not alone. The assumption is that, by so performing the act along with the practitioner, the child will later be able to operate alone: the intersubjective will become intrasubjective.

Guided participation can be contrasted with the learning that Lave and Wenger (1991) call *legitimate peripheral participation,* a process that characterizes various forms of apprenticeship, from that of Vai and Gola tailors to Yucatec midwives, and butchers' apprentices to newcomers in Alcoholics Anonymous. Central to all these forms of apprenticeship is their focus on something other than learning. Apprentices and masters, or rather newcomers and oldtimers, are both involved in activities that have a purpose above and beyond the initiation of newcomers. The tailors, for example, learn by becoming involved in making real garments. In all the instances, the activity as a whole has an end other than the learning of its participants.

In both processes, however, the newcomers do learn. The two processes are similar in three very important respects:

1. Both are based on the notion of learning through performance or engagement, "learning through doing," as one of the instructors in our research kept repeating, as opposed to earlier cognitive notions of learning through receiving bodies of knowledge. "The individual learner is not gaining a discrete body of abstract knowledge (s)he will then transport and reapply in later contexts. Instead, (s)he acquires the skill *to perform by actually engaging in the process*" (Hanks, 1991, p. 15, emphasis added).

2. Both processes are social: instructors and learners collaborate, in a broad sense, and one result is that learners are able to do something at the end that they were unable to do before.

3. In both, learning is achieved through sociocultural mediation of tools and especially linguistic and other semiotic signs. Also, in both kinds of learning the learners do not fully participate. The conditions for performing are attenu-

ated; only some of the task is given over to the learner, and this attenuation (generally a subtle and highly nuanced attenuation) allows for the learning.

On the other hand, there is at least this radical difference between the two processes: in *guided participation* the goal of the activity itself is learning; in *legitimate peripheral participation* the learning is incidental and occurs as part of participation in communities of practice (COP), whose activities are oriented toward practical or material outcomes. This difference has important consequences, as we shall see.

In this chapter and the one that follows, we compare various contexts and conditions that support processes of situated learning. We use the term *facilitated performance* to refer to the circumstances and activities that facilitate learning in university, and to distinguish it from Rogoff's guided participation; we use *attenuated authentic participation* to refer to the closely supervised learning opportunities that students and newcomers experience when they first enter the workplace, and to distinguish that experience from the near-professional practice of legitimate peripheral participation during apprenticeship.

We should note that the movement from guided to legitimate participation does not describe a necessary developmental trajectory (although many people will experience this movement as a sequence as they move toward autonomous professional practice). Rather, facilitated performance and attenuated authentic participation mark occasions or modes of situated learning that fall between the learning focus of guided participation and the institutional pragmatics that govern legitimate peripheral participation. The echo in the names is intended to acknowledge their sources; the difference in wording is intended to reflect the fact that we use these terms in more specialized and possibly narrower ways than those intended by the originators. In what follows, we contrast the contexts and conditions that allow for different types of learning.

DIFFERENCES BETWEEN CONTEXTS
FOR LEARNING

Object of the Activity and Place of Learning

The most striking difference between learning at school and learning at work, one with far-reaching implications, is that the object of the activity in the school context is clearly and explicitly for students to learn (with learning to write as a route to, or specialized instance of, learning). In contrast, the workplace operates as a COP whose activities are focused on material or discursive outcomes, and in which participants are often unaware of the learning that occurs.

Freedman, Adam, and Smart (1994) illustrate the degree to which learning and the learner are the foci of the writing tasks assigned in a university class, even when these tasks were presented as simulations of workplace situations, and the reports elicited ended with recommendations for action. As shown in that article, the real goal of the writing was neither action nor policy, but rather the demonstration that students knew the appropriate arguments to make in order to ground appropriate claims in the relevant arenas (as circumscribed by the nature of the course content). Both students and instructors understood that this demonstration of learning was the goal of the writing. This was contrasted with the action- or policy-orientation of workplace writing produced in the research unit of a government institution.

One consequence of this difference in the goals for the writing is that, in the workplace, our own research and that of others has repeatedly shown that it is often unclear to newcomers *that* they must learn, let alone *what and how* they must learn, and from *whom* they can learn. In the government agencies where we observed, newcomers often asserted that they did not think that they would need to learn to write differently. (See also MacKinnon, 1993.) And when the supervisors were asked whether they considered the novices' learning to be one goal of the tasks they assigned them, their response was an unequivocal: "Hell, NO! They can learn on their own time." (As it turned out, these very supervisors were expert masters and mentors; they simply did not think of learning as implicated in the enterprise because it was not their explicit focal goal.)

Role of Authenticity

Another way of illuminating this difference in orientation is suggested by the following. A key criterion of success in an internship relates to the degree to which the learner sees the task as authentic—that is, one that has consequences in its context. One intern we observed expressed his frustration over being assigned a "make-work project," one that his coworkers did not see as relevant to the operations of the office and whose ultimate audience was as undefined for his supervisor as it was for him. In chapter 10, we hear disaffection expressed by an intern in social work whose supervisor gave him work that seemed unrelated to the real work of the department. "I was essentially isolated from the team," he complains, and thus he cannot see the work as authentic. In the school context, in contrast, any task is seen as authentic insofar as it is assigned by the instructor. From the perspective of the classroom, simulations are as authentic as academic essays or lab reports or book reviews.

Attenuation

In the workplaces we have observed, the assignment of appropriate authentic attenuated tasks to newcomers required skill, subtlety, tact, and imagination on the part of the oldtimer, especially given the complex and multifaceted nature of the work environments. Not every mentor was up to that challenge. Sometimes, newcomers were given routine tasks at the outset, much to their frustration. At other times, however, tasks considerably below the ability and professional orientation of novices were assigned as a way of allowing them enough time to observe the complex operations. More imaginative oldtimers were able to provide interns with authentic and more challenging tasks immediately on their entry, tasks that were both within the competence of very green newcomers and that engaged them in processes that ultimately enabled fuller participation. For example, one intern was asked to take minutes at a round of negotiations; the task was authentic and necessary, it was in her ken, and it allowed her to observe the complex dynamics of the negotiating process as well as giving her an overview of the whole activity in which her work was to play a part. Observing the negotiations helped her understand how the different parts of the task she would be involved in related to the whole. It also opened her eyes to the dynamics of negotiating as well as to the competing value systems at play.

Reflecting on this initial task in her placement, this intern emphasized the value of this experience in that it was relatively easy, familiarized her with a "government format" (notes to file), emphasized the importance of accuracy, "showed them you know when to ask for help," and provided an opportunity to find out about the context of the meetings. A second intern was asked to compare in detail different sets of land claim agreements: the point-for-point careful (and later collaboratively performed) comparisons introduced the newcomer to the whole activity, and engaged the newcomer in thinking through and reorganizing the relevant issues by operating on the discourse that was one material outcome of the activity.

The necessity to involve newcomers in authentic attenuated tasks, however, has certain consequences for the nature of the involvement, consequences that distinguished such learning sharply from school learning. These include both the improvisatory quality of the learning opportunities in the workplace in contrast to the carefully sequenced curriculum possible in the classroom as well as the relative messiness of the workplace context in comparison to the simplified and facilitated context of the classroom. Further consequences arise as attenuation is decreased and newcomers engage in the near-autonomy of legitimate peripheral participation; for example, learning opportunities often occur after performance of tasks, when newcomers and oldtimers review work already completed.

Improvisatory Quality of Learning Opportunities

One consequence of the necessity for authentic participation is something noted by Lave and Wenger (1991) and observed frequently in our work: the highly improvisatory character of the interns' tasks (as opposed to those in the classroom, where a curriculum can be more or less planned in advance—allowing for some degree of improvisation and responsiveness to learners). Consequently, we saw the intern described being pulled away from one task in order to prepare a briefing note for a newly elected government minister.

A negative consequence of the opportunistic quality of learning in the workplace is that, because the tasks are authentic and respond to external demands unrelated to a learner's needs, there are moments when the delicate apportioning of parts of the task must be truncated, and—even in the best internships—the master must take over. Sometimes, there are deadlines to be met; at other times, the supervisor will suddenly find herself short-staffed. And often, the supervisor cannot be certain that the intern can operate under the added pressure. As one intern reflected, "he [the supervisor] would always think about it first before he would ask for my involvement—to see if he thought that I could function under that pressure. And if he thought I couldn't, he would do it himself alone."

To put it another way, there is no possibility for carefully sequencing and designing the course curriculum. The institution of schooling gives instructors a degree of control, allowing them to sequence activities and to simplify tasks. (For example, in an undergraduate law course, we were struck by the sophistication of the sequence of the tasks, such that—among other things—the textual analyses showed increasing degrees of syntactic complexity and genre realization over the course of the year (see Freedman, 1990, 1996).

Messiness of Work Context

As suggested in other studies (Freedman et al., 1994; Dias & Paré, in press) and in the next chapter, even in a university course in which case studies are used, and even when the case studies are not invented but based on actual histories, there is enormous simplification and abstraction from the untidy realities of the everyday world as experienced. No matter how much irrelevance and ambiguity these case histories include, they are still abstractions from the experience of the workplace—abstracted in order to facilitate learning. As Corey (1976) writes:

> In spite of [their realism], it is true that they are not, after all, actual business situations. First, the information comes to the student in neatly written form. Managers in business and government, by contrast, accumulate facts and opinions through memos, conversations, statistical reports, and the public press.
>
> Second, a case is designed to fit a particular unit of class time and to focus on a certain category of problems, for instance, marketing, production, or finance....
>
> Third, a case is a snapshot taken at a point in time. In reality, business problems are often seen as a continuum calling for some action today, further consideration, and action tomorrow. (p. 3)

In other words, the noise is removed and the task is simplified and focused; something like Bereiter and Scardamalia's (1987) procedural facilitation is taking place. The tasks cannot be so simplified in the workplace. It is true that mentors will often model their thinking about issues in such a way as to reveal to novices how to limit and define the problems. It is also true that newcomers may be assigned only a part of the task. The task itself, however, cannot be simplified.

For example, the social and political relations in the workplace context are considerably more complex than in schools, as we demonstrated in chapter 6. Tensions between COPs and among oldtimers must be discerned and then navigated. Some of the complexities of relations are evident in the following extract where a supervisor explains to an intern why the two of them have been having such a difficult time obtaining feedback on a document from a superior: "She was not too concerned, because she was ticked off that she wasn' t invited to the meeting. That's why she wasn' t consistent.... So that was an obstacle to my getting out of [her] what I was looking for." In fact, novices not only have to determine whom to trust as a guide (as we will see), but they also must learn to make that choice without alienating other would-be guides.

Guide-Learner Roles

A further difference between the two contexts for learning derives from the differences in the roles of, and interactions between, guides and learners in the two settings. The roles are more clearly defined in the school setting. The teacher is designated as the authority for the duration of the interaction (recognizing that this duration is relatively short). During internships and apprenticeships, roles are more fluid and indeterminate: there are new oldtimers and old-oldtimers; fresh newcomers and more seasoned newcomers. Furthermore, the expectation is that newcomers will become oldtimers; a possibility entertained only in the fantasy of schoolchildren (in the context of specific classes).

One consequence of this phenomenon for novices in the workplace is that they must learn to discern what their role is to be and from whom they can learn. A phenomenon we observed in a number of settings was the resistance felt by novices or interns to their would-be or could-be guides. Because in some cases there was no clearly sanctioned institutional teaching authority vested in their superiors, and because their supervisors were often relatively new oldtimers, interns often resisted and consequently missed opportunities for learning. One intern, for example, refused to acknowledge the opportunities for learning offered by his supervisor, because of her relative "greenness." That is, he incorporated her revisions to his draft of a document because he had to, but he refused to acknowledge the appropriateness of, and hence to learn from, such editing changes as "land claims" to "land claim agreements," which he kept insisting to us were really synonymous.

Furthermore, as the different terms connote, the relations between oldtimers and newcomers are far more complex, subtle, shifting, and nuanced than the relatively stable and straightforward relations between professors and students. The longer a novice remains in the workplace, the less attenuation is provided and the more attention is shifted from learning to the performance of professional duties. To quote Hanks (1991), "legitimate peripheral participation is not a simple participation structure in which an apprentice occupies a particular role at the edge of a larger process. It is rather an interactive process in which the apprentice engages by simultaneously performing in *several roles*—status subordinate, learning practitioner, sole responsible agent in minor parts of the performance, aspiring expert, and so forth—each implying a different sort of responsibility, a different set of role relations, and a different interactive involvement" (p. 23).

Our observations showed one intern taking on a range of these roles, all in one morning: with respect to the use of technology, he was the expert; when time constraints forced his supervisor to take control of the whole task, the intern's role as a status subordinate was clear; for most of the morning, he operated as a learning practitioner, working collaboratively, but in an attenuated role, with his supervisor; at other points, he was named sole responsible agent for specific tasks (e.g., finding, and contracting work out to, a map-maker). Later, in an interview with us, his supervisor kept stressing the degree to which he, as mentor, learns from newcomers: not only the most current academic theory but also different approaches to complex internal social and political relations.

Evaluation

Earlier we emphasized the fact that school writing is learning-oriented and learner-oriented. To be fair, one must acknowledge the equally pressing institutional reality: to evaluate and hence to rank students. While the instructor's focal goal is that her students learn, that goal is limited by the equally pressing need to grade and rank. This means that, in the end, the university professor has a vested interest in a quality spread, something that necessarily qualifies and limits the degree and the nature of the mentoring and collaborative performance possible. The guide-learner roles in the university are affected by the fact that, in the end and at every point, the guide evaluates the learner.

In the workplace, the shared goal of both newcomer and oldtimer is the production of the best texts possible. There is some evaluation in the workplace, of course, but it is far less frequent and pervasive. And as the newcomer moves toward professional practice—that is, from attenuated to legitimate participation—the oldtimer's role as evaluator is gradually diminished. Eventually, for specific tasks, newcomer and oldtimer are on the same side, working independently or together on a task that will be evaluated by some outsider, and evaluated often in terms of its rhetorical or material success—in persuading others, in effecting action.

One consequence of this is that there is no use of tests and grades, and sparse use of praise and blame. Performance is evaluated by the overall success of the endeavor—the success of the writing, for example, as a rhetorical or social action. One of the interns recognized that his success in producing an initial document had earned him his supervisor's trust and he was then given more significant tasks. "So it was a big test," he said. The reward for success was that novices were entrusted with more responsibility and riskier tasks.

Sites of Learning

Perhaps the most striking distinction between the school and the workplace as contexts for learning, however, is that the sites and moments for learning in the two settings are quite different. Consequently, when students move from university to workplace, because they are alert to one kind of learning, they do not necessarily recognize the opportunities for learning in the new setting.

In the classrooms we observed, the performance was always facilitated as follows: there was a great deal of careful stage managing of the prompt, of the task, and of the discursive context. The writing itself took place either alone, or occasionally in collaboration with peers, with an occasional visit to the professor or teaching assistant for advice. The final submission of the paper by the students almost always meant the end of their involvement with the task.

In the workplace, the initial task itself was less controlled and shaped by the guide; typically, it was initiated and constrained by external sources. There was some collaborative interpretation of the task and often collaborative performance of the task at some stages of the writing. But the most significant difference was that completion of the draft meant the beginning of a long process of iteration.

The most important site for learning in the workplace, as a result, comes during the kind of extensive feedback described by Paradis, Dobrin, and Miller (1985) as "document cycling": "the editorial process by which [supervisors] helped staff members restructure, focus, and clarify their written work" (p. 285). Smart (1993) describes the typical process in a government agency that we observed:

> In all genres, composing processes are structured by a similar cycle of writer/reviewer collaboration. Typically [after composing a draft for review], the writer incorporates rounds of spoken and written feedback from the supervisor into successive revisions until the latter is satisfied. At this point, another round of collaboration usually occurs, involving the writer, the supervisor, and a more senior reviewer. As the collaborative cycle continues, unnecessary technical detail is filtered out, key concepts are defined, and the argument becomes increasingly issue-centered, coherent, and succinct. When the chief of the department decides the text has been refined sufficiently, it is sent to its executive readership. (p. 131)

The intensive and extensive nature of the feedback offered at each stage is suggested by this description offered by a senior executive at a government financial institution we observed:

> When you do things at [this agency], it's a process that someone writes a paper (and it's an important paper—other than a one-pager or two-pager), when they write you a paper, you read it first from a high level—find out if the ideas are there, are the arguments consistent. So, when someone does something for me, I say well, "yeah, you're kinda on the right track." And I say, "Go back and try

this, try that." So, it doesn't get down to the nitty-gritty of the writing at this point. You're still at the, almost the methodological stage, trying to deal with the question that's being posed. And so you go through *a number of iterations*. The person will come back with the paper answering a different question or adding another question to the analysis and it's not until the very end that we'll say, "Now I know all the ideas are there, now I'm going to read it from the perspective of how it's written, are the ideas now expressed clearly."

Another way of looking at the differences between the two settings is this: in the university context, most of the contextual shaping and co-participation took place before the preparation of the first draft; at the workplaces we have observed, although some collaboration took place during the generating and planning, the draft handed in to the supervisor marked the beginning of a long and intense process of responding and revising, a process during which attuned learners could intuit the expectations of the genre in that context and institution. The important point to note is that all the comments are collaborative, not evaluative. The revising itself is an intense period of co-participation where learning could and should take place.

Complicating the fact that the site for learning is different, especially at the revision stage, is the interference from their previous learning patterns that suggests that anything written in response to a draft by a grader is evaluative and final. For these novices entering the workplace, then, the comments written on their drafts often meant negative evaluation and evoked resistance, rather than being recognized as opportunities for learning (and further collaborative performance). The implication of this is that workplace newcomers need to learn to learn again.

LEARNING TO LEARN AGAIN

There is considerable evidence in our research (Freedman, 1987, 1990; Freedman et al., 1994) and that of others (Berkenkotter & Huckin, 1995; Herrington, 1985; McCarthy, 1987; Walvoord & McCarthy, 1993) that university students are expected to learn new genres as they move from class to class. Such learning is both so inevitable and so naturalized that it is hardly commented on by the students (Freedman, 1987). Consequently, in moving to the workplace, the same expectation seems to hold: there may be new genres to be learned, but the modes of learning will be the same. (See initial assurance expressed in Anson & Forsberg, 1990; MacKinnon, 1993.) However, after some time on the job, there are commonly reported feelings of disjuncture and anxiety quite different from those experienced in their schooling (Anson & Forsberg, 1990; Freedman & Adam, 1995; MacKinnon, 1993). It is our claim that these feelings are not so much due to the need to learn new genres (such as memos, briefing notes, reports)—something they have been doing regularly throughout their schooling—but rather due to the need to learn new ways to learn such genres.

Popken (1992) writes about the particular problems associated with discourse transfer. What we observed was a related problem: inappropriate transfer of learning patterns. Many newcomers we observed did not think that they would have to learn at all—and certainly not in new ways. For example, one intern, Julie, viewed each task as though it was set in a university context, with its clearly defined beginning and end, and its clearly demarcated occasions for learning (in class and through assignments). Consequently, she consistently insisted on "getting on with her work," rather than availing herself of the learning opportunity offered her every day by the supervisor who invited her to take a short walk with him and another intern. Every day she refused the opportunity for shared reflection on and learning about what had been happening in the complex political and social rhetorical context of their workplace. It was during these walks that a previous intern had learned how to "read" and interpret the meetings, the interactions, as an insider.

Julie consistently missed these opportunities, misconstruing them as new assignments, rather than as occasions for learning. "I didn't know I was expected to go to that meeting," she said resentfully, when invited to a meeting that would have given her a broader picture of the activity as a whole, and thus would have clarified her specific task. "Was I *supposed* to come?" she asked under her breath in annoyance. In other words, Julie was still mentally situated in the school context, where specific tasks are set out in clearly defined ways, in the context of clearly defined discursive environments (i.e., the assigned readings and the three or four hours a week of lecture and/or seminar).

Another kind of "failure to learn" was evinced by Curtis, who, as described earlier, resisted learning from his supervisor because he felt that she was too "green" an oldtimer, and that her comments in revising were simply matters of personal stylistic preference. Thus, Curtis refused to recognize the legitimacy of changing "land claim agreements" to "land claims," a distinction central to the operation of that particular office. "I'm not making an effort.... They' re going to edit it anyway."

This theme was echoed by a number of interns. Rather than learning from the revisions suggested to their work, revisions to wording that often signified a great deal about how this particular culture viewed the world and the distinctions that were important there, the interns chose to see these changes as idiosyncratic personal preferences that they were being forced to accept but that they could resist learning from. Asked about what she had learned from her supervisor's comments, one intern reflected: "I don't feel so much that it's the government way versus my way. It's just my way and Gill's way and Sandra's way. And my way isn't wrong, and when I'm the Director, I'm gonna write the memo however I want to." One fundamental difference in the two contexts studied, and a key to understanding the learning disjunctures experienced by some newcomers, is the value placed on individualism in the university culture, as opposed to the more collaborative ethos of government agencies and other workplaces. (A negative view would substitute the words "anonymous" or "leveling" for "collaborative.") In the end, all university students are graded individually, even when they collaborate on specific assignments. Transfer of this individualist ethos sometimes interferes with the kind of collaboration necessary for performing and learning in the workplace. There was a kind of egotism in the early interviews with novices or interns: "It's my style, why should I have to change it?" This is exacerbated by the fact that students are not expected to revise their papers in response to their professor's written comments accompanying the grade. The comments are there to justify the grade, rather than serve as an invitation to revise and resubmit.

Furthermore, there is a difference in the nature of the ownership. At least in theory, students' ideas belong to them. Writing a paper is not a shared enterprise between student and professor, and professors are often criticized for plagiarizing from students in a way not conceivable in a workplace. As suggested in Freedman et al. (1994), writers in the government workplace we have observed rely heavily on intertextual references to each others' work (sometimes cited, sometimes not). Employee writing is kept on file, often for frequent consultation; student writing is filed, if at all, at home, and rarely consulted thereafter.

To sum up: in both contexts, the learners learn new genres. The two processes are similar in very important respects: both are based on the notion of learning through performance or engagement—learning through doing, as opposed to earlier cognitive notions of learning through receiving bodies of knowledge. What is entailed for the "teacher" in each setting is, in Hanks' (1991) words, "not giving a discrete body of abstract knowledge" but, instead, creating opportunities where people can learn "to perform by actually engaging in the process" (p. 14).

Common to both contexts as well is the careful control of the learners' involvement and engagement. In each case, the conditions for participation are attenuated: in school, the curriculum is sequenced in terms of order of difficulty, and student performance is facilitated in myriad ways; in the work place, at least initially, only some of the task is given over to the learner, and it is this attenuation (and generally a subtle and highly nuanced attenuation) that allows for the learning. That is, what is learned is learned through activity and through social engagement: instructors and learners collaborate, in a broad sense, and one result is that learners are able to do something at the end that they have not done or been able to do before. In addition, learning in both settings is achieved through sociocultural mediation of tools—especially linguistic and other semiotic signs.

On the other hand, there is this radical difference between the two processes: in one case, that of school-situated facilitated performance, the goal of the activity itself is learning; in the workplace, through processes of attenuated authentic participation, the learning is incidental, and occurs as an integral but tacit part of participation in COP, whose activities are oriented towards practical or material outcomes. The upshot is that, whatever the commonalities, when students leave university to enter the workplace, they not only need to learn new genres of discourse, they need to learn new ways to learn such genres. The two kinds of processes, while sharing certain fundamental features, are different enough that the transition from one setting to the other poses particular problems and senses of disjuncture, anxiety, or displacement. These feelings are inevitable, given the nature of the institutions, and not signs of student or school failure.

CONCLUSION

The distinctions we make in this chapter and the next between facilitated performance, attenuated authentic participation, and legitimate peripheral participation allow us some degree of precision in categorizing and analyzing incidents of situated learning, but the differences between these categories often blur. Thus, if we focus only on the relationship between, and the actions of, newcomers and oldtimers in work settings, we may very well find a kind of collaborative guidance through performance that is at least broadly similar to such guidance in school settings. And more formal learning opportunities in the workplace may place apprentices in situations that are virtually indistinguishable from classroom situations. Alternatively, one can find examples of school interactions that attempt to approximate more closely those of COPs, where the learning is intended to be like that found in instances of attenuated authentic participation or legitimate peripheral participation (see Gutierrez, 1994, Rogoff 1994). There are, after all, classes in which tasks with real-world consequences are selected and where students work in collaborative groups of peers.

Without denying the value of such experiments, nor the possibility of seeing in some mentor–novice relations in the workplace interactions that resemble facilitated performance, our claim is that it is very useful to continue considering facilitated performance, attenuated authentic participation, and legitimate peripheral participation as distinct in important ways, and in ways that privilege no one above the other, but rather reflect the institutional constraints and societal needs expressed in each.

From the perspective of institutional constraints, we must acknowledge, however uncomfortable it may be, that the institutional realities of schooling militate against a total appropriation of the apprenticeship model. A pervasive goal of schooling (not the only goal, but an inevitable one) is that, by the end, students be ranked or slotted. Hubboch (1989) and Petraglia (1995) have each commented on our discipline's deep discomfort with that reality: but denial is a poor refuge. At the very least, this need to grade and evaluate contaminates the relationship between students and teachers, at least to some degree. They may be locked in Elbow's (1986) "embrace of contraries," but at least one pole of the contraries is a push against the kind of collaboration and shared intention that is possible in the workplace.

On the other hand, although we may chafe at these constraints and seek different kinds of interactions, we should acknowledge as well the advantages of schooling, which also have become normalized through their tacitness. Schools do offer the opportunity for an uncontaminated focus on learning and the learner—uncontaminated by concerns for results or material outcomes. This allows for a kind of teaching that is perhaps not possible in the workplace, one which involves sequencing of curriculum and close attention to the learner's pace.

Our choice of the terms *performance* versus *participation* has allowed us to highlight an important contrast. Schools indeed do provide occasions for students to perform, with the attendant implications of display and attention. We must remember, though, that the attention is directed to the learner and the learning—so much so, in fact, that the nature and the degree of facilitation and orchestration are often invisible, even to researchers.

In contrast, the workplace privileges participation: collaborative engagement in tasks whose outcomes take center stage, and where the learning is often tacit and implicit. A subtly different alignment and attunement is at play. Guides and learners play different roles, with differently nuanced strategies for the necessary attenuation of tasks. Our use of *attenuated participation* and *legitimate participation* allows us to distinguish between levels of autonomy, and points to the newcomer's gradual and subtle move toward professional practice, a transition we explore in the following chapter.

10

VIRTUAL REALITIES: TRANSITIONS FROM UNIVERSITY TO WORKPLACE WRITING

In this chapter we consider contexts for learning that further exemplify the theoretical discussion provided in the previous chapter. We have argued that learning is a situated and contingent experience, and that school-based simulations of workplace writing fail to prepare students for professional writing because they cannot adequately replicate the local rhetorical complexity of workplace contexts. By this we do not mean to suggest that course-based case studies are a waste of time, but the goals of such learning opportunities need to be reexamined, especially as they relate to the development of professional writing ability. We believe that course-based case studies provide an essential introduction to the ways of thinking and knowing valued by disciplines and encouraged by the rhetorical practices of those disciplines. In order to learn about professional writing, however, that introduction must be followed by more extensive and integrated workplace experiences, such as work-study programs, internships, on-the-job training, and other forms of transition between school and work.

The learning continuum proposed in chapter 9 describes a range of experiences that provide ever greater distance from the deliberately fashioned educational contexts of the school and ever greater integration into the improvised and often spontaneous learning opportunities of the workplace. (Note: Although the movement from facilitated performance to legitimate peripheral participation does capture the professional development of many who pass through school and into the workplace, it is not a required sequence; some people learn their practice entirely within the workplace, without benefit of the careful scaffolding of facilitated performance.) In describing that transition, we have used the terms *facilitated performance* to refer to the conditions and contexts for teaching and learning in universities, *attenuated authentic participation* to point to the early stages of closely monitored and supervised learning in the workplace, and *legitimate peripheral participation* (Lave & Wenger, 1991) to describe the activities that lead to learning for newcomers who have achieved some degree of autonomy in their workplace involvement.

As the learner moves out from the classroom toward professional practice, the moments and sites of learning become less clearly defined, and certain key features of learning and teaching change. There is a gradual increase in the authenticity of tasks; that is, their consequences and their influence on others and on activity escalates, and there is a parallel growth in their complexity or messiness: workplace tasks lack the exact moments of beginning and ending, the stated evaluation criteria, and the sharp divisions of labor that usually characterize school work. At the same time, there is a steady decrease in explicit attention to learning and in the degree of guidance or attenuation provided; students move from close supervision to autonomous practice as they make the transition from school to work. There are, too, subtle shifts in authority and expertise between learner and teacher; in school, the power and knowledge imbalance is marked, obvious, but newcomers to the workplace often bring certain kinds of expertise (technical, theoretical) that oldtimers who supervise them do not have. A similar shift occurs in terms of evaluation; in school contexts, the learner is evaluated by the teacher, but in the workplace the apprentice and supervisor are assessed together, because newcomer and oldtimer often work as a team. Underlying these changes is a shift from the epistemic function of school writing (the individual student's construction of knowledge) to the collective epistemic and instrumental goals of the workplace (the construction and application of institutional or community knowledge).

In this chapter we look at students learning to write in and for different contexts, some in school, some at work, and some in between. Although the writing tasks in the first two contexts attempted to simulate or suggest aspects of the rhetorical contexts of professional writing, neither could escape their ultimate location within an academic setting. And, it should be noted, neither was presented as an opportunity to learn how to write professionally. Writing in the school contexts was at the service of learning the discipline's values, beliefs, and ways of knowing. Learning occured in the workplace as well, but there writing was at the service of the community. The first three settings described below mark points on a trajectory away from the school and into the workplace; the last, which we describe in greater detail, represents a final stage on that continuum. Our analysis of each stage demonstrates the extent to which learning is contextual and contingent.

LEARNING TO WRITE AT SCHOOL

As explained in the previous chapter, the theoretical frame that accounts for how students learned to write in the university disciplinary classes we observed is best captured by the term facilitated performance. Our argument is that this frame, based on Rogoff's (1990) notion of guided participation, accounts for how university students learn discipline-specific writing in much the same way as guided participation accounts for early child language acquisition or cognitive apprenticeship in middle-class homes.

The most salient commonality is that the guide in both cases, caregiver and teacher, is oriented entirely to the learner and to the learner's learning. In fact, the activity is being undertaken primarily for the sake of the learner, and although the conventions of neither writing nor language are explicitly taught, they are learned because of the carefully shaped context. There is a focused and centered concentration on the learner and the activity which is quite different from what we see in the instances of workplace-based learning described below (and that, as we noted in the previous chapter, is quite different from what Rogoff [1993] and Heath [1983] reported in non-middle-class child-rearing).

Not only is the guide's attention focused on the learner, but the whole social context has been organized by the guide for the sake of the learner. Rogoff's caregiver organizes the storytime experience in much the same way that the instructors we observed orchestrate their courses (within certain temporal, spatial, organizational constraints): readings are set, lectures are delivered, seminars are or are not organized, working groups are or are not set up, assignments are specified—all geared toward enabling the learners to learn certain material.

Further, students did not, in the courses observed, learn to write new genres on the basis of explicit direction by their guides (the instructors and teaching assistants), except in the crudest terms with respect to format, length, and subject matter (Freedman, 1993). Nevertheless the writing was shaped and constrained from the first meeting of the course—that is, from its specification on the course outline and, more significantly, from the first words uttered by the instructor.

Our observations of these classes, and the students composing for them, revealed that learning new genres in the classroom came about as a result of carefully orchestrated processes of collaborative performance between course instructor and students: the students learned through doing, and specifically learned through performing with an attuned expert who structured the curriculum in such a way as to give to the students more and more difficult tasks. The instructor both specified the task and set that task in a rich discursive context. Both the collaborative performance and the orchestration of a richly evocative semiotic context enabled the acquisition and performance of the new genres.

At the beginning of a course in Financial Analysis, for example, the instructor assigned cases to be written up at home and then he himself modeled in class appropriate approaches to the data, identifying key issues and specifying possible recommendations for action. As they attempted to write up the cases themselves at home, the students were "extremely frustrated" because "you have to do a case before you have the tools to know how to do it." "It's like banging your head against a wall." However, the modeling in class, *especially in the context of the students' struggles to find meaning in the data themselves*, gradually enabled the students to make such intellectual moves themselves. At the beginning, "when he would tell us the real issue, we're like—where did that come from?" Then "When you're done and he takes it up in class, you finally know how to do it!" Modeling what the students would later do themselves, the instructor presented a number of cases at the beginning of the course. Like the mother with the storybook, the instructor showed the students first where to look and then what to say, picking out the relevant data from the information in the case:

> "What's the significance of 7 and 8 in the text? Did it add to your thinking about this case?"

> "At what market share restriction would that growth strategy not work?"

> "Assuming best case scenario, what will this company look like in 5 years?"

He constructed arguments, using the warrants of, and based on the values and ideology valorized in, the discipline. Drawing on the simulated purposes for the case, he pointed to the importance of looking at and presenting information in particular ways:

> "As a consultant to the bank, is this a critical value to know?"

> "In real life, you have to quantify this relationship between business risk and financial risk."

After students began presenting the cases themselves orally in class, he provided corrective feedback:

> "Walk people through how you thought about the problem."

> "Let people know what the agenda is and your role."

Gradually students were inducted into the ways of knowing, that is, the ways of construing and interpreting phenomena, valued in that discipline. That is, although they were learning a school genre that bore little resemblance to workplace genres, they were beginning to participate in the type of thinking encouraged by the rhetorical practices of their discipline.

We see in facilitated performance many of the elements specified by Wood, Bruner, and Ross (1976) as functions of the tutor in scaffolding (as quoted in Rogoff, 1990, pp. 93–94). The task is defined by the tutor; the tutor demonstrates an idealized version of the act to be performed; and the tutor indicates or dramatizes the crucial discrepancies between what the child has done and the ideal solution. These processes of collaborative performance offer part of the answer to how the students learned to write the genres expected of them. In addition, the instructor set up a rich discursive context, through his lectures and through the readings, and it is through the mediation of these signs that the students were able to engage appropriately in the tasks set.

Wertsch (1991), drawing on Bakhtin, talks of the power of dialogism, and of echoing (or ventriloquating) of social languages and speech genres. The students that we observed responded—ventriloquistically—to the readings and the professor's discourse, as they worked through the tasks set for them. Initially, they picked up (and transformed in the context of their preexistent conversational patterns) the social language or register they had heard. Here are oral samples culled from the students' conversational interchanges as they worked on producing their case study:

> Allison: I figured this is how we should structure it.... First, how did they get there is the first thing.
>
> Peter: So that's ...
>
> Allison: Business versus financial risk or operations versus debt. Whatever ... Then ... like we will get it from the bankers' perspective.
>
> Peter: Yeah, that's pretty much like what I was thinking too.
>
> Allison: So, right now I have their thing before '78. How do you want it, pre-'78 or post-'78? This is what I did. I went through all....
>
> Peter: Internal comparison and stuff.
>
> ******
>
> Allison: I guess the biggest thing is the debt-to-equity ratio. Notice that? X has way more equity. If you look at Y, their equity compared to their debts is nowhere near, it's not even in the ballpark.
>
> Peter: Which company is it that took a whole bunch of short-term debt?

Then, in the writing of their papers, the conversational syntax, lexicon, and intonational contours of their conversational exchanges disappeared, as they reproduced the discipline-specific terms in the context of academic written English, achieving, thus, the written social register designated by their professor as that of a "financial analyst" (see Freedman et al., 1994). In the final draft of a case study, we find the following:

> Short-term debt restructuring is a necessity. The 60% ratio must be reduced to be more in line with past trends and with the competition. This will be achieved by extension of debt maturities, conversion of debt to equity, reduction of interest rates, as well as deferral of interest payments.

In other words, through the mediation of and appropriation of the social languages provided by the professor's discourse and the readings, the students created the new genres expected of them: ways of knowing became ways of saying. The epistemic social motive of school is met when the professor determines that the discipline's knowledge and ways of knowing are satisfactorily displayed in the completed text; then, a grade is assigned and the text reaches closure.

BETWEEN SCHOOL AND WORK

It is possible to distinguish between school-based attempts to introduce students to disciplinary ways of knowing, such as the case-study assignment described above, and those fuller immersions that occur when students balance their time and attention between the classroom and a workplace. Various forms of such an arrangement may allow students to make forays into work settings, receive visits from practitioners, handle professional documentation, and address actual workplace issues and problems, all in the context of a particular course. Evaluation in these situations, even when there is consultation with practitioners, is primarily an instructor's responsibility. Typically, students in this type of course prepare reports for the workplaces they visit, and representatives of the workplace may be invited to hear and respond to oral presentations of student research results. (Such an assignment is described in chap. 4.)

One of the most successful of this kind of learning experience that we have observed occurred in a 4th-year course in systems analysis. The course engaged students in writing that, in contrast to the simulation of a case study, succeeded in giving them a real experience of workplace discourse, though it was a highly scaffolded and protected introduction. However, as with the case study, there was no explicit writing instruction in the systems analysis course, and no stated intention to teach workplace writing.

The systems analysis course was organized as follows: every year that she teaches the course, the instructor finds six client-organizations who need to have their systems analyzed and redesigned; a total of 30 students are allowed to register, and students are selected by competition; the students are divided into groups of five. Criteria for nomination to specific groups include the following: each group is assigned someone with a background in accounting and another with a background in computing, as well as someone who has a car. A cardinal rule is that friends are to be separated, so that students gain experience working with people that they are not already familiar with or even fond of. Each group is assigned to a separate place of work, and must consequently solve the specific problem in that work environment. In order to do so, and in the course of doing so, they produce the following three kinds of documents:

1. a problem definition document (on the basis of a feasibility study);
2. systems specification document (on the basis of their systems analysis), which includes several alternatives as part of the structured specification;
3. a general design document.

In order to perform these tasks, students must go to the workplace to interview a range of practitioners there, the range determined by the needs and possibilities of that specific work environment. At the first interview, they are accompanied by the course instructor, who guides the interview when necessary and spends considerable time going over what was learned with the students involved.

In addition, each group reports back to the class as a whole three times, giving oral versions of their drafts of each of the three key documents. After these presentations, they receive feedback from the class, hand in their written document to the instructor, and then, at a separately scheduled interview, receive intensive feedback from her as to appropriate revisions. Sometimes further interviews with her are necessary. When she is satisfied, a written document is presented to the client, sometimes accompanied by an oral presentation, if the client so desires. The course is a half-course, the timeline is carefully spelled out at the beginning, and nothing is handed in late.

Clearly, this is school work with a difference, and that difference is the dual exploitation of both the academic and workplace settings. The workplace adds some critical features to the learning context. Perhaps most importantly, it provides authentic tasks. As the professor said about this course (Duxbury & Chinneck, 1993), "the process involves coping systematically with the com-

plexities of the real world, including both human and technological limitations." Students have to "limit the area of study, abstract essential features,
subdivide a complex whole into parts of manageable size and model a real
system to show the relationship among its components." As opposed to traditional lectures in systems analysis and design, which give the students a
tremendous amount of technical information, this course conveys the real-
world people skills needed to be a good systems analyst. The communication
skills, diplomacy and other human issues are not easily transmitted in a book
or in the classroom.

Students gain experience in handling ambiguous situations and in developing solutions subject to real-world constraints. Working with actual problems
also develops analytical skills and problem-solving abilities, gives an understanding of the importance of organizational influences on systems design and
the impact that a user-requested change has on the analysis and design process.

More specifically, the instructor lists some of the strengths of the program
as follows:

> students gain a "more global perspective on the systems analysis process";
> students "learn to work cooperatively in groups"; students learn to "critique each
> other"; the task "enables students to integrate the knowledge gained from other
> business courses."

In comparison to case-study writing, the writing in this course is situated
quite differently along the continuum that is mapped in Table 10.1. Like
case-study writing, this course is situated in an institutional context, to the extent
that it has a course number, it counts as credit toward a degree, and it is
constrained by the time limits of a single semester. But there are important ways
in which it is different, ways that are revealed especially when we think in terms

TABLE 10.1

Changing Aspects of Writing in Three Contexts

	Case-Study	School/Workplace	Internship
1. audience:	instructor; colleagues	client; instructor	supervisor;
2. social motive:	epistemic	epistemic; instrumental	epistemic; instrumental
3. reader's concern:	writer's knowing (value to student)	writer's knowing; value to client	value to collective
4. knowledge:	shared	shared and new	new
5. reader's goal:	evaluation	evaluation; ensure best text	ensure best text; apply knowledge
6. reader's comments:	justify grade	revision-oriented; response	revision-oriented; response
7. closure	grade	grade; indeterminate	indeterminate

of the writing's double social motive, one served by the rhetorical exigences of school work, the other by the exigences of the workplace.

Our analysis of student interactions, composing sessions, and drafts, shows how the systems analysis course offered an interesting hybrid of features, a kind of bridge across the gap between school and work. The audience was both instructor and client. (The instructor was always the first reader and her views, as evaluator, were always important. At the same time, the students always referred to their clients and to their clients' needs and goals in their composing sessions.)

One textual indication of the hybrid nature of this transaction was that students kept having to adjust the amount of shared knowledge they provided: as they went from presenting their documents to class and teacher to preparing the document for their clients, they needed to revise the amount and kind of shared information. A recurrent feature of their revision was the removal of information that they could assume to be shared with their clients.

The social motive of the writing, like that of the workplace, was to recommend real-world action. (On the other hand, an incidental or possibly auxiliary purpose was always kept in mind: an epistemic goal for the writing was recognized by both the instructor and the students in their discussions.) The whole exercise was undertaken in order to learn how to perform in a real-world setting, with real-world constraints. Contrast this with the response, cited in chapter 9, of officers in a government agency who said with some degree of irritation that their novice employees could "learn on their own time." (It's not that learning does not occur; it's that no one sees this as an institutional goal.)

Perhaps the most revealing difference was the changed role of the teacher. Rather than teacher as evaluator, the instructor functioned in the role of supervisor: she collaborated with the students extensively. She accompanied them to the first interview, and discussed the interview with them afterward, carefully pointing to key features and eliciting appropriate understanding. For each piece of writing, she both evaluated (gave a low grade at the beginning) and wrote extensive suggestions for revision, insisting that they revise until they produced the best possible text.

This points to a larger kind of difference. This writing that the students were doing in the systems analysis course was different from typical student writing in that the instructor regarded it as reflecting on her (and the institution) in much the same way that a subordinate's writing in the workplace reflects on the manager. This stands in sharp contrast to most instructors' attitudes toward their students' writing, which is considered to reflect on the students' rather than the teachers' competence.

A related point, explored more fully in chapter 4, is that instructors have a vested interest in a quality spread: it is indeed important that there be some A's (as confirmation that the appropriate teaching has taken place), but it is equally important that there be many B's and C's. Something that underlies all university activity, and that so easily becomes invisible to us in its normalcy, is the institution's function as a gatekeeper. This function is not incidental, something that we must contend with from time to time and can ignore until the actual time for reporting grades; it is pervasive and powerful, shaping the dynamics of the rhetorical exigence in ineluctable fashion.

The writing we observed in the systems analysis course describes a midway point in the gulf between academic and workplace settings. Though based in the university and shaped by some of that institution's epistemic motives, the writing was very much like that of the workplace—in the social roles taken on by writers and readers, in its sense of audience, in its textual features (e.g., shared information, surplus of corroborating detail), and most markedly in the responding and collaborative reading practices of its first reader, the instructor, who served as a guide to the realities of workplace rhetoric, much as a supervising practitioner might. Finally, to return to our comparisons in Table 10.1, we have observed that case-study writers feel closure when the grade is given, and the texts cease to have importance (and often physical existence) at that point. For the systems analysis course, the writing was graded as well, but its existence was not entirely shaped nor ended by that grade: the documents led a continued and indeterminate existence in the clients' workplace. Like written documents we had observed in other workplace settings, their completion indicated their entry into a larger arena where their continued physical existence as documents along with their potential for material consequences could only be guessed at.

The systems analysis course provides a useful perspective into workplace-university differences. At the same time, it points as well to other kinds of programs (not so directly university-based) that might allow for easier and more easily scaffolded transitions to authentic workplace writing contexts: sheltered co-ops, work-study programs, and internships like those described below.

LEARNING TO WRITE AGAIN: ATTENUATED AUTHENTIC PARTICIPATION

Another step away from the university typically locates students in an actual workplace, and involves them in what we have called attenuated authentic participation. During this stage, students work alone, in pairs, or in small groups with a single supervisor. In some cases, interns are evaluated both by university and workplace supervisors, but for the most part the work they do and the texts they author belong to the workplace community. The interns that we observed learning the genres appropriate to the government agencies and social work settings to which they were assigned went through processes that, in some ways, were fundamentally similar to those entailed in the university settings. Common to both kinds of learning was the fact that learning took place as a result of collaboration, in the widest sense, or shared social engagement, as well as the fact that this learning took place through the mediation of sociocultural tools (primarily, but not solely, linguistic signs). There were important differences, however, and these differences are all the more significant for being tacit and implicit, complicating the transition into the workplace, and requiring that students learn in ways quite different from the ways they normally experience in classrooms.

The attenuated authentic participation that characterizes initial workplace experiences includes certain essential components: real but limited tasks, timely assistance, a grasp of rhetorical purposes, and a big picture or overview of the community. In addition, such participation, based as it is in the workplace rather than in the university, must offer the newcomer a sense of membership or belonging and the opportunity to play multiple roles in a variety of workplace relationships. When all these factors are in place, the newcomer is drawn toward mature practice.

We have noted that the participation of newcomers influences the workplace community in ways at once more obvious and more subtle than do course-based work projects, such as the systems analysis course described above. We believe this is a defining characteristic of situated learning in the workplace, marking it as essentially different from school-based learning experiences. A frequent form of influence can be found in the interaction between newcomers and their workplace supervisors (the oldtimers who usually volunteer to work with students). Eileen, one such oldtimer, said: "I still enjoy the feedback from the students and the sharing. I don't really see it as a one-way.... I feel I get a lot back in return." Other comments from supervisors:

I also find that [supervision] helps me to keep fresh in a way. Students obviously see things in a new kind of way and when you've been working in the field for 30 years you tend to see things in one way, so that I find that it keeps me thinking, stimulated. (Risa)

I told her [a social work intern] that I felt when we had joint interviews that I learned from her because it was a different perspective. Questions that she may have thought of asking I just haven't. And also when you're in practice for so many years, sometimes you get quite stuck and you handle interviews the same way. And she was fresh and new and just out—just in school, actually—and the theory is so down pat. (Eliza)

Newcomers also influence the workplace community as a whole. Whereas the work done as part of course-based projects, including student-authored reports, may well be ignored or little valued in the workplace, the work of interns generally contributes to the community's efforts. Newcomers bring new ideas and theories, new approaches and practices, and these can alter the community. When newcomer participation results in a contribution—a meaningful contribution, one that affects and changes the community—newcomers experience a sense of belonging, a sense of membership. This last point is critical. Along with Lave (1991), we see a developing sense of membership as essential to effective workplace learning: "Developing an identity as a member of a community and becoming knowledgeably skillful are part of the same process, with the former motivating, shaping, and giving meaning to the latter, which it subsumes" (p. 65).

The following scene, reconstructed from field notes, is authentic and captures this process of joining the community, as well as many other significant features of workplace learning. Any extended analysis and commentary is in square brackets. The setting is a Canadian government office; Douglas is the learner and Richard is his mentor or supervisor.

Douglas and Richard are observed as they respond to a sudden request to prepare a briefing note on the state of a particular set of negotiations for a new government minister. [Political events such as the appointments of new ministers often interrupt the anticipated flow of business in Canadian government offices. Mentors or supervisors must improvise, if they are to include the learners in the new tasks. Both must be agile.]

Douglas and Richard are standing in front of a desk which has a pile of previous briefing notes and reports on these negotiations. Their task is to develop a new briefing document, summarizing succinctly what the new minister needs to know.

The two discuss the potential content in global terms, brainstorming on a whiteboard, and then they sit down to write. Richard suggests that they work collaboratively. Douglas understands this to mean dividing up the task in two, with each taking responsibility for one half. [Presumably this reflects his notion of collaboration, based on what passed for collaboration as it was undertaken in university.]

Richard corrects this misconception, explaining that he means that they will actually produce the whole text together: the two of them sitting together to generate and compose text, with one person assigned to do the actual inputting. There is some joking and jockeying about who will do the inputting, but Richard decides that Douglas's superior expertise in word-processing (he can use Windows) warrants his taking the seat in front of the computer. [It is not untypical in the workplace for novices to display superior expertise in relevant skills.]

The two proceed to formulate and reformulate text together, with Richard taking the lead and providing feedback to each of Douglas' suggestions, but at the same time constantly eliciting suggestions and listening carefully to Douglas' comments about his own suggestions. The two respond to each other conversationally in a series of half-sentences, which reveals the highly interactive nature of the interchange. Each half-sentence responds to and builds on the previous, so that the product becomes more and more jointly generated. [This kind of interactive generating and composing between a guide and learner is hard to imagine in a school context, even in a tutoring center. The co-participation often reaches a flow at which it is difficult to determine who is suggesting which words.]

Complicating this interactiveness further is the interaction with already extant texts. Each suggestion for the new text is based in large part on the briefing notes and reports that are already available in the documents in front of them, with the words and phrases being modified, echoed, reaccentuated, qualified. [These earlier texts are cultural artifacts, which have been shaped by, and encode, the cultural practices and choices of the organization as it has evolved to that point. In Bakhtin's terms, the words in the new evolving documents are being echoed from the earlier ones, and reaccentuated in the light of the current "speech plan," so that the words become reinfused with slightly different meanings. This dialogism and mediation through cultural artifacts is true of university writing and hence learning as well, but without the complicating factor of the intersubjective activities of guide and learner.]

What we are seeing here is persons-in-activity-with-the-world as mediated through the technological tools (word-processing software) and the cultural artifacts available. The newcomer joins the network of distributed cognition. There is a hermeneutic grappling with notions, and it is sometimes difficult to discover where one thinker's processes ends and the other's begin, and where the new speech plan begins and the influence of older cultural artifacts recedes.

In order to begin feeling like a member of the community, especially in large institutions, social work student interns must quickly gain a picture of the entire collective endeavor and their own place in it. This picture includes the intricate and subtle geography of place and politics: the physical and organizational structure of the community. In the complex world of a large general hospital, for example, this geography includes all of the areas of specialized care, the laboratories, the wards, the hierarchy of the disciplines and individuals that inhabit the institution, and the community's network of complementary and conflicting interests. Eliza, a hospital-based social work supervisor, explains: "I find for the first ... month there's an enormous amount of time spent really just orienting [students] to a hospital situation because that in itself is a complex world." She continues: "What I do is have them go to as many staff meetings and as many of the structured kinds of things that are going on on the unit as possible at the beginning, both staff and patient things, so that they're sort of inundated with people and things happening."

The key to this orientation process is total immersion in the community's activities. Initial learning happens while newcomers are simply observing, or "sitting by Nellie," as it was called when apprentices observed veteran factory hands in the early days of industrialization (Clews & Magnuson, 1996). According to a social work newcomer, Natasha, "my first two weeks was a lot of observation: attending rounds, being introduced to people, and a few meetings." Newcomers are not told what to look for or what to learn; instead, "they're sort of inundated with people and things happening." The questions that arise belong to the students, and the supervisors answer them when the students need answers.

But early in their field placements, most social work students become more than passive observers at meetings or interviews: they respond to telephone calls, research available community resources, speak to medical staff. In short, they are included in community life, rather than studying it from afar. The supervisors we have interviewed spent little or no time preparing students before sending them on errands, giving them small tasks, bringing them to meetings or other events, and asking them to observe elements of practice. Indeed, most had nothing that could be called a deliberate curriculum, or even a set sequence of activities that constituted a learning path.

It is within the workplace community's public settings and in contacts with individuals from other professions in the hospital that the social work newcomers begin to feel like members of their own social work community and of the larger institutional community. They begin to learn the rituals and dynamics of community practice, the subtle tensions of institutional power and influence, and—most importantly for our purposes—they begin to learn about writing. That is, they begin to learn how, where, what, when, and why language occurs in the multiprofessional context of the institution. They participate in the heteroglossia of hospital life, the many specialized discourses about patients. They begin to learn what doctors, nurses, therapists, lab technicians, and psychologists care about, and how their own concerns are in concert or conflict with others. They begin to learn who can speak, when they can speak, and what they can say. They begin to enter the complex social world in which social work texts must operate, the world described in chapter 6.

When supervisors sense that this process has begun, they increase the newcomer's participation by turning cases over to the student. This case load is authentic, because newcomers work with actual people who have real problems, and attenuated, because the cases are not critical or overly difficult and supervisors step in to do or help with some aspects. As we noted in the previous chapter, learning is incidental and occurs as part of participation in the community of practice (COP), whose activities are oriented toward practical or material outcomes. Instruction is secondary to, or a byproduct of, institutional activity. In a sense, there is a reversal of the traditional order of instruction; rather than preceding performance or application, as is usual in school, teaching in the workplace often occurs during or even after the accomplishment of new tasks. As Eileen, a supervisor, noted: "After we do things, particularly do things together, [we] sit down and try to dissect things and I tell him, When I did that, this is what I was thinking." For such teaching to be successful, the oldtimers who act as field educators must carefully engineer and monitor tasks.

As social work interns move out of the initial stage of orientation and observation, and take on the beginnings of a case load, they must begin to produce the regular and occasional documents required by mature practice. In most agencies and institutions, this includes referral forms, assessments, progress reports, transfer and closing summaries, and all the usual rhetorical flora and fauna of institutional life: memos, letters, government forms, and so on. According to Colin, a supervisor: "Students who come here ... should be expected to write all the different reports. It shouldn't be that they're following these cases but don't take on the paper work side of it and only do the clinical side. They should take on ... all the different dimensions of what it means to be a social worker."

Newcomers receive very little advance assistance with this sort of task, although they receive as much feedback as they need, when they need it. Some scaffolding is provided, in the form of a format and some detail, but the newcomer is left to write the report, which must then be cosigned by the supervisor (following a collaborative revision process described below). Interviews, information searches, telephone calls, and other information gathering is done by the newcomer, closely monitored by the supervisor. Much of what is learned in this process is not addressed explicitly. Although we have seen workplace settings where some discourse practices are codified as guidelines, most rhetorical lore is implicit: for example, perhaps no one uses first-person pronouns in certain documents, but that interdiction is nowhere in print and cannot be traced to an authority. A major means of passing along this sort of rhetorical regularity is the practice of sending newcomers to the files to look at previous examples of required documentation, usually under the guidance of a supervisor. A supervisor in a group home for adolescents, Colin, describes the place of files in the abrupt transition from school to the "real world":

> [Students would] be assigned anywhere from three to five cases within the first week or two. And then they'd be told to go and look at the file and to pull the file and to look through and they would see the different kinds of reports that they're expected to do in there.... We basically try and get the students to handle the normal responsibilities of the social worker.... I guess the way I see it, you have to. In some ways, this is a kind of experience to the students of what it's like in the real world.

Reliance on existing texts realizes some of the key criteria for a successful transition, both for the individual and for the community: the newcomer gets to model the texts produced by oldtimers, thus emulating mature practice, and the community gets to reproduce itself, while being revitalized by the unique contributions of each newcomer. Again, no explicit discipline-wide, or even agency-wide, policy on training appears to be in effect, and yet supervisor after supervisor does the same thing: sends the student newcomers to the files. Supervisors are careful to exploit the newcomer's early struggles with aspects of practice, because they offer what teachers often call "a teachable moment": a fortuitous opportunity to offer guidance. Eliza, a supervisor, explains: "Well, I think my basic philosophy is that you, as much as possible, try to allow the student[s] to go with it on their own, to have as much freedom—unless they run into, or you feel they're going to run into, real snags, at which point you intervene, or help, or support, or do for, or whatever." Again, opportunities to write appear to be apt moments for introducing newcomers to the subtleties of community life and practice, and a form of "document cycling" (Paradis, Dobrin, & Miller, 1985; Smart, 1993) provides plenty of opportunities, as this excerpt from an interview with Natasha, a student, indicates:

> I would do my assessments, [the supervisor] would look at them and then give me her feedback and suggestions and, uh, areas that might be reworked or what have you. So it was essentially like that: [the supervisor] sort of like corrected me, "here's it back, and let's talk about it and discuss."

In the workplace, as Natasha points out, the emphasis is different: "Something that we highlighted as a goal, in our initial contract, was to look at my writing and improve my writing skills. You know, not so much the grammar and the spelling, but the skill of writing in the field." Certainly, the rhetorical sophistication described by Glenn, a student newcomer, in the following interview excerpt seems tied closely to particular workplace circumstances:

> I began to learn how to be more concise, more focused in my writing. My supervisor at the [agency] tried to teach me how to say a lot but not very much, meaning, you know, there are certain innuendoes to what I was saying, um, while protecting certain things of confidentiality between myself and my client.

To "say a lot but not very much" demonstrates a rhetorical skill that cannot be taught outside a context and practice in which those measurements make sense. What constitutes an "innuendo"? For whom will the text "say a lot" without saying "very much," and what is too much? What is the worker-client relationship, and how would it be affected by breaking the standards of confidentiality, some of which are universally prescribed by law and others which are local and largely tacit? These are questions that have no answer outside of particular circumstances, and the generalities about confidentiality that are offered in a school setting are likely to mean little in the field, where each worker-client relationship is different, and where the secrets of a person's life are defined by who reads reports and for what purpose. These lessons, the subtleties of culture, are learned in the centripetal pull of authentic attenuated participation, as the newcomer gradually transforms into an oldtimer.

To sum up: typically, early in the newcomer's workplace experience, learning takes place through engagement in active processes, guidance by mentors, and mediation through cultural tools. In this respect, the learning is like that of the university setting. What is different is the nature of the interactive co-participation and collaboration between mentor and learner; the improvisatory nature of the task; its authenticity and ecological validity in a larger context (the institution and indeed society as a whole); and the varied and shifting roles played by mentor and learner. Furthermore, there is no deliberate attention paid to the learner's learning; all attention is directed to the task at hand and its successful completion.

LATER STAGES: LEGITIMATE PERIPHERAL PARTICIPATION

In a final stage between school and full mature practice, students in the workplace begin to work autonomously. Even in their initial forays into the field as undergraduates, social work students are often expected to take on a version of mature practice. Colin, a supervisor we interviewed put it this way: "I'm a believer in trying to engage a student immediately in terms of doing and participating in clinical work. So as soon as the student comes in, literally the first day of placement, I have two cases on my desk waiting for her.... I think that the most important thing to start off with is the case right away." When social work students reach the senior undergraduate or graduate level and enter their final field placements, or when they complete their programs and enter the profession, their experience even more closely resembles traditional apprenticeship in professional practice. Guidance is decreased, responsibility increased, and the newcomer blends into the community. This is the stage of legitimate peripheral participation:

> Once I began, my supervisor said, "Here's a case," gave me some background and said, "Go ahead." To me that was great.... I wanted to learn to ... have my own style and this was a great way for me to do it. It was a learning experience and I have achieved my goal. So, for me, that autonomy was good for me. (Kate)

As we note in the previous chapter, Hanks (1991) describes legitimate peripheral participation as "an interactive process in which the apprentice engages by simultaneously performing in several roles—status subordinate, learning practitioner, sole responsible agent in minor parts of the performance, aspiring expert, and so forth—each implying a different sort of responsibility, a different set of role relations, and a different interactive involvement" (p. 23). These factors were conspicuously missing from the following negative experience, a field placement that did not engage the newcomer Spiro in legitimate peripheral participation:

> In my experience at [agency], I was essentially isolated from the team. There was no team to go to. Even though I was a "member" [gestures to indicate quotation marks] of the team, I was not officially interacting with any of the team.... I think that to feel you're on side you need to be with colleagues and to exchange clinical impressions, to learn from others ... with their vast experience, I think, is essential.
>
> Q: Did you do any writing?
>
> A: [Yes, but] it was very confusing because it wasn't clear as to what exactly they wanted. So I would get back, you know, I would submit [the report] to my supervisor and my supervisor would look at it and most of the parts were okay. There were some parts that just needed total revision. Why I couldn't know this beforehand is beyond me.... the expectations of my field work, my written work, was I would say, generally unclear. So I think the demand is left up to trial and error, I suppose.... But it never really clicks in until the time comes when you're

actually writing it yourself and you know the family or you have a good impression of where the family is at.

Lave and Wenger (1991) argue that learning is "an evolving form of membership" (p. 53); learning is thwarted when the learner is isolated, as was the student quoted above. He wrote a report and even received guidance from a supervisor, but the writing was out of context, he was not a member of a community and therefore had no role or responsibility, and the activity involved no authentic interaction. Compare this to another internship experience (excerpts from two interviews with the same student, Raymond):

> The first two weeks I was completely disoriented. The hospital was very intimidating to me. I was lost. I didn't know where to go and I didn't really feel grounded at all, so I felt lost.... But then when I got my first case, I was able to feel a little more oriented and more like I had a role here.

> [By] participating in rounds ... I'm understanding I guess the culture of it all. I'm feeling a part of it more than an outsider.... The culture, you know, it's a big system, and there's a culture that goes on; like in rounds talking about patients, and the language that's used.... And I guess I feel validated in a way I guess, you know, that what I'm doing, it's not just superficial, on a superficial level.... now I just feel more involved and more part of it.

Like Lave and Wenger (1991), we see this movement toward membership as critical to the workplace learning experience. Knowledge is inseparable from a sense of identity and a sense of location within a group; and knowledge-making is always a collaborative activity. Engagement in the activities that produce the group's specialized knowledge leads to membership in the group. Spiro, a social work student we cited earlier, describes the collaboration:

> Q: How are you learning to do [assessment reports]?

> A: There are several ways.... assessment workers do the same thing: gathering your information; gathering your data from the file material; doing interviews with people that have been involved with the child—whether it's a child care worker, a social worker, you get a different perspective on the problems; team feedback, because I present the case and get feedback on it, and based on the feedback we try to address the problems or the issues; and individuals—consultation with [fellow student], for example.

Note the changes that occur in this student's account of learning how to write a regular agency document: initially, he reports what others do; then he switches to the generic "you"; next he presents the case and gets feedback; and, finally, the team ("we") addresses the problem. Consider, too, the extensive interaction: with other texts, with child care and social workers, with team members, and with a fellow student. There is a sense here of membership, of working with others in partnership. Spiro elaborates on his field experience:

> We would have assessment team meetings, and there were various aspects within the assessment process that needed some clarification. Besides, I did the first couple of them with [fellow student].... We basically shared a lot of ideas and that was a very interesting process, that was. And we would pull our supervisor aside, too, and bounce off ideas, and other colleagues. So we had resources. We could access our team. We could access our supervisor.... I was put, and [fellow student] was put, in a situation where we have to respond ... not only to the family but ... to the Director of Assessment—what the requirements, policies, and things of that nature need to reflect. We have to respond to the Director of Professional Services.... I think it's very important to respond to what the social worker needs to know and what the child care worker needs to know. So, we're writing basically to a family of professionals that need to know where to go with this case.

Here, unmistakably, is a newcomer engaged in legitimate peripheral participation. He is a member of a team, operating as an equal (but still under supervision), and he is situated within the network of actions, interests, and individuals that constitute this COP. His tasks are no longer attenuated, and though reports are still cosigned at this late stage, they are rarely much revised by supervisors. The student's focus is on achieving a goal, on doing something with his text, on performing mature practice.

CONCLUSION

Our observations of school and workplace learning and writing have made us cautious about making generalizations. Clearly, learning is profoundly situated, as is writing: learning to write in particular contexts is indistinguishable from learning to participate in the full range of actions that constitute the activity in those contexts. As we argued in the previous chapter, students who move from university to the workplace and fail to recognize the differences in learning contexts and conditions risk missing the point. However, as the discussion in this chapter makes clear, there are ways to help student newcomers experience the practitioner's rhetorical life and, in so doing, learn something about workplace writing.

A condition central to the experiences of professional writing described in this chapter was their authenticity, or virtual rhetorical reality: the students in the two workplace settings had a real impact, they actually influenced action.

Another important and closely related condition was the primacy of instrumentality. The students obviously learned something from their experience, but the learning was secondary to, or a by-product of, the instrumental purpose of their writing. Perhaps most importantly, the students' experiences were carefully monitored, scaffolded, and controlled by oldtimers who took advantage of specific moments of uncertainty or confusion to offer relevant advice. It is this careful balancing between actual practice and timely instruction that we feel characterizes successful transitions into workplace writing.

11

CONTEXTS FOR WRITING: UNIVERSITY AND WORK COMPARED

In this closing chapter we return to the question we began with. What are the relations between writing in university and writing in the workplace? It may have struck readers that for a book about writing, surprisingly little writing, in the usual sense of texts, gets quoted and discussed. But that, of course, reflects the way we have had to refocus our operating notions of what writing is, in the way that we explained in our first two chapters, toward a vision of a complex network of activities in which composition represents only one strand. Even the texts themselves, we have found, derive their meaning as much from the activity systems in which they are embedded as from their denotational content. Most of our attention and discussion has, therefore, focused on what surrounds writing. Given our question, we should be concerned with writing-in-place; but *place* takes on richer dimensions than we generally visualize: physical and temporal location; social space (other actors immediately present and implicated to various degrees; past or future actors, interested, mediating, on and off the page), cultural-historical settings, institutional ways; the page itself, its appearance and its place alongside other pages; text accompanying or within graphical displays, texts as records in filing cabinets and on library shelves; and virtual space, transient on screen but etched on disks and CDS and retrievable.

The theoretical concepts we have relied on for our explanations hint as well at location: concepts such as *situated learning, distributed cognition, genre as social action, genre sets, legitimate peripheral participation* in *communities of practice,* and *activity systems*—concepts that contextualize writing. Writing, it turns out and in a manner of speaking, will be known by the company it keeps.

Because writing is so bound up in situation, the title of this book is not as hyperbolic as it appears. Writing at school and writing at work are indeed worlds apart; and the lesson that can be drawn from that realization is on the face of it considerably disconcerting. It seems reasonable to us that universities should be expected, among other things, to prepare people for the world of work, and not least for writing at work. Because with few exceptions writing is a medium deployed in both worlds, such preparation is not an unreasonable expectation. And it is precisely such an expectation that makes acting, the second term in our title, critical. Writing *is* acting; but in Activity Theory terms, writing at work and writing in school constitute two very different *activities*, one primarily epistemic and oriented toward accomplishing the work of schooling, and the other primarily an instrumental and often economic activity, and oriented accordingly toward accomplishing the work of an organization. In that light, one activity, writing in school, is not necessarily preparation for successfully undertaking the other activity, writing at work. In such light also, we can argue that both activities can function effectively in their respective systems without necessarily bridging their two worlds.

One might legitimately argue that whereas the two worlds of school and work are indeed apart, it is the people who cross between them who transport and translate what they have learned as writers from one domain to the other. Our book is an argument against (at least the facile versions of) such notions, what Joliffe (1994) calls "the myth of transcendence." It helps here to recall and adapt the phrase we cite from Wertsch in chapter 2 and to speak of the writer not as an isolated agent (or of writing not as an isolated act) but as person-acting-in-context-with-cultural-tools (primary tools such as language, but also architectural drawings, scholarly journals, word-processing programs and analytical software, clients' records, the telephone, and fax). Such tools carry with them stored knowledge, ways of acting, generic information that prescribes or makes convenient certain ways of writing and precludes others. Such tools again place the writer: whether writing alone or with others, the writer is in a role, is situated in an organization or institution, among people, in a dialogic relationship with other texts, constrained or extended by the writing instruments—on computer within an electronic network, for instance—or by the physical setting, at a desk within an institution with supervisors who oversee one's writing, within a cultural setting where writing is one other means of making one's mark or the sole means, within communities that impose a history of genres, institutional values and habits; in social settings with other writers where text is communally created; or on the borders of intersecting and often conflicting activity systems or communities of practice (COPs). As one of the titles of a chapter in Dias and Paré (in press) suggests, *we write where we are.* Location, it would appear, is (almost) everything.

But people do move between those worlds of school and work; so we need to ask how we might act in university settings to ease the transition from writing as a school-going activity to writing as a work activity, and as well how workplaces might change to help newcomers accomplish those ends. In considering those questions, we need to recapitulate how these two worlds compare as contexts for writing.

COMPARING DOMAINS
IN TERMS OF READING PRACTICES

For our purposes here, we need do no more than draw on our observations from previous chapters. School writing practices, we have argued, are dominated by the epistemic motive and the need to rank. Such motives also ensure that school-produced texts are read very differently from the ways in which work-produced texts are read by their intended readers. Thus school texts will ordinarily receive no more than one reading. While teachers may provide written comments with or without a grade, those comments generally have the effect of justifying the grade rather than suggesting a reworking of the text. Notions of writing to inform one's readers and of reading as dialogic are largely inoperative or subverted within the teacher–student relationship. We know that many conscientious teachers try to establish something more like normal "life-world" communications by the way they set and respond to assignments; but this minority is working against the grain of prevailing expectations. In the workplace, on the other hand, "document cycling" (Paradis, Dobrin, & Miller, 1985; Smart, 1993) is common practice. Many texts have multiple readers, all of whom may have different reasons for reading, and each of whom may read selectively. Texts produced for school, however cursory the reading, are read more or less in their entirety. As well, such texts have, so to speak, a limited shelf life. They must be produced, read, and graded within a specified time frame, and unlike workplace texts, they will not likely enter a process of filing, referencing, and cross-referencing, or be inserted into a documentary record.

COMPARING DOMAINS
IN TERMS OF "INTERTEXTUAL DENSITY"

We hypothesize that workplace writing, by contrast with students' writing in universities, is marked by complexity and density of intertextual connection, a connectedness that is just as real and significant between writing and speech, where there is no visible evidence for it, as it is between co-inscribed writing and drawing, where there is. Workplaces emerge from our study as dense webs of intertextual connections, some of them signaled and explicit (or manifest, Fairclough, 1992, p. 104) and some implicit (or constitutive, *ibid.*), with new texts echoing or following the conventions of existing ones. To trace these connections is to make visible both the epistemic (knowledge- and idea-making) and the interpersonal structures that constitute central elements of a work context.

The most school-like of the work settings we have studied is the central financial institution. It is school-like in the central role accorded to the evaluation by superiors of the written papers of subordinates, and also in that the material for the papers, the content that undergoes written analysis, is itself already a symbolic artifact. The writers work entirely from charts, tables, and written text and never from observation of economic activities out in the world. The symbolic media employed, moreover—mathematical notations, graphs, and computer codes—are ones that are central also to mainstream academic disciplines. And although the quantity and thoroughness of the supervisor's feedback on the writer's draft are greater than most students could expect, the relations obtaining between the two texts of the draft and the commentary (whether written or spoken) are similar in some respects to those one would find in the university. They may draw attention, for instance, to weak logic or ineffective ordering, or to the need for different emphases or more frequent "signposting."

Further, while the written texts are ultimately action-oriented—they are needed for decisions in which the institution will exercise vast governmental power—they are not individually intended to instigate action. Rather, they build the knowledge on which informed action may be based, and in that, too, they resemble academic texts.

What seem radically different are the other sorts of consideration that inform the supervisor's commentary. Whereas the professor's sense of what is necessary and appropriate derives from "the literature," or from the curriculum, or from a sense of what is currently valued in the written transactions of the discipline, the intertext on which the supervisor draws is more varied and more diffuse. On the one hand she, and perhaps her immediate work team, may have a particular view of the economy and policy that they are keen for top management to espouse. On the other, she knows what is wanted in the institution, its current concerns, agendas and sensitivities, by "having her finger on the pulse," and that in turn means being *au courant* not only with the documents that are currently central to policy-making but also with feelings and attitudes that may be communicated through informal conversation, through gossip and through facial expressions, sighs and the like at meetings and cocktail parties. In order to contribute effectively to the writing of a text that will leave her in a good light when it passes up the line, she needs to be an effective reader of the signs that are circulating in the institution in many media. The text, moreover, must be shaped with an eye to the range of responses it will occasion and the emotional, interpersonal, and political as well as strictly informational reverberations it will cause throughout the network. It is in this sense of its implicatedness in a complex multisymbolic communicative web that the written workplace text is, despite its superficial similarities as a paper that gets evaluated, very different in essence from a student's economics paper.

If this school/work difference is so apparent in the professional sphere that seems closest to school, it seems likely to appear even more markedly in our other professional disciplines—in social work, for instance, where the practitioners are writing about real people and interpreting the entire constellation of symbolic performances through which they present, and in architecture, where the practitioner is involved in a vast symbolic web that encompasses technical, legal, professional, and financial spheres and embraces large numbers of players and a great variety of communicative means. It is because of this depth of intertextual allusion and this range of association with other communicative processes that the sparsest-looking workplace texts may mean more richly than the most densely-referenced student paper. Student interns and newcomers are unlikely to gain easy or immediate access to what may pass as "common knowledge" within workplace communities. Learning to manage the relationships that enable fuller participation in such communities, moreover, may be one of the crucial transitional learning tasks for novice professionals.

WORKPLACE FUNCTIONS OF WRITING NOT FOUND IN SCHOOL: THE COMPLEXITY OF WORKPLACE WRITING

Because most of the purposes and necessities of work are absent from the classroom, there are numerous functions that academic writing is never called on to serve. First, students have no need to produce legally valid records, nor occasion to perform acts for which they will be held to account. Their writing rarely serves purposes of record in any sense that relates to legal or financial accountability. Nor do their texts have performativity, in the sense of realizing speech acts such as orders or requests.

At work, written texts regularly serve as records, in at least three different ways. The recorded information may be what counts; thus, an architect's diary may confirm in later dispute that the initial error in the placing of a steel wall had been 100 mm. Or the written text may constitute evidence of the architect's professional activities; so notebook entries, along with sketches and date-coded photographs, might establish that the architect did indeed visit the site on a certain date. This is the sort of record commonly referred to as a paper-trail. Alternatively, the text may have been the vehicle by which a speech act was performed, such as an instruction to the contractor. The surviving text is simply a trace of the act, the linguistic material and not the utterance itself, which was an event in history; the text's performative work was accomplished in its original delivery. The function of the preservation of the signed and dated text, however, is to provide legally compelling proof that the act took place.

Secondly, both students and professionals use writing to keep track, but there are major differences in what has to be tracked, arising from the circumstance that a professional's dealings may be with many individuals, institutions, and jobs whereas a student's are largely with one client per course (the teacher) and multiple sources of learning material, such as notes made in class, class materials, textbooks, library books, and journals. Whereas a student's Post It notes and slips of paper may mainly represent bits of information (e.g., points noted from books, references, etc.), the professional's notes often represent individuals, agencies, and involvements with whom he or she has some inter-active relationship. The professional is required to take action that will affect the people and states of affairs that the bits of paper represent; and those external entities are also liable to change without notice, occasioning new and unpre-dicted demands for action.

These conditions of professional work have time and space implications. The action that the professional has to undertake in relation to the different jobs and responsibilities often has to take place in a particular sequence. *This* has to happen before *that* can; what happens in relation to involvement B depends on what first happens in involvement A; and in the meantime Party X may do something quite unexpected that will affect both. The tracking problems faced by professionals may involve more intricate and shifting representations than those faced by students. Both groups have recourse to writing to help them, but the demands on professionals result in specialized uses of writing that are more developed and elaborated than anything we may observe in a student's study-bedroom.

This writing behavior is not unaffected by the fact that the physical space in which professionals write is not their own but their employer's. Whereas students write for the most part either in libraries that are an open resource outside the supervisor's (the teacher's) surveillance or in their own accommodation, the professional has a workspace or room in the institution's building, alongside his or her colleagues. This proximity naturally increases the density of communication within the domain, in ways that affect writing: drafts may be casually passed around and discussed, for instance, so that the written text readily becomes part of the shared network of meanings and may readily surface, in quotation or allusion, in the speech or from the pens and printers of colleagues. Writing may also circulate as part of the process of its composition and authorization. Those who pass it, from their own desk to that of a colleague, have thereby participated in the production of the text even though they may not have added anything except their initials, and become in part answerable for it ("has that been across your desk?").

We have already noted in chapter 8 how the professional's office space itself, including wall and furniture surfaces, is co-opted in the production, organization, and dissemination of text.

In general the social and multiparticipant nature of professional work generates a multitude of writing behaviors that occur with great regularity in the workplace but are more or less unknown in the university. An example would be when someone photocopies an incoming fax (of which classrooms, incidentally, experience rather few), highlights a passage, scribbles a comment at the side and passes the document to a colleague, who may write a further comment and pass it on again. Photocopying in general performs very different functions in the two environments. Bear in mind that for A to photocopy a document written by B and to pass it to C is a fresh act of written communication, even though no new text has been generated. In the office, copying everything to everyone is a simple way of keeping everyone in the picture and confirming continuing common membership in the task. But although the recipients receive the same text, they do not necessarily receive the same message, first because their different locations within the activity system lead them to read from different perspectives, and secondly because the intertextual connections in terms of which meanings are constructed may be different for different participants. Individuals bring different discursive histories to the framing of the text because they have previously been involved in different dialogic exchanges. This is a situation that skillful workplace writers can turn to their advantage (as we saw with the example of the Site Instruction in chap. 8).

Genre and the Pressure to Conserve

Given the complexity and liveliness of the workplace, we might expect that there will be exigences that call for improvisation; yet the likelihood of such inventiveness is often diminished by institutional guidelines for certain conventional features, in-house formal structures, and readers' expectations that enforce such observance. Those several readers and multiple readings within the workplace may not only support but also police the production of texts. In some organizations such readings are intended primarily to ensure that the design and content conform to company policy as outlined in company documents. When Ledwell-Brown (in press), a research associate on our project, examined the responses of managers to the written reports of their subordinates in order to determine the extent to which those responses reflected company goals and values, she concluded that managers' responses were indeed closely tied to those goals and values, which included the company's goal to maintain its status as the leader in its manufacturing field, its pride in its long institutional history, the company's expectation of employees' loyalty and dedication to its goals, a strong hierarchical line of authority and decision making justified by tradition and past success, and bolstered by company procedures manuals and regular performance appraisals. As one manager said, "One of the things that makes the company what it is ... we try to do the things that brought us where we are—and we do them the same way ... not that we don't ever want to change." In other words, genres in this organization are the genres that have worked in the past and apparently continue to get things done.

Allied with such concerns is company-wide practice to record and document decisions and the several steps toward them. "What's not on paper doesn't exist!" is an oft-cited maxim of a former vice-president. Putting it on paper "makes it official." Such documentation, in turn, serves as the memory of the company for newcomers and provides models for current reports. It can also provide justification for past decisions if and whenever such decisions are reviewed, and can be an instrument, however benign, of regulation and surveillance. Newcomers must know the lore of the company, particularly a widely-held belief that its success is related to "the way we do things here," before they decide such controlling practices merely deny individual creativity and initiative (see chap. 6 for a description of the complex accountabilities at work in professional contexts).

We may recall, however, that students learn in school to submit to and accommodate a variety of such expectations and sometimes contradictory (among courses) demands as a matter of expedience. More often than not school writing genres are tightly specified, designed to further certain learning goals, monitor learning, and standardize grading. And even when the specifications are not spelled out, they are often implicitly operative. Such expectations provide the basis for most of the writing done in school and generate stable structures for the specifically school-related tasks of defining, shaping, and displaying knowledge. Modifications of the genre are unlikely to occur at the initiative of the students. Unlike workplace writers, for instance, the economists in the Bank of Canada who began their formal report to the governor of the Bank with an epigraph from the Rolling Stones (Smart, 1998), a conspicuous shift from the format of preceding reports, the abbreviated tenure of students within a course and their overall subordinate status as such, do not afford them easy familiarity with a discipline and its conventions or the degree of comfort and freedom to experiment that comes from fellowship and full participation.

UNIVERSITY AND WORKPLACE AS ACTIVITY SYSTEMS

Activity theory has helped us identify a key distinction in the way we regard writing. We need to distinguish in our discussion between writing as an *activity*—an ongoing activity as it is generically conceived when we speak, for instance, of scholarly and non-scholarly writing, or literary writing, or written communication, or the history of writing and so on—and writing as an *action* or an *operation* in an activity system, be that activity system work, school-going, recreation or law-making. It is easy in discussion to conflate writing as the generic *activity* with writing as an *action* (or as an *operation*, which is how we most often know and practice writing). It is writing as *action* that we have largely been concerned with in this book. What we have observed at the variety of sites we have studied is writing as an *action*, contributing to and, therefore, defined by a larger ongoing activity (be it economic forecasting in a central bank or ensuring the social and medical good of hospital patients) and embodying place, time, history, tools, situation, cultural, disciplinary, institutional knowledge and conventions, and especially, the several agents in the situations that occasion the writing: the writer, current and prospective readers, cowriters and other collaborators, all part of a larger activity system and driven by motives that are not necessarily identical and drawn by objectives that may often conflict. Thus, we have not generalized from *actions* of writing in the activity system called social work to designating an *activity* called social work writing, because we have observed no such activity as a cultural reality; the *actions* of writing in social work within their social surround contribute rather to other activities, ones that are recognized and named within the culture, such as record-keeping, child protection in the justice system, or hospital care.

Writing by students in university as an *action* can be directed variously by the goals of getting a good grade by conforming to set guidelines, or defining and exploring a new concept in a satisfying way, or ensuring completion of the task by a set deadline. Thus, when our analysis reveals that students' motives (the desire for higher grades, for instance) lead to actions that subvert teachers' desire to promote learning through the writing tasks they design and assign, we may plan to forestall such contradictory actions by considering them in the context of the larger activity system called the university. Taking that wider perspective, we may find, for instance, that competing demands from other courses and tuition costs that force students into part-time employment may necessitate some students bypassing the built-in learning processes and writing primarily to meet the letter of the assignment.

Such an analysis when extended to transitional (university to workplace) situations may help explain how student interns in the workplace, or new employees for that matter, may not recognize that they need not only to modify their writing *as action* but to redefine the goals and criteria for their writing by locating it within an entirely different activity system. So they may not realize how much of workplace knowledge is tacit rather than explicit, how much the written text is implicated in a complex, multisymbolic communicative web, and that their moving into full participation may be much more a process of enculturation and much less a matter of transferring school learning or receiving deliberate instruction. Interns and newcomers as they participate in shared activities internalize that culture's way of doing things, norms as well as knowledge, embodied as well in the mediating tools, which include language and technical artifacts such as computers and accounting systems. These are points to be considered when university programs are evaluated in terms of how well they prepare graduates for the workplace.

PRACTICAL CONSIDERATIONS

Probably because it seems so obvious, we have not sufficiently emphasized a central function of writing, a dimension of writing's epistemic function, the way that writing makes inner speech overt and functions as a means of thinking. It may also be because people who talk about writing seem to be talking most often about writing as an outcome, a product, something to be read by others, a record to return to. Perhaps we need to shift the balance by pointing to how writing is not only the end product of thinking but also the means; and as such writing may contribute to the realization of an architectural drawing, as we saw in chapter 5, or help marshal arguments for a key decision without figuring as such in the final outcome. When we ask then what might be learned in university about writing that is transferable to the workplace, it is this use of writing that we need to value highly. It is this use that can be cultivated as habit and engaged across the curriculum rather than in specialized courses on writing: using writing to register fleeting impressions, sketch transient ideas, notebooks for and of the mind, texts not always intended to be revisited and, having accomplished their immediate function, out of the way and seemingly superfluous.

Case-study writing is often proposed as the kind of university exercise that is likely to have carry-over effects. While case studies help students learn key concepts and apply general principles to very specific situations, those situations are defined as instances-for-practice-in-education. Situations that students are likely to encounter in the workplace are not only experienced quite differently; they are often less sharply defined; they are dynamic, in flux, and very much located in institutional histories, personal relationships, and local, temporal events. What else is portable regarding writing in the transition from university to workplace? Certainly, skills related to portable tools: computer-related skills, including keyboarding, word-processing, and spreadsheet skills, language fluency, abilities related to using and designing forms, charts, and other kinds of graphic displays. Oral skills and the social skills valued in group work ought to carry over as well. Again, we need to remind ourselves that such skills will be modified in transition; for instance, an individual's fluency will be severely retarded in the workplace if he or she lacks rhetorical savvy. Although we must concede that producing English sentences is something students ought to be able to do, a failure to do so is less of an issue with students in their final years. Their problems are less sentence-level problems and more ones of rhetoric. Schools by the very nature of the epistemic demands they make on language may effectively promote general language development: a high level of syntactic and lexical sophistication, the ability to produce continuous text and manage flow and difficult transitions, adjusting to different rhetorical contexts and therefore some degree of stylistic flexibility and sensitivity, a concern for verbal economy.

However, there are certain assumptions about the portability of writing skills from university to workplace that need to be rethought because they ignore the ecology of the workplace. The workplace does not enact the values of a liberal civil society that are often proclaimed as guiding principles for the classroom: a place where vulnerable people are afforded protection, are free to speak and given space to speak whether they are contributing or not; where people are required to listen to everybody; where the criterion for discourse is authenticity with a minimum of distortion. Taking an idealized, global view of what we do may not work in an organization. Thus, when we advocate teaching problem-solving strategies and techniques for collaboration as preparation for work-place writing, we may be assuming too easily a workplace setting imbued with a corporate ethic of working in teams and sharing, where bosses welcome new ideas and are not wary of being outshone by upstart juniors. Moreover, workplaces do not afford the time or incentive for the tentative-ness that is encouraged in classrooms. At the same time, the political dynamics of classrooms are very different from those of the workplace: achievement in school is measured by how much better you perform than your competitors, and non-performance in collaborative groups is not likely to be penalized.

Despite these differences, we ought not underestimate the value to the workplace of what happens in schools. Schools afford space and time to acquire and fully understand theoretical concepts required for the workplace, concepts that can be learned, if at all, only on the run in the workplace and in the context of other work. Schools provide the opportunity as well, at certain levels at least, for learners to be critical of received notions, to consider alternatives, to speculate and hypothesize—options that are likely to be regarded as disruptive or simply unwarranted in most workplaces. Our experience is that such benefits of schooling do not go unrecognized in the workplace: interns are valued in the workplace for their awareness of recent theory, and encouraged to share their knowledge with full-time professionals.

Learning in University and in the Workplace

There is scope for really fruitful partnerships between people in university who are reflexive about writing, teaching, and learning processes and those people responsible for education and training in the workplace; however, we have to first admit certain kinds of complications.

- Can we subject oldtimers and the work they do to critical analysis?

Workplace writers are far more skilled and accomplished than they themselves or their managers acknowledge. Because writing is, in Activity Theory terms, most often operational (or as Polanyi puts it, held in subsidiary rather than focal awareness), workplace writers are not deliberately attentive to their writing habits or practices. Such inattentiveness might result from what Fairclough (1995) calls the "naturalization of ideology"—a process by which the values and choices involved in particular discourse formulations disappear through habit or familiarity. Or it might work against the interests of participants to "notice" discourse practices, either because they are in no position to change them or because they benefit from them and do not wish to expose or alter the power imbalances the practices engender and maintain (see Segal, Paré, Brent, & Vipond, 1998).

• Novices and interns who enter workplaces with critical attitudes can be disruptive and even abrasive.

Whereas universities encourage and provide time for dissenting voices and debate, as well as consideration of alternatives, workplaces may consider such practices unproductive, if not disruptive. Interns and novices should proceed cautiously, aware of the conservative nature of most institutions and the function that discourse plays in that conservation process. There is also a danger in introducing novice employees too early in their training to critical approaches to work practices. Until they are fully socialized into the workplace, they do not necessarily see the justification for certain practices, and must expect resistance to suggestions of change, especially when offered self-righteously. Fruitful interaction often occurs after interns or newcomers have gained sufficient experience to able to discern what it is they need to know and who is most likely to provide the information they need.

• Are we helping students and interns by asking them to innovate?

Although taking initiatives is often the corporate ideal presented to all employees, especially in large corporations, the reality often is that taking a critical stance is not rational behavior with high survival value for most employees at many levels, who wish to do no more than get through the day or satisfy immediate needs and demands. An idealized, global view of the corporation's goals and functions, while worth recalling from time to time, may prove to have little applicability to day to day activities.

• Professionalization comes at a cost to self-identity.

To illustrate: social work supervisors often discourage interns from using "I" in social work reporting on the grounds that it is not professional; our hunch is that by not using "I," social workers disguise their personal identity under professional makeup and distance their personal selves from the work they do. Thus, social work interns and graduates who see themselves as agents of change will be functioning as agents but not the ones they expected to be. As we have seen, as soon as they begin using the genres of the agency, they buy into the ideology; they learn to live with contradiction. Such professional genres construct subject positions that may not accord with their goals; not to be too dramatic, they fragment the personality. It is the price of professionalization, so that they may do things as professionals that they are not prepared to do as persons.

BRIDGING THE GAP

Given the theoretical orientations we began with and the perspectives we have employed, we are not surprised that writing at school and at work is indeed happening in two different worlds. Because workplace writing is so deeply embedded in workplace practices and cultures and is not normally identified as a distinct work practice, it should seem rather anomalous that in most school settings, writing assumes a distinct identity and seeming autonomy. Courses dedicated to the teaching of writing were until recently exceptional outside the North American context, and whereas there are good historical and cultural reasons for their institution and prevalence in North America (see Berlin, 1996, and Russell, 1991, for instance), a view of writing as integrally woven into disciplinary knowing and integrally bound up within action and activity (as an operation, in Activity Theory terms) appears to us to be a plausible explanation for the dearth of writing courses outside North America. In other words, people are assumed to learn to write by doing things with writing; that is, as writing becomes increasingly operational, a means rather than an end.

It seems reasonable that the embeddedness of writing in workplace practices ought to be replicated in school settings as well, if it isn't for the fact that the process of education does often operate on a model of detaching skills and practices from their workaday settings in order to teach them effectively. Such encapsulation (Engeström, 1991) of knowledge and skills is quite likely a deterrent rather than an aid to learning to write. If as we argue, writing is a by-product of other activities, a means for getting something else done, we ought to consider how we might engage students in activities that commit them to write as necessary means—but only as a means not an end. If there is one major, obvious-seeming way in which educational courses might prepare people better for the demands of writing at work, it is through constituting the class as a working group with some degree of complexity, continuity, and interdependency of joint activity. Such arrangements will go some way toward realizing the far richer communicative relations that contextualize writing in the workplace.

REFERENCES

Ackerman, J. & Oates, S. (1996). Image, text, and power in architectural design and workplace writing. In A. H. Duin & C. J. Hansen (Eds.), *Nonacademic writing: Social theory and technology* (pp.81–121). Mahwah, NJ: Lawrence Erlbaum Associates.

Anderson, P. V. (1985). What survey research tells us about writing at work. In L.Odell & D. Goswami (Eds.), *Writing in non-academic settings* (pp.3–83). New York: Guilford.

Anderson, P. V., Brockmann, R. J., & Miller, C. R. (Eds.). (1983). *New essays in technical and scientific communication: Research, theory, and practice.* Farmingdale, NY: Baywood.

Anson, C. N. & Forsberg, L. L. (1990). Moving beyond the academic community: Transitional stages in professional writing. *Written Communication,* 7 (2), 200–231.

Austin, J. L. (1962). *How to do things with words.* Oxford: Clarendon Press.

Bakhtin, M. M. (1981). *The dialogic imagination: Four essays by M. M. Bakhtin.* (M. Holquist, Ed., C. Emerson and M. Holquist, Trans.). Austin: University of Texas Press.

Bakhtin, M. M. (1986). *Speech genres and other late essays.* (C. Emerson & M. Holquist, Eds., V. W. McGee, Trans.). Austin, TX: University of Texas Press.

Bataille, R. R. (1982). Writing in the world of work: What our graduates report. *College Composition and Communication,* 33, 276–282.

Bateson, G. (1972). Steps to an ecology of mind: *A revolutionary approach to man's understanding of himself.* New York: Ballantine.

Bazerman, C. (1979). Written language communities: Writing in the context of reading. (Educational Resources Information Center Publication No. 232 159).

Bazerman, C. (1988). *Shaping written knowledge: The genre and activity of the experimental article in science.* Madison: University of Wisconsin Press.

Bazerman , C. (1994). Systems of genres. In A. Freedman & P. Medway (Eds.), *Genre and the new rhetoric* (pp. 79–101). London: Taylor & Francis.

Bazerman, C. & Paradis, J. (1991a). Introduction. In C. Bazerman & J. Paradis (Eds.), *Textual dynamics of the professions* (pp. 3–10). Madison: University of Wisconsin Press.

Bazerman, C. & Paradis, J. (Eds.). (1991b). *Textual dynamics of the professions: Historical and contemporary studies of writing in professional communities.* Madison: University of Wisconsin Press.

Bereiter, C. & Scardamalia, M. (1987). *The psychology of writing.* Hillsdale, NJ: Lawrence Erlbaum Associates.

Berkenkotter, C. & Huckin, T. N. (1995). *Genre knowledge in disciplinary communication: Cognition/culture/power.* Hillsdale, NJ: Lawerence Erlbaum Associates.

Berlin, J. A. (1987). *Rhetoric and reality: Writing instruction in American colleges, 1900–1985.* Carbondale & Edwardsville, IL: Southern Illinois University Press.

Berlin, J. A. (1986). *Rhetorics, poetics, and cultures: Refiguring college English studies.* Urbana, IL: National Council of Teachers of English.

Bitzer, L. F. (1968). On the classification of discourse performances. *Rhetorical Society Quarterly,* 7, 31–40.

Bourdieu, P. (1977). *Outline of a theory of practice* (R. Nice, Trans.). London: Cambridge University Press. (Original work published 1972).

236

Bourdieu, P. (1993). *Sociology in question* (R. Nice, Trans.). London: Sage Publications. (Original work published 1984)

Bourdieu, P., & Passeron, J. C. (1977). *Reproduction in education, society, and culture.* London: Sage.

Brand, N., & White, J. O. (1976). *Legal writing: A strategy of persuasion.* New York: St. Martin's Press.

Brandt, D. (1990). *Literacy as involvement: The acts of writers, readers, and text.* Carbondale, IL: Southern Illinois Univesity Press.

Brandt, D. (1992). The cognitive and the social: An ethnomethodological approach to writing process research. *Written communication, 9,* 315–351.

Bristol, M. C. (1936). *Handbook on social case recording.* Chicago: University of Chicago Press.

Britton, J., Burgess, T., Martin, N., McLeod, A., & Rosen, H. (1975). *The development of writing abilities, 11–18.* London: Macmillan Education.

Brown, A. L., Ash, D., Rutherford, K., Nakagawa, K., Gordon, A., & Campione, J. C. (1993). *Distributed expertise in the classroom.* In G. Salomon (Ed.), Distributed cognitions: Psychological and educational considerations. (pp. 188–228). Cambridge: Cambridge University Press.

Brown, J. (1988). A survey of writing practices in management. *English Quarterly, 21,* 7–18.

Brown, V. (1993). Decanonizing discourses: Textual analysis and the history of economic thought. In W. Henderson, T. Dudley-Evans, & R. Backhouse (Eds.), *Economics and language* (pp. 64–84). London: Routledge.

Burke, K. (1957). *The philosophy of literary form* (Rev. Abr. ed.). New York: Vintage.

Burke, K. (1950). *A rhetoric of motives.* Berkeley, CA: University of California Press.

Chandler, D. (1992). The phenomenology of writing by hand. *Intelligent Tutoring Media, 3* (2/3), 65–74.

Clark, G. (1990). *Dialogue, dialectic, and conversation: A social perspective on the function of writing.* Carbondale and Edwardsville: Southern Illinois University Press.

Clews, R., & Magnuson, H. (1996, June). Theory and practicum: Bridging the gap. Paper presented at the meeting of the Social Work Field Education Conference, Hamilton, ON.

Coe, R. M. (1986, May). Process, form, and social reality. Paper presented at the 4th International Conference on the Teaching of English, Canadian Council of Teachers of English, Ottawa, Canada.

Coe, R. M. (1987). An apology for form; or, who took the form out of the process? *College English, 49,* 13–28.

Coe, R. M. (1994). "An arousing and fulfilment of desires": The rhetoric of genre in the process era—and beyond. In A. Freedman & P. Medway (Eds.), *Genre and the new rhetoric* (pp. 181–190). London: Taylor & Francis.

Cole, M. (1991). Conclusion. In L. B. Resnick, J. M. Levine, & D. T. Teasley (Eds), *Perspectives on socially shared cognition* (pp. 398–417). Washington, DC: American Psychological Association.

Cole, M., & Engeström, Y. (1993). A socio-cultural approach to distributed cognition. In G. Salomon (Ed.), *Distributed cognitions: Psychological and education considerations* (pp. 1 46). Cambridge: Cambridge University Press

Cooper, M. M. (1996). Foreword. In A. Duin & C. Hansen (Eds.), *Nonacademic writing: Social theory and technology* (pp. ix–xii). Mahwah, NJ: Lawrence Erlbaum Associations.

Cope, B., & Kalantzis, M. (Eds.). (1993). The *powers of literacy: A genre approach to teaching writing.* London: Falmer.

Corbin, C. I. (1992). Writing and the design student: Strategies for initiating the process. *Proceedings of the 1991 Southeast Regional ACSA Conference* (pp.177–183). Charlotte, NC: UNCC College of Architecture.

Corey, R. C. (1976). *The use of cases in management education*. Boston, MA: Harvard Business School, Publishing Division.

de Saussure, F. (1967). *Cours de linguistique Générale*. Wiesbaden: Otto Harrassowitz. (Original work published 1916).

Devitt, A. (1991). Intertextuality in tax accounting. In C. Bazerman & J. Paradis (Eds.), *Textual dynamics of the professions* (pp. 336–357). Madison, WI: University of Wisconsin Press.

Dias, P. (1987). *Making sense of poetry: Patterns in the process*. Ottawa: Canadian Council of Teachers of English.

Dias, P. X., & Paré, A. (Eds.). (in press). *Transitions: Writing in academic and workplace settings*. Cresskill, NJ: Hampton.

Doheny-Farina, S. (1985). Writing in an emerging organization: An ethnographic study. *Written Communication, 3*, 158–185.

Douglas, M. (1986). *How institutions think*. Syracuse, NY: Syracuse University Press.

Driskill, L.P. (1989). Understanding the writing context in organizations. In M. Kogen (Ed.), *Writing in the business professions* (pp. 125–145). Urbana, IL: National Council of Teachers of English.

Duguay, P., & Longworth, D. (1997). Macroeconomic models and policy making at the Bank of Canada. Paper presented at the 10th Anniversary Congress of the Tinbergen Institute, Amsterdam.

Duguay, P., & Poloz, S. (1994). The role of economic projections in Canadian monetary policy formulation. *Canadian Public Policy - Analyse des Politiques, 20*, 189–199.

Duin, A.H., & Hansen, C. J. (1996). *Nonacademic writing: Social theory and technology*. Mahwah, NJ: Lawrence Erlbaum Associates.

Duxbury, L., & Chinneck, J. (1993). The practicum approach to the teaching of systems analysis and design: A view from the trenches. Paper presented at Administrative Services Association of Canada, Lake Louise, Alberta.

Ede, L., & Lunsford, A. (1984). Audience addressed/audience invoked: The role of audience in composition theory and pedagogy. *College Composition and Communication, 35*, 155–171.

Ede, L., & Lunsford, A. (1990). *Singular texts/plural authors: Perspectives on collaborative writing. Carbondale and Edwardsville*: Southern Illinois University Press.

Elbow, P. (1986). *Embracing contraries: Explorations in learning and teaching*. New York: Oxford University Press.

Emig, J. (1971). *The composing processes of twelfth graders*. (Research Report No. 13). Urbana, IL: National Council of Teachers of English.

Engeström, Y. (1991) *Non scolae sed vitae discimus*: Toward overcoming the encapsulation of learning. *Learning and Instruction, 1*, 243–259.

Engeström, Y. (1993). Developmental studies of work as a testbench of activity theory: The case of primary care medical practice. In S. Chaiklin & J. Lave (Eds.), Understanding practice: *Perspectives on activity and context* (pp.64–103). Cambridge: Cambridge University Press.

Engeström, Y. (1997, March). Talk, text, and instrumentality in collaborative work: An activity-theoretical perspective. Paper Presented at the Annual Meeting of the Conference on College Composition and Communication, Phoenix, AZ.

Engeström, Y., Engeström, R., & Kärkkäinen, M. (1995). Polycontextuality and boundary crossing in expert cognition: Learning and problem solving in complex work activities. *Cognition and Instruction, 5,* 319–336.

Ericsson, K. A., & Simon, H.A. (1985). *Protocol analysis: Verbal reports as data.* Cambridge, MA: MIT Press.

Faigley, L. (1986). Competing theories of process: A critique and a proposal. *College English, 48,* 527–542.

Faigley, L. (1992). *Fragments of rationality: Postmodernity and the subject of composition.* Pittsburgh: University of Pittsburgh Press.

Faigley, L., & Miller, T. (1982). What we learn from writing on the job. *College English, 44,* 557–569.

Fairclough, N. (1992). *Discourse and social change.* Cambridge: Polity Press.

Fairclough, N. (1995). *Critical discourse analysis: The critical study of language.* London: Longman.

Fitzgerald, P. (1985). *Looking at Law.* Ottawa: Bybooks.

Fleck, L. (1979). *Genesis and development of a scientific fact* (F. Bradley & T. Trenn, Trans.). Chicago: University of Chicago Press. (Original work published 1935).

Flower, L. (1977). Problem-solving strategies and the writing process. *College English, 39,* 449–461.

Flower, L., & Hayes, J. R. (1981). A cognitive process theory of writing. *College Composition and Communication, 32,* 365–387.

Flower, L. S., Hayes, J. R., & Swarts, H. (1980). *Revising functional documents: The scenario principle* (Tech. Rep. No. 10). Pittsburgh, PA: Carnegie-Mellon University.

Foucault, M. (1979). *Discipline and punish: The birth of the prison* (A. Sheridan, Trans.). New York: Harper.

Freadman, A. (1987). Anyone for tennis? In I. Reid (Ed.), *The place of genre in learning: Current debates* (pp. 91–124)). Geelong, Australia: Deaken University Press.

Freedman, A. (1987). Learning to write again: Discipline-specific writing at university. *Carleton Papers in Applied Language Studies, 4,* 95–115.

Freedman, A. (1990). Reconceiving genre. *Texte (9),* 279–292.

Freedman, A. (1993). Show and tell? The role of explicit teaching in learning new genres. *Research in the Teaching of English,* 27, 222–251.

Freedman, A. (1996). Argument as genre and genres of argument. In D. Berrill (Ed.), *Perspectives on written argumentation* (pp. 91–120). Cresskill, NJ: Hampton Press.

Freedman, A., Adam, C., & Smart, G. (1994). Wearing suits to class: Simulating genres and simulations as genre. *Written Communication, 11,* 192–226.

Freedman, A., & Adam, C. (1995, March). Learning and teaching new genres: New literacies, new responsibilities. Paper presented at the annual meeting of the Conference on College Composition and Communication, Washington, DC.

Freedman, A., & Adam, C. (in press). Write where you are: How do we situate learning to write? In P. X. Dias & A. Paré (Eds.), *Transitions: Writing in academic and workplace settings.* Cresskill, NJ: Hampton.

Freedman, A., & Medway, P., (Eds.). (1994a). *Genre and the new rhetoric.* London and Bristol, PA: Taylor & Francis.

Freedman, A., & Medway, P., (Eds.). (1994b). Learning and teaching genre. Portsmouth, NH: Boynton-Cook/ Heinemann.

Freedman, A., & Pringle, I. (Eds.). (1979). *Reinventing the rhetorical tradition*. Ottawa, ON: Canadian Council of Teachers of English.

Geertz, C. (1983). *Local knowledge: Further essays in interpretive anthropology*. New York: Basic Books.

Giltrow, J., & Valiquette, M. (1994). Genres and knowledge: Students writing in the disciplines. In A. Freedman & P. Medway (Eds.), *Learning and teaching genre* (pp. 47–62). Portsmouth, NH: Heinemann.

Goodman, J., Fairey, J., & Paul, V. (1992). The word and the freshman design student: Word and image in form and imagination. *Proceedings of the 1991 Southeast Regional ACSA Conference* (pp.184–187). Charlotte, NC: UNCC College of Architecture.

Graves, D. H. (1984). *A researcher learns to write*. Exeter: Heinemann.

Gutierrez, K. (1994, April). Laws of possibility: Reconstituting classroom activity for Latino children. Paper presented at AERA, New Orleans, LA.

Halliday, M. A. K. (1975). *Learning how to mean: Explorations in the development of language*. London: Edward Arnold.

Halliday, M. A. K. (1985). An *introduction to functional grammar*. London: Edward Arnold.

Hanks , W. F. (1991). Foreword. In J. Lave & E. Wenger (Eds.), *Situated learning: Legitimate peripheral participation* (pp. 13–24). Cambridge: Cambridge University Press.

Heath, S. B. (1983). *Ways with words: Language, life, and work in communities and classrooms*. New York: Cambridge University Press.

Hebden, J. E. (1986). Adopting an organization's culture: The socialization of graduate trainees. *Organizational Dynamics, 15*, 54–72.

Herndl, C. G. (1993). Teaching discourse and reproducing culture: A critique of research and pedagogy in professional and non-academic writing. *College Composition and Communication, 44* (3), 349–363

Herndl, C. G. (1996). The transformation of critical ethnography into pedagogy, or the vicissitudes of traveling theory. In A. Duin & C. Hansen (Eds.), *Nonacademic writing: Social theory and technology* (pp. 17–33). Mahwah, NJ: Lawrence Erlbaum Associates.

Herrington, A. (1985). Writing in academic settings: A study of the contexts for writing in two college chemical engineering courses. *Research in the Teaching of English, 19*, 331–59.

Hillocks, G., Jr. (1986). *Research on written composition: New directions for teaching*. Urbana, IL: National Conference on Research English & Educational Resources Information Center Clearinghouse on Reading and Communication Skills.

Hubboch, S. (1989, Fall/Winter). Confronting the power in empowering students. *The Writing Instructor, 35*–44.

Huckin, T. N. (1992). Context-sensitive text analysis. In G. Kirsch & P. A. Sullivan (Eds.), *Methods and methodology in composition research* (pp. 84–104). Carbondale and Edwardsville: Southern Illinois University Press.

Hunt, K. W. (1970). Syntactic maturity in school children and adults. *Monographs of the Society for Research in Child Development, 35* (1), entire issue.

Hutchins, E. (1993). Learning to navigate. In S. Chaiklin & J. Lave (Eds.), *Understanding practice: Perspectives on activity and context* (pp. 35–63). Cambridge: Cambridge University Press.

Jakobson, R. (1987). Linguistics and poetics. In K. Pomorska & S. Rudy (Eds.), *Language in literature* (pp. 62–94). Cambridge, MA: Harvard University Press.

Johnson, A. G. (1995) *The Blackwell dictionary of sociology*. Cambridge, MA: Blackwell.

Joliffe, D.A. (1994). The myth of transcendence and the problem of the "Ethics" essay in college writing instruction. In P. A. Sullivan & D. J. Qualley (Eds.), *Pedagogy in the age of politics: Writing and reading (in) the academy* (pp. 183–194). Urbana, IL: National Council of Teachers of English.

Kinneavy, J. L. (1971). *A theory of discourse.* Englewood Cliffs, NJ: Prentice-Hall.

Knoblauch, C. H. (1980). Intentionality in the writing process. *College Composition and Communication, 31,* 153–159.

Kress, G. (1982). *Learning to write.* London: Routledge & Kegan Paul.

Kress, G., & van Leeuwen, T. (1996). *Reading images: The grammar of visual design.* London: Routledge.

Kristeva, J. (1986) Word, dialogue and novel. In T. Moi (Ed.), *The Kristeva reader* (pp. 34–61). Oxford: Blackwell.

Latour, B., & Woolgar, S. (1986). *Laboratory life: The social construction of scientific facts.* 2nd edition. Beverly Hills, CA: Sage.

Lave, J. (1988). *Cognition in practice: Mind, mathematics and culture in everyday life.* Cambridge: Cambridge University Press.

Lave, J. (1991). Situating learning in communities of practice. In L. B. Resnick, J. M. Levine, and D. T. Teasley (Eds.), *Perspectives on socially shared cognition* (pp. 63–82). Washington, DC: American Psychological Association.

Lave, J. & Wenger, E. (1991). *Situated learning: Legitimate peripheral participation.* Cambridge: Cambridge University Press.

Ledwell-Brown, J. (1993). *Reader responses to writing in a business setting: A study of managers' responses to writing in an organizational culture.* Unpublished doctoral dissertation, McGill University.

Ledwell-Brown, J. (in press). Organizational cultures as contests for learning to write. In P. Dias & A. Paré (Eds.), *Transitions: Writing in academic and workplace settings.* Cresskill, NJ: Hampton.

LeFevre, K. B. (1987). *Invention as a social act.* Carbondale and Edwardsville: Southern Illinois University Press.

Leont'ev, A. N. (1981). The problem of activity in psychology. In J. V. Wertsch (Ed.), *The concept of activity in Soviet psychology* (pp. 37–71). Armonk, NY: Sharpe.

Lunsford, A., & Ede, L. (1990). *Singular texts/plural authors: Perspectives on collaborative writing.* Carbondale: University of Southern Illinois Press.

MacDonald, S. P. (1992). A method for analyzing sentence-level differences in disciplinary knowledge making. *Written Communication, 9 (4),* 533–569.

MacKinnon, J. (1993). Becoming a rhetor: Developing writing ability in a mature, writing-intensive organization. In R. Spilka (Ed.). *Writing in the workplace: New research perspectives* (pp. 41–55). Carbondale, IL: Southern Illinois University Press.

Martin, R. (1992). *Writing in the design disciplines.* Minneapolis, MN: University of Minneapolis, Center for Interdisciplinary Studies of Writing.

Matthews, H. (1992). Writing for designers: A strategy for teaching. *Proceedings of the 1991 Southeast Regional ACSA Conference* (pp.173–176). Charlotte, NC: UNCC College of Architecture.

McCann, R. (1992). Through the looking glass: Writing as a method of experiential design. *Proceedings of the 1991 Southeast Regional ACSA Conference* (pp.197–203). Charlotte, NC: UNCC College of Architecture.

McCarthy, L. P. (1987). A stranger in strange lands: A college student writing across the curriculum. *Research in the Teaching of English, 21*, 233–265.

McCarthy, L. P., & Gerring, J. P. (1994). Revising psychiatry's charter document: DSM-IV. *Written Communication, 11*, 147–192.

Medway, P. (1996). Writing, speaking, drawing: The distribution of meaning in architects' communication. In M. Sharples & T. van der Geest (Eds.), *The New writing environment: Writers at work in a world of technology* (pp. 25–42). London: Springer Verlag.

Miller, C. (1994). Genre as social action. In A. Freedman & P. Medway (Eds.), *Genre and the new rhetoric* (pp. 23–42). London: Taylor & Francis.

Mishler, E.G. (1986). *Research interviewing*. Cambridge, MA: Harvard University Press.

Morris, C. (1971) *Writings on the general theory of signs*. Cambridge, MA: MIT Press.

Murray, D. (1980). Writing as process: How writing finds its own meaning. In T. R. Donovan & B. W. McClelland (Eds.), *Eight approaches to teaching composition* (pp. 3–20). Urbana, IL: National Council of Teachers of English.

Myers, G. (1985). Texts as knowledge claims: The social construction of two biologists' articles. *Social Studies of Science, 15*, 593–630.

Myers, G. (1989). The pragmatics of politeness in scientific articles. *Applied Linguistics, 10*, 1–35.

Nardi, B. (1992). Studying context: A comparison of activity theory, situated action models, and distributed cognition. Proceedings of the East-West HCI Conference (pp. 352–359). St Petersburg, Russia.

Nickerson, R. S. (1993). On the distribution of cognition: Some reflections. In G. Salomon (Ed.), *Distributed cognitions: Psychological and educational considerations* (pp. 229–261). Cambridge: Cambridge University Press.

Nystrand, M. (1989). A social-interactive model of writing. *Written Communication, 6*, 66–85.

Odell, L., & Goswami, D. (1982). Writing in a non-academic setting. *Research in the Teaching of English, 16*, 201–223.

Odell, L., & Goswami, D. (Eds.). (1985). *Writing in nonacademic settings*. New York: Guilford.

Paradis, J., Dobrin, D., & Miller, R. (1985). Writing at Exxon Ltd.: Notes on the writing environment of an R & D organization. In L. Odell & D. Goswami (Eds.), *Writing in non academic settings* (pp. 281–308). New York: Guilford.

Paré, A. (1991a). *Writing in social work: A case study of a discourse community*. Unpublished doctoral dissertation, McGill University, Montreal.

Paré, A. (1991b). Ushering "audience" out: From oration to conversation. *Textual Studies in Canada, 1*, 45–64.

Paré, A. (1993). Discourse regulations and the production of knowledge. In R. Spilka (Ed.), *Writing in the workplace: New research perspectives* (pp.111–123). Carbondale, IL: Southern Illinois University Press.

Paré, A. (in press). Writing as a way into social work: Genre sets, genre systems, and distributed cognition. In P.X. Dias & A. Paré (Eds.), *Transitions: Writing in academic and workplace settings*. Cresskill, NJ: Hampton.

Paré, A., & Smart, G. (1994). Observing genres in action: Towards a research methodology. In A. Freedman & P. Medway (Eds.), *Genre and the new rhetoric* (pp. 146–154). London and Bristol, PA: Taylor & Francis.

Park, D. (1982). The meanings of "audience." *College English, 44*, 247–257.

Peirce, C. (1931/1958). *Collected papers of Charles Sanders Peirce* (Vols. 1–6, C. Hartshorne & P. Weiss, Eds.; Vols. 7–8, A.W. Burks, Ed.). Cambridge, MA: Harvard University Press.

Petraglia, J. (1995). Spinning like a kite: A closer look at the pseudotransactional function of writing. *Journal of Advanced Composition, 15* (1), 19–33.

Polanyi, M. (1958). *Personal knowledge: Towards a post-critical philosophy.* Chicago, IL: University of Chicago Press.

Popken, R. (1992). Genre transfer in developing adult writers. *Focuses, 5,* 3–17.

Rafoth, B., & Rubin, D. (Eds.). (1989). *The social construction of written communication.* Norwood, NJ: ABLEX.

Reither, J., & Vipond, D. (1989). Writing as collaboration. *College English, 51,* 855–867.

Renshaw, P. D. (1992). Reflecting on the experimental context: Parents' interpretations of the education motive during teaching episodes. In L. T. Winegar & J. Valsiner (Eds.), *Children's development within social context.* Vol. 2: Research and Methodology (pp. 53–74). Hillsdale, NJ: Lawrence Erlbaum Associates.

Resnick, L. B., Levine, J. M., & Teasley, S. D. (Eds.). (1991). *Perspectives on socially shared cognition.* Washington, DC: American Psychological Association.

Rogoff, B. (1990). *Apprenticeship in thinking.* New York: Oxford University Press.

Rogoff, B. (1991). Social interaction as apprenticeship in thinking: Guided participation in spatial planning. In L. Resnick, J. Levine, & S. Teasley (Eds.), *Perspectives on socially shared cognition* (pp. 349 364). Washington, DC: American Psychological Association.

Rogoff, B. (1993, April). Guided participation of children and their families. Paper presented at the American Educational Research Association Conference, Atlanta, GA.

Rogoff, B. (1994, April). Models of teaching and learning. Development through participation. Paper presented at the American Educational Research Association Conference, New Orleans, LA.

Rosenblatt, L. (1978). *The reader, the text, the poem.* Carbondale, IL: Illinois University Press.

Rush, J., & Evers, F. (1986). *Making the match: Canada's university graduates and corporate employers.* Montreal: Corporate-Higher Education Forum.

Rush, J., & Evers, F. (1991). *Report on making the match: Phase two.* Montreal: Corporate-Higher Education Forum.

Russell, D. R. (1991). *Writing in the academic disciplines, 1870–1990: A curricular history.* Carbondale: Southern Illinois University Press.

Russell, D. R. (1997). Rethinking genre in school and society: An activity theory analysis. *Written Communication, 14*(4), 504–554.

Salomon, G. (1993). Introduction. In G. Salomon (Ed.), *Distributed cognitions: Psychological and education considerations* (pp. xi–xxi). Cambridge: Cambridge University Press.

Schryer, C. F. (1994). The lab vs. the clinic: Sites of competing genres. In A. Freedman & P. Medway (Eds.), *Genre and the new rhetoric* (pp. 105–124). London and Bristol, PA: Taylor & Francis.

Segal, J., Paré, A., Brent, D., & Vipond, D. (1998). The researcher as missionary: Problems with rhetoric and reform in the disciplines. *College Composition and Communication, 50,* 71–90.

Selzer, J. (1983). The composing processes of an engineer. *College Composition and Communication, 34,* 178 187.

Shaughnessy, M. (1977). *Errors and expectations: A guide for the teacher of basic writing.* New York: Oxford University Press.

Sheffield, A. E. (1920). *The social case history: Its construction and content.* New York: Russell Sage Foundation.

Smagorinsky, P., & Coppock, J. (1994). Cultural tools and the classroom context: An exploration of an artistic response to literature. *Written Communication, 11* (3), 283–310.

Smart, G. (1985). Writing to discover structure and meaning in the world of business. *Carleton Papers in Applied Language Studies, 2,* 3–44.

Smart, G. (1989). A social view of genre: Some implications for teaching. *Inkshed, 8,* 9–12.

Smart, G. (1993). Genre as community invention: A central bank's response to its executives' expectations as readers. In R. Spilka (Ed.), *Writing in the workplace: New research perspectives* (pp. 124–140). Carbondale, IL: Southern Illinois University Press.

Smart, G. (1998). An *ethnographic study of knowledge-making in a central bank: The interplay between writing and economic modeling.* Unpublished doctoral dissertation, McGill University.

Smith, D. (1974). The social construction of documentary reality. *Sociological Inquiry, 44,* 257–268.

Sommers, N. (1980). Revision strategies of student writers and experienced adult writers. *College Composition and Communication, 31,* 378–88.

Spilka, R., (1990). Orality and literacy in the workplace. *Journal of Business and Technical Communication, 4,* 44–67.

Spilka, R. (Ed). (1993). *Writing in the workplace: New research perspectives.* Carbondale and Edwardsville: Southern Illinois University Press.

Suleiman, S. R., & Crossman, I. (Eds.). (1980). *The reader in the text: Essays on audience and interpretation.* Princeton, NJ: Princeton University Press.

Swales, J. (1990). *Genre analysis: English in academic and research settings.* Cambridge: Cambridge University Press.

Taylor, C. (1985). *Human agency and language: Philosophical papers 1.* Cambridge: Cambridge University Press.

Taylor, C. (1989). *Sources of the self: The making of modern identity.* Cambridge, MA: Harvard University Press.

Thiessen, G. (1995, April). Interview with Peter Gzowski. *CBC Morningside.*

Todorov, T. (1984). *Mikhail Bakhtin: The dialogical principle* (Wlod Godzich, Trans.). Minneapolis: University of Minnesota Press.

Tompkins, J. P. (Ed.). (1980). *Reader response criticism: From formalism to post- structuralism.* Baltimore, MD: John Hopkins University Press.

Toulmin, S. (1958). *The uses of argument.* Cambridge: Cambridge University Press.

Toulmin, S., Rieke, R., & Janik, A. (1979). *An introduction to reasoning.* New York: Macmillan.

Upchurch, D. A. (1993). *Writing in the design curriculum: Alternative routes to the imagination: A collection of student writing 1992–93.* Muncie, Indiana: Ball State University, College of Architecture and Planning.

Voloshinov, V. (1986). *Marxism and the philosophy of language.* Cambridge, MA: Harvard University Press.

Vygotsky, L. (1978). *Mind in society: The development of higher psychological processes.* Cambridge, MA: Harvard University Press.

Vygotsky, L. S. (1981a). The genesis of higher mental functions. In J. V. Wertsch (Ed.), *The concept of activity in Soviet psychology* (pp. 144–188). Armonk, NY: M. E. Sharpe.

Vygotsky, L.S. (1981b). The instrumental method in psychology. In J. V. Wertsch (Ed.), *The concept of activity in Soviet psychology* (pp. 134–143). Armonk, NY: M. E. Sharpe.

Vygotsky, L. S. (1986). *Thought and language*. Translation newly revised and edited by Alex Kosulin. Cambridge, MA: MIT Press.

Waern, Y. (1979). *Thinking aloud during reading: A descriptive model and its application* (Report No. 546). Stockholm: Department of Psychology, University of Stockholm.

Walvoord, B., & McCarthy, L. P. (1993). *Thinking and writing in college: A naturalistic study of students in four disciplines*. Urbana, IL: National Council of Teachers of English.

Wertsch, J. V. (Ed.). (1981). *The concept of activity in Soviet psychology*. Armonk, NY: M. E.Sharpe.

Wertsch, J. V. (1985). *Vygotsky and the social formation of mind*. Cambridge, MA: Harvard University Press.

Wertsch, J. V. (1991). *Voices of the mind: A sociocultural approach to mediated action*. Cambridge, MA: Harvard University Press.

Wertsch, J. V., Minick, N., & Arns, F. J. (1984). The creation of context in joint problem-solving. In B. Rogoff & J. Lave (Eds.), *Everyday cognition: Its development in social context* (pp. 151–171). Cambridge, MA: Harvard University Press.

Wertsch, J. V., Tulviste, P., & Hagstrom, F. (1993). A sociocultural approach to agency. In E. A. Forman, N. Minick, & C. A. Stone (Eds.), *Contexts for learning: Sociocultural dynamics in children's development* (pp. 336–357). New York and Oxford: Oxford University Press.

Willard, C. A. (1982). Argument fields. In J. R. Cox & C. A. Willard (Eds.), *Advances in argumentation theory and research* (pp. 27–77). Carbondale, IL: Southern Illinois University Press.

Williams, R. (1976). Keywords: *A vocabulary of culture and society*. London: Fontana Press.

Winsor, D. (1989). An engineer's writing and the corporate construction of knowledge. *Written Communication, 6*, 270–285.

Winsor, D. (1994). Invention and writing in technical work. *Written Communication, 11* (2), 227–250.

Witte, S. P. (1992). Context, text, intertext: Toward a constructivist semiotic of writing. *Written Communication, 9* (2), 237–308.

Wood, C. C. (1992). *A study of the graphical mediating representations used by collaborative authors*. Brighton: University of Sussex School of Cognitive and Computing Science.

Wood, D., Bruner, J. S., & Ross, S. G. (1976). The role of tutoring in problem-solving. *Journal of Child Psychology and Psychiatry, 17*, 89–100.

AUTHOR INDEX

SUBJECT INDEX

A

Academic writing, *see* University writing
Activity systems, 65, 66–67, 114
    University and Workplace writing:
        bridge between, 230–231
Activity Theory, 23–28, 67, 123, 177
    genre theory, 46
    University writing, 65, 67–68, 233
    Management Strategies course, 69–76,
        79
    architectural practice, 180
    writing, 223
Architects, 152
    division of labor with architectural tech-
        nologists, 157
Architectural activity at school and work,
        see also Architectural practice,
        177–179
Architectural education, 82–84, 177–178
    design notebook, 98–102
    design studies, 102–103
    language connection, 106–107
    writing about architecture, 84–85
    writing as architecture, 107–111
    writing for architecture, 85–107
Architectural practice, *see also* Architec-
        tural activity in school and work,
        151–182
Activity Theory, 180

architects and architectural technolo-
        gists, 152
    division of labor, 157
    complexity of the job, 166–168
genres, 153–156
    conceptual design, 154–155
    construction, 156
    contracts, 153–154
    renovation of old buildings, 156
    working drawings and specifica-
        tions, 155–156
metafunctions of texts, 157
modes of communication, 160–162
writing, 161, 180–182
    careful judgment, 165–166
    complexity, 175–177
    epistemic purpose, 160, 181
    experience of architects, 168–169
    increase, 169–171
    learning architectural genres,
        171–175
    multifunctionality, 175–177
    persuasive function, 164–165
    rhetorical demands, 162–168
    social relations, 166
Architectural technologists, 152
    division of labor with architects, 157
Architecture and writing, 84–111
AT, *see* Activity Theory
Attenuated authentic performance (Work-
        place), 188, 199, 200, 201–202,
        216–217

249